INFORMATION
RETRIEVAL

INFORMATION RETRIEVAL

RETRIEVAL

Second Edition

C. J. van Rijsbergen B.Sc. Ph.D. M.B.C.S.

Computer Laboratory,
University of Cambridge

BUTTERWORTHS
London   Boston
Sydney Durban Wellington Toronto

United Kingdom	**Butterworth & Co (Publishers) Ltd**
London	88 Kingsway, WC2B 6AB
Australia	**Butterworths Pty Ltd**
Sydney	586 Pacific Highway, Chatswood, NSW 2067
	Also at Melbourne, Brisbane, Adelaide and Perth
Canada	**Butterworth & Co (Canada) Ltd**
Toronto	2265 Midland Avenue, Scarborough, Ontario, M1P 4S1
New Zealand	**Butterworths of New Zealand Ltd**
Wellington	77-85 Customhouse Quay, 1
	T & W Young Building, CPO Box 472
South Africa	**Butterworth & Co (South Africa) Ltd**
Durban	152-154 Gale Street
USA	**Butterworth (Publishers) Inc**
Boston	19 Cummings Park, Woburn, Massachusetts 01801

First published 1975
Second edition 1979

© Butterworth & Co (Publishers) Ltd, 1979

ISBN 0 408 70929 4

British Library Cataloguing in Publication Data

Van Rijsbergen, C. J.
Information retrieval. — 2nd ed.
1. Information storage and retrieval systems
I. Title
029.7   Z699   78-40725
ISBN 0-408-70929-4

Printed in Great Britain by
The Whitefriars Press Ltd, London and Tonbridge

PREFACE TO THE SECOND EDITION

The major change in the second edition of this book is the addition of a new chapter on probabilistic retrieval. This chapter has been included because I think this is one of the most interesting and active areas of research in information retrieval. There are still many problems to be solved so I hope that this particular chapter will be of some help to those who want to advance the state of knowledge in this area. All the other chapters have been updated by including some of the more recent work on the topics covered. In preparing this new edition I have benefited from discussions with Bruce Croft, David Harper, Stephen Robertson and Karen Sparck Jones. I am grateful to the University of Cambridge Computer Laboratory for providing me with the facilities for carrying out the work. Finally, I am indebted to the Royal Society for supporting me on their Scientific Information Research Fellowship.

C.J.v.R.

PREFACE TO THE FIRST EDITION

The material of this book is aimed at advanced undergraduate information (or computer) science students, postgraduate library science students, and research workers in the field of IR. Some of the chapters, particularly Chapter 6*, make *simple* use of a little advanced mathematics. However, the necessary mathematical tools can be easily mastered from numerous mathematical texts that now exist and in any case references have been given where the mathematics occur.

I had to face the problem of balancing clarity of exposition with density of references. I was tempted to give large numbers of references but was afraid they would have destroyed the continuity of the text. I have tried to steer a middle course and not compete with the *Annual Review of Information Science and Technology*.

Normally one is encouraged to cite only works that have been published in some readily accessible form such as a book or periodical. Unfortunately much of the interesting work in IR is contained in technical reports and Ph.D. theses. For example most of the work done on the SMART system at Cornell is available only in reports. Luckily many of these are now available through the National Technical Information Service (U.S.) and University Microfilms (U.K.). I have not avoided using these sources although if the same material is accessible more readily in some other form I have given it preference.

I should like to acknowledge my considerable debt to many people and institutions that have helped me. Let me say first that they are responsible for many of the ideas in this book but that only I wish to be held responsible. My greatest debt is to Karen Sparck Jones who

---

* This is Chapter 7 in the second edition.

taught me to research information retrieval as an experimental science. Nick Jardine and Robin Sibson taught me about the theory of automatic classification. Cyril Cleverdon is responsible for forcing me to think about evaluation. Mike Keen helped by providing data. Gerry Salton has influenced my thinking about IR considerably, mainly through his published work. Ken Moody had the knack of bailing me out when the going was rough and encouraging me to continue experimenting. Juliet Gundry is responsible for making the text more readable and clear. Bruce Croft, who read the final draft, made many useful comments. Ness Barry takes all the credit for preparing the manuscript. Finally, I am grateful to the Office of Scientific and Technical Information for funding most of the early experimental work on which the book is based; to the King's College Research Centre for providing me with an environment in which I could think, and to the Department of Information Science at Monash University for providing me with the facilities for writing.

C.J.v.R

CONTENTS

One

INTRODUCTION

Information retrieval is a wide, often loosely-defined term but in these pages I shall be concerned only with automatic information retrieval systems. Automatic as opposed to manual and information as opposed to data or fact. Unfortunately the word information can be very misleading. In the context of information retrieval (IR), information, in the technical meaning given in Shannon's theory of communication, is not readily measured (Shannon and Weaver[1]). In fact in many cases, one can adequately describe the kind of retrieval by simply substituting 'document' for 'information'. Nevertheless, 'information retrieval' has become accepted as a description of the kind of work published by Cleverdon, Salton, Sparck Jones, Lancaster and others. A perfectly straightforward definition along these lines is given by Lancaster[2]: 'Information retrieval is the term conventionally, though somewhat inaccurately, applied to the type of activity discussed in this volume. An information retrieval system does not inform (i.e. change the knowledge of) the user on the subject of his inquiry. It merely informs on the existence (or non-existence) and whereabouts of documents relating to his request.' This specifically excludes Question–Answering systems as typified by Winograd[3] and those described by Minsky[4]. It also excludes data retrieval systems such as used by, say, the stock exchange for on-line quotations.

To make clear the difference between data retrieval (DR) and information retrieval (IR), I have listed in Table 1.1 some of the distinguishing properties of data and information retrieval. One may want to criticise this dichotomy on the grounds that the boundary

TABLE 1.1. DATA RETRIEVAL OR INFORMATION RETRIEVAL?

	Data Retrieval (DR)	*Information Retrieval* (IR)
Matching	Exact match	Partial match, best match
Inference	Deduction	Induction
Model	Deterministic	Probabilistic
Classification	Monothetic	Polythetic
Query language	Artificial	Natural
Query specification	Complete	Incomplete
Items wanted	Matching	Relevant
Error response	Sensitive	Insensitive

between the two is a vague one. And so it is, but it is a useful one in that it illustrates the range of complexity associated with each mode of retrieval.

Let us now take each item in the table in turn and look at it more closely. In data retrieval we are normally looking for an exact match, that is, we are checking to see whether an item is or is not present in the file. In information retrieval this may sometimes be of interest but more generally we want to find those items which partially match the request and then select from those a few of the best matching ones.

The inference used in data retrieval is of the simple deductive kind, that is, aRb and bRc then aRc. In information retrieval it is far more common to use inductive inference; relations are only specified with a degree of certainty or uncertainty and hence our confidence in the inference is variable. This distinction leads one to describe data retrieval as deterministic but information retrieval as probabilistic. Frequently Bayes' Theorem is invoked to carry out inferences in IR, but in DR probabilities do not enter into the processing.

Another distinction can be made in terms of the classifications that are likely to be useful. In DR we are most likely to be interested in a monothetic classification, that is, one with classes defined by objects possessing attributes both necessary and sufficient to belong to a class. In IR such a classification is on the whole not very useful, in fact more often a polythetic classification is what is wanted. In such a classification each individual in a class will possess only a proportion of all the attributes possessed by all the members of that class. Hence no attribute is necessary nor sufficient for membership to a class.

The query language for DR will generally be of the artificial kind, one with restricted syntax and vocabulary, in IR we prefer to use natural language although there are some notable exceptions. In DR the query is generally a complete specification of what is wanted, in IR it is invariably incomplete. This last difference arises partly from the fact

2

that in IR we are searching for relevant documents as opposed to exactly matching items. The extent of the match in IR is assumed to indicate the likelihood of the relevance of that item. One simple consequence of this difference is that DR is more sensitive to error in the sense that, an error in matching will not retrieve the wanted item which implies a total failure of the system. In IR small errors in matching generally do not affect performance of the system significantly,

Many automatic information retrieval systems are *experimental*. I only make occasional reference to *operational* systems. Experimental IR is mainly carried on in a 'laboratory' situation whereas operational systems are commercial systems which charge for the service they provide. Naturally the two systems are evaluated differently. The 'real world' IR systems are evaluated in terms of 'user satisfaction' and the price the user is willing to pay for its service. Experimental IR systems are evaluated by comparing the retrieval experiments with standards specially constructed for the purpose. I believe that a book on *experimental* information retrieval, covering the design and evaluation of retrieval systems from a point of view which is independent of any particular system, will be a great help to other workers in the field and indeed is long overdue.

Many of the tecniques I shall discuss will not have proved themselves incontrovertibly superior to all other techniques, but they have promise and their promise will only be realised when they are understood. Information about new techniques has been so scattered through the literature that to find out about them you need to be an expert before you begin to look. I hope that I will be able to take the reader to the point where he will have little trouble in implementing some of the new techniques. Also, that some people will then go on to experiment with them, and generate new, convincing evidence of their efficiency and effectiveness.

My aim throughout has been to give a complete coverage of the more important ideas current in various special areas of information retrieval. Inevitably some ideas have been elaborated at the expense of others. In particular, emphasis is placed on the use of automatic classification techniques and rigorous methods of measurement of effectiveness. On the other hand, automatic content analysis is given only a superficial coverage. The reasons are straightforward, firstly the material reflects my own bias, and secondly, no adequate coverage of the first two topics has been given before whereas automatic content analysis has been documented very well elsewhere. A subsidiary reason for emphasising automatic classification is that little appears to be known or understood about it in the context of IR so that research workers are loath to experiment with it.

The structure of the book

The introduction presents some basic background material, demarcates the subject and discusses loosely some of the problems in IR. The chapters that follow cover topics in the order in which I would think about them were I about to design an experimental IR system. They begin by describing the generation of machine representations for the information, and then move on to an explanation of the logical structures that may be arrived at by clustering. There are numerous methods for representing these structures in the computer, or in other words, there is a choice of file structures to represent the logical structure, so these are outlined next. Once the information has been stored in this way we are able to search it, hence a discussion of search strategies follows. The chapter on probabilistic retrieval is an attempt to create a formal model for certain kinds of search strategies. Lastly, in an experimental situation all of the above will have been futile unless the results of retrieval can be *evaluated*. Therefore a large chapter is devoted to ways of measuring the effectiveness of retrieval. In the final chapter I have indulged in a little speculation about the possibilities for IR in the next decade.

The two major chapters are those dealing with automatic classification and evaluation. I have tried to write them in such a way that each can be read independently of the rest of the book (although I do not recommend this for the non-specialist).

Outline

Chapter 2: Automatic Text Analysis—contains a straightforward discussion of how the text of a document is represented inside a computer. This is a superficial chapter but I think it is adequate in the context of this book.

Chapter 3: Automatic Classification—looks at automatic classification methods in general and then takes a deeper look at the use of these methods in information retrieval.

Chapter 4: File Structures—here we try and discuss file structures from the point of view of someone primarily interested in information retrieval.

Chapter 5: Search Strategies—gives an account of some search strategies when applied to document collections structured in different ways. It also discusses the use of feedback.

Chapter 6: Probabilistic Retrieval—describes a formal model for enhancing retrieval effectiveness by using sample information about the frequency of occurrence and co-occurrence of index terms in the relevant and non-relevant documents.

Chapter 7: Evaluation—here I give a traditional view of the measurement of effectiveness followed by an explanation of some of the more promising attempts at improving the art. I also attempt to provide foundations for a theory of evaluation.

Chapter 8: The Future—contains some speculation about the future of IR and tries to pinpoint some areas of research where further work is desperately needed.

Information retrieval

Since the 1940s the problem of information storage and retrieval has attracted increasing attention. It is simply stated: we have vast amounts of information to which accurate and speedy access is becoming ever more difficult. One effect of this is that relevant information gets ignored since it is never uncovered, which in turn leads to much duplication of work and effort. With the advent of computers, a great deal of thought has been given to using them to provide rapid and intelligent retrieval systems. In libraries, many of which certainly have an information storage and retrieval problem, some of the more mundane tasks, such as cataloguing and general administration, have successfully been taken over by computers. However, the problem of effective retrieval remains largely unsolved.

In principle, information storage and retrieval is simple. Suppose there is a store of documents and a person (user of the store) formulates a question (request or query) to which the answer is a set of documents satisfying the information need expressed by his question. He can obtain the set by reading all the documents in the store, retaining the relevant documents and discarding all the others. In a sense, this constitutes 'perfect' retrieval. This solution is obviously impracticable. A user either does not have the time or does not wish to spend the time reading the entire document collection, apart from the fact that it may be physically impossible for him to do so.

When high speed computers became available for non-numerical work, many thought that a computer would be able to 'read' an entire document collection to extract the relevant documents. It soon became apparent that using the natural language text of a document not only caused input and storage problems (it still does) but also left unsolved the intellectual problem of characterising the document content. It is conceivable that future hardware developments may make natural language input and storage more feasible. But automatic characterisation in which the software attempts to duplicate the human process of 'reading' is a very sticky problem indeed. More specifically 'reading' involves attempting to extract information, both syntactic and semantic, from the text and using it to decide whether each document is relevant or not to a particular request. The difficulty is not only knowing how to extract the information but also how to use it to decide relevance. The comparatively slow progress of modern linguistics on the semantic front and the conspicuous failure of machine translation (Bar-Hillel[5]) show that these problems are largely unsolved.

The reader will have noticed that already, the idea of 'relevance' has slipped into the discussion. It is this notion which is at the centre of information retrieval. The purpose of an automatic retrieval strategy is to retrieve all the *relevant* documents at the same time retrieving as few of the *non-relevant* as possible. When the characterisation of a document is worked out, it should be such that when the document it represents is relevant to a query, it will enable the document to be retrieved in response to that query. Human indexers have traditionally characterised documents in this way when assigning index terms to documents. The indexer attempts to anticipate the kind of index terms a user would employ to retrieve each document whose content he is about to describe. Implicity he is constructing queries for which the document is relevant. When the indexing is done automatically it is assumed that by pushing the text of a document or query through the same automatic analysis, the output will be a representation of the content, and if the document is relevant to the query, a computational procedure will show this.

Intellectually it is possible for a human to establish the relevance of a document to a query. For a computer to do this we need to construct a model within which relevance decisions can be quantified. It is interesting to note that most research in information retrieval can be shown to have been concerned with different aspects of such a model.

An information retrieval system

Let me illustrate by means of a black box what a typical IR system would look like. The diagram shows three components: input, processor and output. Such a trichotomy may seem a little trite, but the components constitute a convenient set of pegs upon which to hang a discussion.

Starting with the input side of things. The main problem here is to obtain a representation of each document and query suitable for a computer to use. Let me emphasise that most computer-based retrieval

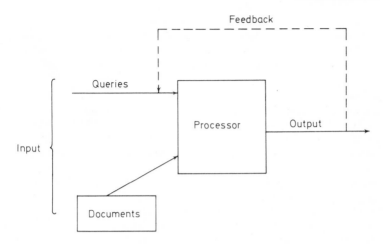

Figure 1.1. A typical IR system

systems store only a representation of the document (or query) which means that the text of a document is lost once it has been processed for the purpose of generating its representation. A *document representative* could, for example, be a list of extracted words considered to be significant. Rather than have the computer process the natural language, an alternative approach is to have an artificial language within which all queries and documents can be formulated. There is some evidence to show that this can be effective (Barber *et al.*[6]). Of course it presupposes that a user is willing to be taught to express his information need in the language.

When the retrieval system is on-line it is possible for the user to change his request during one search session in the light of a sample retrieval, thereby it is hoped improving the subsequent retrieval run. Such a procedure is commonly referred to as *feedback*. An example of a sophisticated on-line retrieval system is the MEDLINE system (McCarn and Leiter[7]). I think it is fair to say that it will be only a short time before all retrieval systems will be on-line.

Secondly, the processor, that part of the retrieval system concerned with the retrieval process. The process may involve structuring the information in some appropriate way, such as classifying it. It will also involve performing the actual retrieval function, that is, executing the search strategy in response to a query. In the diagram the documents have been placed in a separate box to emphasise the fact that they are not just input but can be used during the retrieval process in such a way that their structure is more correctly seen as part of the retrieval process.

7

Finally, we come to the output, which is usually a set of citations or document numbers. In an operational system the story ends here. However, in an experimental system it leaves the evaluation to be done.

IR in perspective

This section is not meant to constitute an attempt at an exhaustive and complete account of the historical development of IR. In any case it would not be able to improve on the accounts given by Cleverdon[8] and Salton[9]. Although information retrieval can be subdivided in many ways, it seems that there are three main areas of research which between them make up a considerable portion of the subject. They are: content analysis, information structures, and evaluation. Briefly the first is concerned with describing the contents of documents in a form suitable for computer processing; the second with exploiting relationships between documents to improve the efficiency and effectiveness of retrieval strategies; the third with the measurement of the effectiveness of retrieval.

Since the emphasis in this book is on a particular approach to document representation, I shall restrict myself here to a few remarks about its history. I am referring to the approach pioneered by Luhn[10]. He used frequency counts of words in the document text to determine which words were sufficiently significant to represent or characterise the document in the computer (more details about this in the next chapter). Thus a list of what might be called 'keywords' was derived for each document. In addition the frequency of occurrence of these words in the body of the text could also be used to indicate a degree of significance. This provided a simple weighting scheme for the 'keywords' in each list and made available a document representative in the form of a 'weighted keyword description'.

At this point it may be convenient to elaborate on the use of 'keyword'. It has become common practice in the IR literature to refer to descriptive items extracted from text as *keywords* or *terms*. Such items are often the outcome of some process such as, for example, the gathering together of different morphological variants of the same word. In this book keyword and term will be used interchangeably.

The use of statistical information about distributions of words in documents was further exploited by Maron and Kuhns[11] and Stiles[12] who obtained statistical associations between keywords. These associations provided a basis for the construction of a thesaurus as an aid to retrieval. Much of this early research was brought together with the publication of the 1964 Washington Symposium on *Statistical Association Methods for Mechanized Documentation* (Stevens *et al.*[13]).

Sparck Jones has carried on this work using measures of association between keywords based on their frequency of co-occurrence (that is, the frequency with which any two keywords occur together in the same document). She has shown[14] that such related words can be used effectively to improve recall, that is, to increase the proportion of the relevant documents which are retrieved. Interestingly, the early ideas of Luhn are still being developed and many automatic methods of characterisation are based on his early work.

The term information structure (for want of better words) covers specifically a logical organisation of information, such as document representatives, for the purpose of information retrieval. The development in information structures has been fairly recent. The main reason for the slowness of development in this area of information retrieval is that for a long time no one realised that computers would not give an acceptable retrieval time with a large document set unless some logical structure was imposed on it. In fact, owners of large data-bases are still loath to try out new organisation techniques promising faster and better retrieval. The slowness to recognise and adopt new techniques is mainly due to the scantiness of the experimental evidence backing them. The earlier experiments with document retrieval systems usually adopted a serial file organisation which, although it was efficient when a sufficiently large number of queries was processed simultaneously in a batch mode, proved inadequate if each query required a short real time response. The popular organisation to be adopted instead was the inverted file. By some this has been found to be restrictive (Salton[15]). More recently experiments have attempted to demonstrate the superiority of clustered files for on-line retrieval.

The organisation of these files is produced by an automatic classification method. Good[16] and Fairthorne[17] were among the first to suggest that automatic classification might prove useful in document retrieval. Not until several years later were serious experiments carried out in document clustering (Doyle[18]; Rocchio[19]). All experiments so far have been on a small scale. Since clustering only comes into its own when the scale is increased it is hoped that this book may encourage some large scale experiments by bringing together many of the necessary tools.

Evaluation of retrieval systems has proved extremely difficult. Senko[20] in an excellent survey paper states: 'Without a doubt system evaluation is the most troublesome area in ISR . . .', and I am inclined to agree. Despite excellent pioneering work done by Cleverdon et al.[21] in this area, and despite numerous measures of effectiveness that have been proposed (see Robertson[22, 23] for a substantial list), a general theory of evaluation had not emerged. I attempt to provide foundations for such a theory in Chapter 7 (page 168).

9

In the past there has been much debate about the validity of evaluations based on relevance judgments provided by erring human beings. Cuadra and Katter[24] supposed that relevance was measurable on an ordinal scale (one which arises from the operation of rank-ordering) but showed that the position of a document on such a scale was affected by external variables not usually controlled in the laboratory. Lesk and Salton[25] subsequently showed that a dichotomous scale on which a document is either relevant or non-relevant, when subjected to a certain probability of error, did not invalidate the results obtained for evaluation in terms of *precision* (the proportion of retrieved documents which are relevant) and *recall* (the proportion of relevant documents retrieved). Today effectiveness of retrieval is still mostly measured in terms of precision and recall or by measures based thereon. There is still no adequate statistical treatment showing how appropriate significance tests may be used (I shall return to this point in the Chapter on Evaluation, page 178). So, after a few decades of research in this area we basically have only precision and recall, and a working hypothesis which states, quoting Cleverdon[26]: 'Within a single system, assuming that a sequence of sub-searches for a particular question is made in the logical order of expected decreasing precision, and the requirements are those stated in the question, there is an inverse relationship between recall and precision, if the results of a number of different searches are averaged.'

Effectiveness and efficiency

Much of the research and development in information retrieval is aimed at improving the effectiveness and efficiency of retrieval. Efficiency is usually measured in terms of the computer resources used such as core, backing store, and C.P.U. time. It is difficult to measure efficiency in a machine independent way. In any case it should be measured in conjunction with effectiveness to obtain some idea of the benefit in terms of unit cost. In the previous section I mentioned that effectiveness is commonly measured in terms of precision and recall. I repeat here that *precision* is the ratio of the number of relevant documents retrieved to the total number of documents retrieved, and *recall* is the ratio of the number of relevant documents retrieved to the total number of relevant documents (both retrieved and not retrieved). The reason for emphasising these two measures is that frequent reference is made to retrieval effectiveness but its detailed discussion is delayed until Chapter 7. It will suffice until we reach that chapter to think of retrieval effectiveness in terms of precision and recall. It would have been possible to give the chapter on evaluation before any of the other material but this, in my view, would have been like putting the cart before the horse. Before we can appreciate the evaluation of observations we need to understand what gave rise to the observations. Hence I have delayed discussing evaluation until some understanding of what makes an information retrieval system tick has been gained. Readers not satisfied with this order can start by first reading Chapter 7 which in any case can be read independently.

Bibliographic remarks

The best introduction to information retrieval is probably got by reading some of the early papers in the field. Luckily many of these have now been collected in book form. I recommend for browsing the books edited by Garvin[27], Kochen[28], Borko[29], Schecter[30] and Saracevic[31]. It is also worth noting that some of the papers cited in *this* book may be found in one of these collections and be therefore readily accessible. A book which is well written and can be read without any mathematical background is one by Lancaster[2]. More recently a number of books have come out entirely devoted to information retrieval and allied topics, they are Doyle[32], Salton[33], Paice[34], and Kochen[35]. In particular the latter half of Doyle's book makes interesting reading since it describes what work in IR was like in the early days (the late 1950s to early 1960s). A critical view of information storage and retrieval is presented in the paper by Senko[20]. This paper is more suitable for people with a computer science background, and is particularly worth reading because of its healthy scepticism of the whole subject. Readers more interested in information retrieval in a library context should read Vickery[36].

One early publication worth reading which is rather hard to come by is the report on the Cranfield II project by Cleverdon *et al.*[21] This report is not really introductory material but constitutes in my view one of the milestones in information retrieval. It is an excellent example of the experimental approach to IR and contains many good ideas which have subsequently been elaborated in the open literature. Time spent on this report is well spent.

Papers on information retrieval have a tendency to get published in journals on computer science and library science. There are, however, a few major journals which are largely devoted to information retrieval. These are, *Journal of Documentation, Information Storage and*

11

Retrieval*, and *Journal of the American Society for Information Science.*

Finally, every year a volume in the series *Annual Review of Information Science and Technology* is edited by C. A. Cuadra. Each volume attempts to cover the new work published in information storage and retrieval for that year. As a source of references to the current literature it is unsurpassed. But they are mainly aimed at the practitioner and as such are a little difficult to read for the uninitiated.

References

1. SHANNON, C. E. and WEAVER, W., *The Mathematical Theory of Communication,* University of Illinois Press, Urbana (1964)
2. LANCASTER, F. W., *Information Retrieval Systems: Characteristics, Testing and Evaluation,* Wiley, New York (1968)
3. WINOGRAD, T., *Understanding Natural Language,* Edinburgh University Press, Edinburgh (1972)
4. MINSKY, M., *Semantic Information Processing,* MIT Press, Cambridge, Massachusetts (1968)
5. BAR-HILLEL, Y., *Language and Information. Selected Essays on their Theory and Application,* Addison-Wesley, Reading, Massachusetts (1964)
6. BARBER, A. S., BARRACLOUGH, E. D. and GRAY, W. A. 'On-line information retrieval as a scientist's tool', *Information Storage and Retrieval,* **9,** 429–440 (1973)
7. McCARN, D. B. and LEITER, J., 'On-line services in medicine and beyond', *Science,* **181,** 318–324 (1973)
8. CLEVERDON, C. W., 'Progress in documentation. Evaluation of information retrieval systems', *Journal of Documentation,* **26,** 55–67 (1970)
9. SALTON, G., 'Automatic text analysis', *Science,* **168,** 335–343 (1970)
10. LUHN, H. P., 'A statistical approach to mechanised encoding and searching of library information', *IBM Journal of Research and Development,* **1,** 309–317 (1957)
11. MARON, M. E. and KUHNS, J. L., 'On relevance, probabilistic indexing and information retrieval', *Journal of the ACM,* **7,** 216–244 (1960)
12. STILES, H. F., 'The association factor in information retrieval', *Journal of the ACM,* **8,** 271–279 (1961)
13. STEVENS, M. E., GIULIANO, V. E. and HEILPRIN, L. B., *Statistical Association Methods for Mechanised Documentation,* National Bureau of Standards, Washington (1964)
14. SPARCK JONES, K., *Automatic Keyword Classification for Information Retrieval,* Butterworths, London (1971)
15. SALTON, G., Paper given at the 1972 NATO Advanced Study Institute for on-line mechanised information retrieval systems (1972)
16. GOOD, I. J., 'Speculations concerning information retrieval', Research Report PC-78, IBM Research Centre, Yorktown Heights, New York (1958)
17. FAIRTHORNE, R. A., 'The mathematics of classification', *Towards Information Retrieval,* Butterworths, London, 1–10 (1961)

* Now called *Information Processing and Management.*

18. DOYLE, L. B., 'Is automatic classification a reasonable application of statistical analysis of text?', *Journal of the ACM,* **12,** 473–489 (1965)
19. ROCCHIO, J. J., 'Document retrieval systems–optimization and evaluation'. Ph.D. Thesis. Harvard University. Report ISR-10 to National Science Foundation, Harvard Computation Laboratory (1966)
20. SENKO, M. E., 'Information storage and retrieval systems'. In *Advances in Information Systems Science,* (Edited by J. Tou) Plenum Press, New York (1969)
21. CLEVERDON, C. W., MILLS, J. and KEEN, M., *Factors Determining the Performance of Indexing Systems,* Vol. I, *Design,* Vol. II, *Test Results,* ASLIB Cranfield Project, Cranfield (1966)
22. ROBERTSON, S. E., 'The parameter description of retrieval tests', Part 1; The basic parameters, *Journal of Documentation,* **25,** 1–27 (1969)
23. ROBERTSON, S. E., 'The parametric description of retrieval tests', Part 2; Overall measures, *Journal of Documentation,* **25,** 93–107 (1969)
24. CUADRA, A. C. and KATTER, R. V., 'Opening the black box of "relevance" ', *Journal of Documentation,* **23,** 291–303 (1967)
25. LESK, M. E. and SALTON, G., 'Relevance assessments and retrieval system evaluation', *Information Storage and Retrieval,* **4,** 343–359 (1969)
26. CLEVERDON, C. W., 'On the inverse relationship of recall and precision', *Journal of Documentation,* **28,** 195–201 (1972)
27. GARVIN, P. L., *Natural Language and the Computer,* McGraw-Hill, New York (1963)
28. KOCHEN, M., *The Growth of Knowledge–Readings on Organisation and Retrieval of Information,* Wiley, New York (1967)
29. BORKO, H., *Automated Language Processing,* Wiley, New York (1967)
30. SCHECTER, G., *Information Retrieval: A Critical View,* Academic Press, London (1967)
31. SARACEVIC, T., *Introduction to Information Science,* P.R. Bowker, New York and London (1970)
32. DOYLE, L. B., *Information Retrieval and Processing,* Melville Publishing Co., Los Angeles, California (1975)
33. SALTON, G., *Dynamic Information and Library Processing,* Prentice-Hall, Englewoods Cliffs, N.J. (1975)
34. PAICE, C. D., *Information Retrieval and the Computer,* Macdonald and Jane's, London (1977)
35. KOCHEN, M., *Principles of Information Retrieval,* Melville Publishing Co., Los Angeles, California (1974)
36. VICKERY, B. C., *Techniques of Information Retrieval,* Butterworths, London (1970)

Two

AUTOMATIC
TEXT ANALYSIS

Introduction

Before a computerised information retrieval system can actually
operate to retrieve some information, that information must have
already been stored inside the computer. Originally it will usually have
been in the form of documents. The computer, however, is not likely to
have stored the complete text of each document in the natural language
in which it was written. It will have instead, a document representative
which may have been produced from the documents either manually or
automatically.

The starting point of the text analysis process may be the complete
document text, an abstract, the title only, or perhaps a list of words
only. From it the process must produce a document representative in a
form which the computer can handle.

The developments and advances in the process of representation
have been reviewed every year by the appropriate chapters of Cuadra's
Annual Review of Information Science and Technology*. The reader is
referred to them for extensive references. The emphasis in this Chapter
is on the statistical (a word used loosely here: it usually simply implies
counting) rather than linguistic approaches to automatic text analysis.
The reasons for this emphasis are varied. Firstly, there is the limit on
space. Were I to attempt a discussion of semantic and syntactic
methods applicable to automatic text analysis, it would probably fill
another book. Luckily such a book has recently been written by Sparck
Jones and Kay[2]. Also Montgomery[3] has written a paper surveying

---

* Especially see the recent review by Damerau[1].

14

linguistics in information science. Secondly, linguistic analysis has proved to be expensive to implement and it is not clear how to use it to enhance information retrieval. Part of the problem has been that very little progress has been made in formal semantic theory. However, there is some reason for optimism on this front, see for example Keenan[4, 5]. Undoubtedly a theory of language will be of extreme importance to the development of intelligent IR systems. But, to date no such theory has been sufficiently developed for it to be applied successfully to IR. In any case satisfactory, possibly even very good, document retrieval systems can be built without such a theory. Thirdly, the statistical approach has been examined and tried ever since the days of Luhn and has been found to be moderately successful.

This chapter therefore starts with the original ideas of Luhn on which much of automatic text analysis has been built, and then goes on to describe a concrete way of generating document representatives. Furthermore, ways of exploiting and improving document representatives through weighting or classifying keywords are discussed. In passing, some of the evidence for automatic indexing is presented.

Luhn's ideas

In one of Luhn's[6] early papers he states: 'It is here proposed that the frequency of word occurrence in an article furnishes a useful measurement of word significance. It is further proposed that the relative position within a sentence of words having given values of significance furnish a useful measurement for determining the significance of sentences. The significance factor of a sentence will therefore be based on a combination of these two measurements.'

I think this quote fairly summarises Luhn's contribution to automatic text analysis. His assumption is that frequency data can be used to extract words and sentences to represent a document.

Let f be the frequency of occurence of various word types in a given position of text and r their rank order, that is, the order of their frequency of occurrence, then a plot relating f and r yields a curve similar to the hyperbolic curve in *Figure 2.1*. This is in fact a curve demonstrating Zipf's Law[7]* which states that the product of the frequency of use of words and the rank order is approximately constant. Zipf verified his law on American Newspaper English. Luhn used it as a null hypothesis to enable him to specify two cut-offs, an

* Also see, Fairthorne, R. A., 'Empirical hyperbolic distributions (Bradford–Zipf–Mandelbrot) for bibliometric description and prediction,' *Journal of Documentation*, **25**, 319–343 (1969).

upper and a lower (see *Figure 2.1*), thus excluding non-significant words. The words exceeding the upper cut-off were considered to be common and those below the lower cut-off rare, and therefore not contributing significantly to the content of the article. He thus devised a counting technique for finding significant words. Consistent with this he assumed that the resolving power of significant words, by which he meant the ability of words to discriminate content, reached a peak at a rank order position half way between the two cut-offs and from the peak fell off in either direction reducing to almost zero at the cut-off points. A certain arbitrariness is involved in determining the cut-offs. There is no oracle which gives their values. They have to be established by trial and error.

It is interesting that these ideas are really basic to much of the later work in IR. Luhn himself used them to devise a method of automatic abstracting. He went on to develop a numerical measure of significance for sentences based on the number of significant and non-significant words in each portion of the sentence. Sentences were ranked according to their numerical score and the highest ranking were included in the abstract (extract really). Edmundson and Wyllys[8] have gone on to generalise some of Luhn's work by normalising his measurements with respect to the frequency of occurrence of words in general text.

There is no reason why such an analysis should be restricted to just words. It could equally well be applied to stems of words (or phrases) and in fact this has often been done.

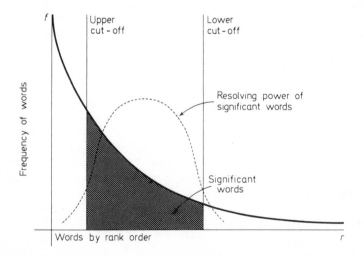

Figure 2.1. A plot of the hyperbolic curve relating f, the frequency of occurrence and r, the rank order (Adapted from Schultz[44] page 120)

Generating document representatives—conflation

Ultimately one would like to develop a text processing system which by means of computable methods with the minimum of human intervention will generate from the input text (full text, abstract, or title) a document representative adequate for use in an automatic retrieval system. This is a tall order and can only be partially met. The document representative I am aiming for is one consisting simply of a list of class names, each name representing a class of words occurring in the *total* input text. A document will be indexed by a name if one of its *significant* words occurs as a member of that class.

Such a system will usually consist of three parts: (1) removal of high frequency words, (2) suffix stripping, (3) detecting equivalent stems.

The removal of high frequency words, 'stop' words or 'fluff' words is one way of implementing Luhn's upper cut-off. This is normally done by comparing the input text with a 'stop list' of words which are to be removed.

Table 2.1 gives a portion of such a list, and demonstrates the kind of words that are involved. The advantages of the process are not only that non-significant words are removed and will therefore not interfere during retrieval, but also that the size of the total document file can be reduced by between 30 and 50 per cent.

The second stage, suffix stripping, is more complicated. A standard approach is to have a complete list of suffixes and to remove the longest possible one.

Table 2.2 lists some suffixes. Unfortunately, context free removal leads to a significant error rate. For example, we may well want UAL removed from FACTUAL but not from EQUAL. To avoid erroneously removing suffixes context rules are devised so that a suffix will be removed only if the context is right. 'Right' may mean a number of things:

(1) the length of remaining stem exceeds a given number; the default is usually 2;

(2) the stem-ending satisfies a certain condition, e.g. does not end with Q.

Many words, which are equivalent in the above sense, map to one morphological form by removing their suffixes. Others, unluckily, though they are equivalent, do not. It is this latter category which requires special treatment. Probably the simplest method of dealing with it is to construct a list of equivalent stem-endings. For two stems to be equivalent they must match except for their endings, which themselves must appear in the list as equivalent. For example stems such as ABSORB- and ABSORPT- are conflated because there is an

17

TABLE 2.1

A	CANNOT	INTO	OUR	THUS
ABOUT	CO	IS	OURS	TO
ABOVE	COULD	IT	OURSELVES	TOGETHER
ACROSS	DOWN	ITS	OUT	TOO
AFTER	DURING	ITSELF	OVER	TOWARD
AFTERWARDS	EACH	LAST	OWN	TOWARDS
AGAIN	EG	LATTER	PER	UNDER
AGAINST	EITHER	LATTERLY	PERHAPS	UNTIL
ALL	ELSE	LEAST	RATHER	UP
ALMOST	ELSEWHERE	LESS	SAME	UPON
ALONE	ENOUGH	LTD	SEEM	US
ALONG	ETC	MANY	SEEMED	VERY
ALREADY	EVEN	MAY	SEEMING	VIA
ALSO	EVER	ME	SEEMS	WAS
ALTHOUGH	EVERY	MEANWHILE	SEVERAL	WE
ALWAYS	EVERYONE	MIGHT	SHE	WELL
AMONG	EVERYTHING	MORE	SHOULD	WERE
AMONGST	EVERYWHERE	MOREOVER	SINCE	WHAT
AN	EXCEPT	MOST	SO	WHATEVER
AND	FEW	MOSTLY	SOME	WHEN
ANOTHER	FIRST	MUCH	SOMEHOW	WHENCE
ANY	FOR	MUST	SOMEONE	WHENEVER
ANYHOW	FORMER	MY	SOMETHING	WHERE
ANYONE	FORMERLY	MYSELF	SOMETIME	WHEREAFTER
ANYTHING	FROM	NAMELY	SOMETIMES	WHEREAS

ANYWHERE	FURTHER	NEITHER	SOMEWHERE	WHEREBY
ARE	HAD	NEVER	STILL	WHEREIN
AROUND	HAS	NEVERTHELESS	SUCH	WHEREUPON
AS	HAVE	NEXT	THAN	WHEREVER
AT	HE	NO	THAT	WHETHER
BE	HENCE	NOBODY	THE	WHITHER
BECAME	HER	NONE	THEIR	WHICH
BECAUSE	HERE	NOONE	THEM	WHILE
BECOME	HEREAFTER	NOR	THEMSELVES	WHO
BECOMES	HEREBY	NOTHING	THEN	WHOEVER
BECOMING	HEREIN	NOW	THENCE	WHOLE
BEEN	HEREUPON	NOWHERE	THERE	WHOM
BEFORE	HERS	OF	THEREAFTER	WHOSE
BEFOREHAND	HERSELF	OFF	THEREBY	WHY
BEHIND	HIM	OFTEN	THEREFORE	WILL
BEING	HIMSELF	ON	THEREIN	WITH
BELOW	HIS	ONCE	THEREUPON	WITHIN
BESIDE	HOW	ONE	THESE	WITHOUT
BESIDES	HOWEVER	ONLY	THEY	WOULD
BETWEEN	I	ONTO	THIS	YET
BEYOND	IE	OR	THOSE	YOU
BOTH	IF	OTHER	THOUGH	YOUR
BUT	IN	OTHERS	THROUGH	YOURS
BY	INC	OTHERWISE	THROUGHOUT	YOURSELF
CAN	INDEED		THRU	YOURSELVES

19

TABLE 2.2

ABILITIES	ALISES	ANCIAL	ARISABILITY	ASISINGFUL
ABILITY	ALISING	ANCIALS	ARISABLE	ASISINGLY
ABLE	ALISINGFUL	ANCIES	ARISATION	ASISINGS
ABLED	ALISINGLY	ANCING	ARISATIONS	ASIZABLE
ABLEDLY	ALISINGS	ANCINGFUL	ARISE	ASIZE
ABLENESS	ALISM	ANCINGLY	ARISED	ASIZED
ABLENESSES	ALISMS	ANCINGS	ARISEDLY	ASIZEDLY
ABLER	ALIST	ANCY	ARISER	ASIZER
ABLES	ALISTIC	ANEOUS	ARISES	ASIZES
ABLING	ALISTICALLY	ANEOUSLY	ARISING	ASIZING
ABLINGFUL	ALISTICISM	ANEOUSNESS	ARISINGFUL	ASIZINGFUL
ABLINGLY	ALISTICISMS	ANT	ARISINGLY	ASIZINGLY
ABLY	ALISTICS	ANTANEOUS	ARISINGS	ASIZINGS
ACEOUS	ALISTS	ANTANEOUSLY	ARISM	ASM
ACEOUSLY	ALITIES	ANTED	ARISMS	ASMS
ACEOUSNESS	ALITY	ANTEDLY	ARIST	AST
ACEOUSNESSES	ALIZATION	ANTIALITIES	ARISTIC	ASTIC
ACIES	ALIZATIONAL	ANTIALITY	ARISTICISM	ASTICAL
ACIDOUS	ALIZATIONALLY	ANTIALNESS	ARISTICISMS	ASTICALLY
ACIDOUSLY	ALIZATIONS	ANTIALNESSES	ARISTICS	ASTICISM
ACIOUSNESS	ALIZE	ANTIC	ARISTS	ASTICISMS
ACIOUSNESSES	ALIZED	ANTICISM	ARITIES	ASTICS
ACITIES	ALIZEDLY	ANTICISMS	ARITY	ASTMENT
ACITY	ALIZER	ANTICS	ARIZABILITIES	ASTMENTS
ACY	ALIZES	ANTING	ARIZABILITY	ASTRIES

AE	ALIZING	ANTINGFUL	ARIZABLE	ASTRY
AGE	ALIZINGFUL	ANTINGLY	ARIZATION	ASTS
AGED	ALIZINGLY	ANTINGS	ARIZATIONS	ASY
AGEDLY	ALIZINGS	ANTLY	ARIZE	ATA
AGER	ALLED	ANTMENT	ARISED	ATABILITIES
AGES	ALLEDLY	ANTMENTS	ARISEDLY	ATABILITY
AGING	ALLIC	ANTRESS	ARIZER	ATABLE
AGINGFUL	ALLICALLY	ANTRESSES	ARIZES	ATABLES
AGINGLY	ALLICISM	ANTRY	ARIZING	ATABLY
AIC	ALLICISMS	ANTS	ARIZINGFUL	ATAL
AICAL	ALLICS	AR	ARIZINGLY	ATE
AICALLY	ALLING	ARIAL	ARIZINGS	ATED
AICALS	ALLINGFUL	ARIALS	ARLY	ATEDLY
AICISM	ALLINGLY	ARIAN	AROID	ATELY
AICISMS	ALLMENT	ARIANS	AROIDS	ATENESS
AICS	ALLY	ARIC	ARS	ATENESSES
AL	ALMENT	ARICISM	ARY	ATER
ALISATION	ALNESS	ARICISMS	ASIS	ATES
ALISATIONAL	ALNESSES	ARICS	ASISE	ATIC
ALISATIONALLY	ALS	ARIES	ASISEABLE	ATICAL
ALISATIONS	ANCE	ARILINESS	ASISED	ATICALLY
ALISE	ANCED	ARILY	ASISEDLY	ATICISM
ALISED	ANCEDLY	ARINESS	ASISER	ATICISMS
ALISEDLY	ANCER	ARINESSES	ASISES	ATICS
ALISER	ANCES	ARISABILITIES	ASISING	ATING

entry in the list defining B and PT as equivalent stem-endings if the preceding characters match.

The assumption (in the context of IR) is that if two words have the same underlying stem then they refer to the same concept and should be indexed as such. This is obviously an over-simplification since words with the same stem, such as NEUTRON and NEUTRALISE, sometimes need to be distinguished. Even words which are essentially equivalent may mean different things in different contexts. Since there is no cheap way of making these fine distinctions we put up with a certain proportion of errors and assume (correctly) that they will not degrade retrieval effectiveness too much.

It is inevitable that a processing system such as this will produce errors. Fortunately experiments have shown that the error rate tends to be of the order of 5 per cent (Andrews[9]). Lovins [10,11] using a slightly different approach to stemming also quotes errors of the same order of magnitude.

My description of the three stages has been deliberately undetailed, only the underlying mechanism has been explained. An excellent description of a conflation algorithm, based on Lovins' paper[10] may be found in Andrews[9], where considerable thought is given to implementation efficiency.

Surprisingly, this kind of algorithm is not core limited but limited instead by its processing time.

The final output from a conflation algorithm is a set of classes, one for each stem detected. A class name is assigned to a document if and only if one of its members occurs as a significant word in the text of the document. A document representative then becomes a list of class names. These are often referred to as the documents *index terms* or *keywords*.

Queries are of course treated in the same way. In an experimental situation they can be processed at the same time as the documents. In an operational situation, the text processing system needs to be applied to the query at the time that it is submitted to the retrieval system.

Indexing

An *index* language is the language used to describe documents and requests. The elements of the index language are *index terms,* which may be *derived* from the text of the document to be described, or may be arrived at independently. Index languages may be described as *pre-coordinate* or *post-coordinate,* the first indicates that terms are coordinated at the time of indexing and the latter at the time of

22

searching. More specifically, in pre-coordinate indexing a logical combination of any index terms may be used as a label to identify a class of documents, whereas in post-coordinate indexing the same class would be identified at search time by combining the classes of documents labelled with the individual index terms.

One last distinction, the vocabulary of an index language may be *controlled* or *uncontrolled*. The former refers to a list of approved index terms that an indexer may use, such as for example used by MEDLARS. The controls on the language may also include hierarchic relationships between the index terms. Or, one may insist that certain terms can only be used as adjectives (or qualifiers). There is really no limit to the kind of syntactic controls one may put on a language.

The index language which comes out of the conflation algorithm in the previous section may be described as uncontrolled, post-coordinate and derived. The vocabulary of index terms at any stage in the evolution of the document collection is just the set of all conflation class names.

There is much controversy about the kind of index language which is best for document retrieval. The recommendations range from the complicated relational languages of Farradane *et al.*[12] and the Syntol group (see Coates[13] for a description) to the simple index terms extracted by text processing systems just described. The main debate is really about whether automatic indexing is as good as or better than manual indexing. Each can be done to various levels of complexity. However, there seems to be mounting evidence that in both cases, manual and automatic indexing, adding complexity in the form of controls more elaborate than index term weighting do not pay dividends. This has been demonstrated by the results obtained by Cleverdon *et al.*[14], Aitchison *et al.*[15], Comparative Systems Laboratory[16] and more recently Keen and Digger[17]. The message is that uncontrolled vocabularies based on natural language achieve retrieval effectiveness comparable to vocabularies with elaborate controls. This is extremely encouraging, since the simple index language is the easiest to automate.

Probably the most substantial evidence for automatic indexing has come out of the SMART Project (1966). Salton[18] recently summarised its conclusions: '... on the average the simplest indexing procedures which identify a given document or query by a set of terms, weighted or unweighted, obtained from document or query text are also the most effective'. Its recommendations are clear, automatic text analysis should use weighted terms derived from document excerpts whose length is at least that of a document abstract.

The document representatives used by the SMART project are more sophisticated than just the lists of stems extracted by conflation. There

23

is no doubt that stems rather than ordinary word forms are more effective (Carroll and Debruyn[19]). On top of this the SMART project adds index term weighting, where an index term may be a stem or some concept class arrived at through the use of various dictionaries. For details of the way in which SMART elaborates its document representatives see Salton[20].

In the next sections I shall give a simple discussion of the kind of frequency information that may be used to weight document descriptors and explain the use of automatically constructed term classes to aid retrieval.

Index term weighting

Traditionally the two most important factors governing the effectiveness of an index language have been thought to be the *exhaustivity* of indexing and the *specificity* of the index language. There has been much debate about the exact meaning of these two terms. Not wishing to enter into this controversy I shall follow Keen and Digger[17] in giving a working definition of each.

For any document, *indexing exhaustivity* is defined as the number of different topics indexed, and the *index language specificity* is the ability of the index language to describe topics precisely. Keen and Digger further define *indexing specificity* as the level of precision with which a document is *actually* indexed. It is very difficult to quantify these factors. Human indexers are able to rank their indexing approximately in order of increasing exhaustivity or specificity. However, the same is not easily done for *automatic* indexing.

It is of some importance to be able to quantify the notions of indexing exhaustivity and specificity because of the predictable effect they have on retrieval effectiveness. It has been recognised (Lancaster[21]) that a high level of exhaustivity of indexing leads to high recall* and low precision*. Conversely a low level of exhaustivity leads to low recall and high precision. The converse is true for levels of indexing specificity, high specificity leads to high precision and low recall, etc. It would seem, therefore, that there is an optimum level of indexing exhaustivity and specificity for a given user population.

Quite a few people (Sparck Jones[22, 23], Salton and Yang[24]), have attempted to relate these two factors to document collection statistics. For example, exhaustivity can be assumed to be related to the number of index terms assigned to a given document, and specificity related to the number of documents to which a given term is assigned in a given

---

* These terms are defined in the introduction on page 10.

collection. The importance of this rather vague relationship is that the two factors are related to the *distribution* of *index terms* in the collection. The relationships postulated are consistent with the observed trade-off between precision and recall just mentioned. Changes in the number of index terms per document lead to corresponding changes in the number of documents per term and vice versa.

I am arguing that in using distributional information about index terms to provide, say, index term weighting we are really attacking the old problem of controlling exhaustivity and specificity.

If we go back to Luhn's original ideas, we remember that he postulated a varying discrimination power for index terms as a function of the rank order of their frequency of occurrence, the highest discrimination power being associated with the middle frequencies. His model was proposed for the selection of significant terms from a document. However, the same frequency counts can be used to provide a weighting scheme for the individual terms in a document. In fact there is a common weighting scheme in use which gives each index term a weight directly proportional to its frequency of occurrence in the document. At first this scheme would appear to be inconsistent with Luhn's hypothesis that the discrimination power drops off at higher frequencies. However, referring back to *Figure 2.1,* the scheme would be consistent if the upper cut-off is moved to the point where the peak occurs. It is likely that this is in fact what has happened in experiments using this particular form of weighting.

Attempts have been made to apply weighting based on the way the index terms are distributed in the entire collection. The index term vocabulary of a document collection often has a Zipfian distribution, that is, if we count the number of documents in which each index term occurs and plot them according to rank order then we obtain the usual hyperbolic shape. Sparck Jones[22] showed experimentally that if there are N documents and an index term occurs in n of them then a weight of $\log(N/n) + 1$ leads to more effective retrieval than if the term were used unweighted. If indexing specificity is assumed to be inversely proportional to the number of documents in which an index term occurs then the weighting can be seen to be attaching more importance to the more specific terms.

The difference between the last mode of weighting and the previous one may be summarised by saying that document frequency weighting places emphasis on content description whereas weighting by specificity attempts to emphasise the ability of terms to discriminate one document from another.

Salton and Yang[24] have recently attempted to combine both methods of weighting by looking at both *inter* document frequencies and *intra* document frequencies. Their conclusions are really an extension of those reached by Luhn. By considering both the total frequency of occurrence of a term and its distribution over the documents, that is, how many times it occurs in each document, they were able to draw several conclusions. A term with high total frequency of occurrence is not very useful in retrieval irrespective of its distribution. Middle frequency terms are most useful particularly if the distribution is skewed. Rare terms with a skewed distribution are likely to be useful but less so than the middle frequency ones. Very rare terms are also quite useful but come bottom of the list except for the ones with a high total frequency. The experimental evidence for these conclusions is insufficient to make a more precise statement of their merits.

Salton and his co-workers have developed an interesting tool for describing whether an index is 'good' or 'bad'. They assume that a good index term is one which, when assigned as an index term to a collection of documents, renders the documents as dissimilar as possible, whereas a bad term is one which renders the documents more similar. This is quantified through a *term discrimination value* which for a particular term measures the increase or decrease in the average dissimilarity between documents on the removal of that term. Therefore a good term is one which on removal from the collection of documents leads to a decrease in the average dissimilarity (adding it would hence lead to an increase), whereas a bad term is one which leads on removal to an increase. The idea is that a greater separation between documents will enhance retrieval effectiveness but that less separation will depress retrieval effectiveness. Although superficially this appears reasonable what really is required is that the relevant documents become less separated in relation to the non-relevant ones. Experiments using the term discrimination model have been reported[25, 26]. A connection between term discrimination and *inter* document frequency has also been made supporting the earlier results reported by Salton, Wong and Yang[27]. The main results have been conveniently summarised by Yu and Salton[28], where also some formal proofs of retrieval effectiveness improvement are given for strategies based on frequency data. For example, the inverse document frequency weighting scheme described above, that is assigning a weight proportional to $\log (N/n) + 1$, is shown to be formally more effective than not using these weights. Of course to achieve a proof of this kind some specific assumptions about how to measure effectiveness and how to match documents with queries have to be made. They also establish the effectiveness of a technique used to conflate low frequency terms, which increases recall, and of a technique used to combine high frequency terms into phrases, which increases precision.

26

Probabilistic indexing

In the past few years a detailed quantitative model for automatic indexing based on some statistical assumptions about the distribution of words in text has been worked out by Bookstein, Swanson, and Harter[29, 30, 31]. The difference between the terms *word-type* and *word-token* is crucial to the understanding of their model. A token instantiates a type, so that it is possible to refer to the occurrence of a world-type WAR; then a particular occurrence at one point in the text of a document (or abstract) will be a word-token. Hence 'the frequency of occurrence of word *w* in a document' means the number of word-tokens occurring in that document corresponding to a unique word-type. The type/token qualification of a word will be dropped whenever the context makes it clear what is meant when I simply refer to a 'word'.

In their model they consider the difference in the distributional behaviour of words as a guide to whether a word should be assigned as an index term. Their starting point has been the much earlier work by Stone and Rubinoff[32], Damerau[33], and Dennis[34] who showed that the statistical behaviour of 'speciality' words was different from that of 'function' words. They found that function words were closely modelled by a Poisson distribution over all documents whereas specialty words did not follow a Poisson distribution. Specifically, if one is looking at the distribution of a function word *w* over a set of texts then the probability, $f(n)$, that a text will have n occurrences of the function word *w* is given by

$$f(n) = \frac{e^{-x}x^n}{n!}$$

In general the parameter x will vary from word to word, and for a given word should be proportional to the length of the text. We also interpret x as the mean number of occurrences of the *w* in the set of texts.

The Bookstein–Swanson–Harter model assumes that specialty words are 'content-bearing' whereas function words are not. What this means is that a word randomly distributed according to a Poisson distribution is not informative about the document in which it occurs. At the same time the fact that a word does *not* follow a Poisson distribution is assumed to indicate that it conveys information as to what a document is about. This is not an unreasonable view: knowing that the specialty word WAR occurs in the collection one would expect it to occur only in the relatively few documents that are about WAR. On the other hand, one would expect a typical function word such as FOR to be randomly distributed.

27

The model also assumes that a document can be about a word to *some degree*. This implies that in general a document collection can be broken up into subsets; each subset being made up of documents that are about a given word to the *same degree*. The fundamental hypothesis made now is that a content-bearing word is a word that distinguishes more than one class of documents with respect to the extent to which the topic referred to by the word is treated in the documents in each class. It is precisely these words that are the candidates for index terms. These content-bearing words can be mechanically detected by measuring the extent to which their distributions deviate from that expected under a Poisson process. In this model the status of one of these content words within a subset of documents of the same 'aboutness' is one of non-content-bearing, that is, within the given subset it does not discriminate between further subsets.

Harter[31] has identified two assumptions, based upon which the above ideas can be used to provide a method of automatic indexing. The aim is to specify a rule that for any given document will assign it index terms selected from the list of candidates. The assumptions are:

(1) The probability that a document will be found relevant to a request for information on a subject is a function of the relative extent to which the topic is treated in the document.
(2) The number of tokens in a document is a function* of the extent to which the subject referred to by the word is treated in the document.

In these assumptions a 'topic' is identified with the 'subject of the request' and with the 'subject referred to by the word'. Also, only single word requests are considered, although Bookstein and Kraft[35] in a more recent paper have attempted an extension to multi-word requests. The indexing rule based on these assumptions indexes a document with word *w* if and only if the probability of the document being judged relevant to a request for information on *w* exceeds some cost function. To calculate the required probability of relevance for a content-bearing word we need to postulate what its distribution would look like. We know that it cannot be a single Poisson distribution, and that it is intrinsic to a content-bearing word that it will distinguish between subsets of documents differing in the extent to which they treat the topic specified by the word. By assumption (2), within one of these subsets the distribution of a content-bearing can however be described by a Poisson process. Therefore if there are only two such

---

* Although Harter[31] uses 'function' in his wording of this assumption I think 'measure' would have been more appropriate.

subsets differing in the extent to which they are about a word w then the distribution of w can be described by a mixture of two Poisson distributions. Specifically, with the same notation as before we have

$$f(n) = \frac{p_1 e^{-x_1} x_1^{\,n}}{n!} + \frac{(1-p_1) e^{-x_2} x_2^{\,n}}{n!}$$

here p_1 is the probability of a random document belonging to one of the subsets and x_1 and x_2 are the mean occurrences in the two classes. This expression shows why the model is sometimes called the *2-Poisson model*. It is important to note that it describes the statistical behaviour of a content-bearing word over two classes which are 'about' that word to different extents, these classes are not necessarily the relevant and non-relevant documents although by assumption (1) we can calculate the probability of relevance for any document from one of these classes. It is the ratio

$$\frac{p_1 e^{-x_1} x_1^{\,k}}{p_1 e^{-x_1} x_1^{\,k} + (1-p_1) e^{-x_2} x_2^{\,k}}$$

that is used to make the decision whether to assign an index term w that occurs k times in a document. This ratio is in fact the probability that the particular document belongs to the class which treats w to an average extent of x_1 given that it contains exactly k occurrences of w. This ratio is compared with some cost function based on the cost a user is prepared to attach to errors the system might make in retrieval. The details of its specification can be found in the cited papers.

Finally although tests have shown that this model assigns 'sensible' index terms, it has not been tested from the point of view of its effectiveness in retrieval. Ultimately that will determine whether it is acceptable as a model for automatic indexing.

Discrimination and/or representation

There are two conflicting ways of looking at the problem of characterising documents for retrieval. One is to characterise a document through a representation of its contents, regardless of the way in which other documents may be described, this might be called *representation without discrimination*. The other way is to insist that in characterising a document one is discriminating it from all, or potentially all, other documents in the collection, this we might call *discrimination without representation*. Naturally, neither of these extreme positions is assumed in practice, although identifying the two is useful when thinking about the problem of characterisation.

In practice one seeks some sort of optimal trade-off between representation and discrimination. Traditionally this has been attempted through balancing indexing exhaustively against specificity. Most automatic methods of indexing can be seen to be a mix of representation versus discrimination. In the simple case of removing high frequency words by means of a 'stop' word list we are attempting to increase the level of discrimination between document. Salton's methods based on the discrimination value attempts the same thing. However it should be clear that when removing possible index terms there must come a stage when the remaining ones cannot adequately represent the contents of documents any more. Bookstein–Swanson–Harter's formal model can be looked upon as one in which the importance of a term in representing the contents of a document is balanced against its importance as a discriminator. They in fact attempt to attach a cost function to the trade-off between the two.

The emphasis on representation leads to what one might call a document-orientation: that is, a total preoccupation with modelling what the document is about. This approach will tend to shade into work on artificial intelligence, particularly of the kind concerned with constructing computer models of the contents of any given piece of natural language text. The relevance of this work in AI, as well as other work, has been conveniently summarised by Smith[36].

This point of view is also adopted by those concerned with defining a concept of 'information', they assume that once this notion is properly explicated a document can be represented by the 'information' it contains[37].

The emphasis on discrimination leads to a query-orientation. This way of looking at things presupposes that one can predict the population of queries likely to be submitted to the IR system. In the light of data about this population of queries one can then try and characterise documents in an optimal fashion. Recent work attempting to formalise this approach in terms of utility theory has been done by Maron and Cooper[38, 39], although it is difficult to see at this stage how it might be automated.

Automatic keyword classification

Many automatic retrieval systems rely on thesauri to modify queries and document representatives to improve the chance of retrieving relevant documents. Salton[40] has experimented with many different kinds of thesauri and concluded that many of the simple ones justify themselves in terms of improved retrieval effectiveness.

In practice many of the thesauri are constructed manually. They have mainly been constructed in two ways:

(1) words which are deemed to be about the same topic are linked;
(2) words which are deemed to be about related things are linked.

The first kind of thesaurus connects words which are intersubstitutible, that is, it puts them into equivalence classes. Then one word could be chosen to represent each class and a list of these words could be used to form a controlled vocabulary. From this an indexer could be instructed to select the words to index a document, or the user could be instructed to select the words to express his query. The same thesaurus could be used in an automatic way to identify the words of a query for the purpose of retrieval.

The second kind of thesaurus uses semantic links between words to, for example, relate them hierarchically. The manually constructed thesaurus used by the MEDLARS system is of this type.

However, methods have been proposed to construct thesauri automatically. Whereas the manual thesauri are semantically based (e.g. they recognise synonyms, more general, or more specific relationships) the automatic thesauri tend to be syntactically and statistically based. Again the use of syntax has proved to be of little value so I shall concentrate on the statistical methods. These are based mainly on the patterns of co-occurrence of words in documents. These 'words' are often the descriptive items which were introduced earlier as terms or keywords.

The basic relationship underlying the automatic construction of keyword classes is as follows. If keyword a and b are substitutible for one another in the sense that we are prepared to accept a document containing one in response to a request containing the other, this will be because they have the same meaning or refer to a common subject or topic. One way of finding out whether two keywords are related is by looking at the documents in which they occur. If they tend to co-occur in the *same* documents the chances are that they have to do with the same subject and so can be substituted for one another.

It is not difficult to see that based on this principle a classification of keywords can be automatically constructed, of which the classes are used analogously to those of the manual thesaurus mentioned before. More specifically we can identify two main approaches to the use of keyword classifications:

(1) replace each keyword in a document (and query) representative by the name of the class in which it occurs;
(2) replace each keyword by all the keywords occurring in the class to which it belongs.

If we think of a simple retrieval strategy as operating by matching on the descriptors, whether they be keyword names or class names, then 'expanding' representatives in either of these ways will have the effect of increasing the number of matches between document and query, and hence tends to improve recall*. The second way will improve precision as well. Sparck Jones[41] has reported a large number of experiments using automatic keyword classifications and found that in general one obtained a better retrieval performance with the aid of automatic keyword classification than with the unclassified keywords alone.

Unfortunately even here the evidence has not been conclusive. The work by Minker *et al.*[42] has not confirmed the findings of Sparck Jones, and in fact they have shown that in some cases keyword classification can be detrimental to retrieval effectiveness. Salton[43], in a review of the work of Minker *et al.*, has questioned their experimental design which leaves the question of the effectiveness of keyword classification still to be resolved by further research.

The discussion of keyword classifications has by necessity been rather sketchy. Readers wishing to pursue it in greater depth should consult Sparck Jones's book[41] on the subject. We shall briefly return to it when we discuss automatic classification methods in Chapter 3.

Normalisation

It is probably useful at this stage to recapitulate and show how a number of *levels* of *normalisation* of text is involved in generating document representatives. At the lowest level we have the document which is merely described by a string of words. The first step in normalisation is to remove the 'fluff' words. We now have what traditionally might have been called the 'keywords'. The next stage might be to conflate these words into classes and describe documents by sets of class names which in modern terminology are the keywords or index terms. The next level is the construction of keyword classes by automatic classification. Strictly speaking this is where the normalisation stops.

Index term weighting can also be thought of as a process of normalisation, if the weighting scheme takes into account the number of different index terms per document. For example we may wish to ensure that a match in one term among ten carries more weight than one among twenty. Similarly, the process of weighting by frequency of occurrence in the total document collection is an attempt to normalise document representatives with respect to expected *frequency* distributions.

* Recall is defined in the introduction.

Bibliographic remarks

The early work of H. P. Luhn has been emphasised in this chapter. Therefore, the reader may like to consult the book by Schultz [44] which contains a selection of his papers. In particular, it contains his 1957 and 1958 papers cited in the text. Some other early papers which have had an impact on indexing are Maron and Kuhns [45], and its sequel in Maron [46]. The first paper contains an attempt to construct a probabilistic model for indexing. Batty [47] provides useful background information to the early work on automatic keyword classification. An interesting paper which seems to have been largely ignored in the IR literature is Simon [48]. Simon postulates a stochastic process which will generate a distribution for word frequencies similar to the Zipfian distribution. Doyle [49] examines the role of statistics in text analysis. A recent paper by Sparck Jones [50] compares many of the different approaches to index term weighting. A couple of state-of-the-art reports on automatic indexing are Stevens [51] and Sparck Jones [52]. Salton [53] has compiled a report containing a theory of indexing. Borko [54] has provided a convenient summary of some theoretical approaches to indexing. For an interesting attack on the use of statistical methods in indexing, see Ghose and Dhawle [55].

References

1. DAMERAU, F. J., 'Automated language processing', *Annual Review of Information Science and Technology,* **11,** 107–161 (1976)
2. SPARCK JONES, K. and KAY, M., *Linguistics and Information Science,* Academic Press. New York and London (1973)
3. MONTGOMERY, C. A., 'Linguistics and information science', *Journal of the American Society for Information Science,* **23,** 195–219 (1972)
4. KEENAN, E. L., 'On semantically based grammar', *Linguistic Inquiry,* **3,** 413–461 (1972)
5. KEENAN, E. L., *Formal Semantics of Natural Language,* Cambridge University Press (1975)
6. LUHN, H. P., 'The automatic creation of literature abstracts', *IBM Journal of Research and Development,* **2,** 159–165 (1958)
7. ZIPF, H. P., *Human Behavior and the Principle of Least Effort,* Addison-Wesley, Cambridge, Massachusetts (1949)
8. EDMONDSON, H. P. and WYLLYS, R. E., 'Automatic abstracting and indexing survey and recommendations', *Communications of the ACM,* **4,** 226–234 (1961)
9. ANDREWS, K., 'The development of a fast conflation algorithm for English'. Dissertation submitted for the Diploma in Computer Science, University of Cambridge (unpublished) (1971)
10. LOVINS, B. J., 'Development of a stemming algorithm'. *Mechanical Translation and Computational Linguistics,* **11,** 22–31 (1968)
11. LOVINS, B. J., 'Error evaluation for stemming algorithms as clustering algorithms', *Journal of the American Society for Information Science,* **22,** 28–40 (1971)

12. FARRADANE, J., RUSSELL, J.M. and YATES-MERCER, A., 'Problems in information retrieval. Logical jumps in the expression of information', *Information Storage and Retrieval*, **9**, 65–77 (1973)

13. COATES, E. J., 'Some properties of relationships in the structure of indexing languages', *Journal of Documentation*, **29**, 390–404 (1973)

14. CLEVERDON, C. W., MILLS, J. and KEEN, M., *Factors Determining the Performance of Indexing Systems*, Vol. I, *Design*, Vol. II, *Test Results*, ASLIB Cranfield Project, Cranfield (1966)

15. AITCHISON, T. M., HALL, A. M., LAVELLE, K. H. and TRACY, J. M., *Comparative Evaluation of Index Languages*, Part I, *Design*, Part II, *Results*, Project INSPEC, Institute of Electrical Engineers, London (1970)

16. Comparative Systems Laboratory, *An Inquiry into Testing of Information Retrieval Systems*, 3 Vols. Case-Western Reserve University (1968)

17. KEEN, E. M. and DIGGER, J. A., *Report of an Information Science Index Languages Test*, Aberystwyth College of Librarianship, Wales (1972)

18. SALTON, G., 'Automatic text analysis', *Science*, **168**, 335–343 (1970)

19. CARROLL, J. M. and DEBRUYN, J. G., 'On the importance of root-stem truncation in word-frequency analysis', *Journal of the American Society for Information Science*, **21**, 368–369 (1970)

20. SALTON, G., *Automatic Information Organization and Retrieval*, McGraw-Hill, New York (1968)

21. LANCASTER, F. W., *Information Retrieval Systems: Characteristics, Testing and Evaluation*, Wiley, New York (1968)

22. SPARCK JONES, K., 'A statistical interpretation of term specificity and its application in retrieval', *Journal of Documentation*, **28**, 11–21 (1972)

23. SPARCK JONES, K., 'Does indexing exhaustivity matter?', *Journal of the American Society for Information Science*, **24**, 313–316 (1973)

24. SALTON, G. and YANG, C. S., 'On the specification of term values in automatic indexing', *Journal of Documentation*, **29**, 351–372 (1973)

25. SALTON, G., YANG, C. S. and YU, C. T., 'A theory of term importance in automatic text analysis', *Journal of the American Society for Information Science*, **26**, 33–44 (1975)

26. SALTON, G., WONG, A. and YU, C. T., 'Automatic indexing using term discrimination and term precision measurements', *Information Processing and Management*, **12**, 43–51 (1976)

27. SALTON, G., WONG, A. and YANG, S. S., 'A vector space model for automatic indexing', *Communications of the ACM*, **18**, 613–620 (1975)

28. YU, C. T. and SALTON, G., 'Effective information retrieval using term accuracy', *Communications of the ACM*, **20**, 135–142 (1977)

29. BOOKSTEIN, A. and SWANSON, D. R., 'Probabilistic models for automatic indexing', *Journal of the American Society for Information Science*, **25**, 312–318 (1974)

30. BOOKSTEIN, A. and SWANSON, D. R., 'A decision theoretic foundation for indexing', *Journal of the American Society for Information Science*, **26**, 45–50 (1975)

31. HARTER, S. P., 'A probabilistic approach to automatic keyword indexing, Part 1: On the distribution of speciality words in a technical literature, Part 2: An algorithm for probabilistic indexing', *Journal of the American Society for Information Science*, **26**, 197–206 and 280–289 (1975)

32. STONE, D. C. and RUBINOFF, M., 'Statistical generation of a technical vocabulary', *American Documentation*, **19**, 411–412 (1968)

33. DAMERAU, F. J., 'An experiment in automatic indexing', *American Documentation*, **16**, 283–289 (1965)

34. DENNIS, S. F., 'The design and testing of a fully automatic indexing–searching system for documents consisting of expository text', In: *Information Retrieval: A Critical Review* (Edited by G. Schecter), Thompson Book Co., Washington D.C., 67–94 (1967)
35. BOOKSTEIN, A. and KRAFT, D., 'Operations research applied to document indexing and retrieval decisions', *Journal of the ACM*, **24**, 418–427 (1977)
36. SMITH, L. C., 'Artificial intelligence in information retrieval systems', *Information Processing and Management*, **12**, 189–222 (1976)
37. BELKIN, N. J., 'Information concepts for information science', *Journal of Documentation*, **34**, 55–85 (1978)
38. MARON, M. E., 'On indexing, retrieval and the meaning of about', *Journal of the American Society for Information Science*, **28**, 38–43 (1977)
39. COOPER, W. S. and MARON, M. E., 'Foundations of probabilistic and utility-theoretic indexing', *Journal of the ACM*, **25**, 67–80 (1978)
40. SALTON, G., 'Experiments in automatic thesaurus construction for information retrieval', *Proceedings IFIP Congress 1971*, **TA-2**, 43–49 (1971)
41. SPARCK JONES, K., *Automatic Keyword Classification for Information Retrieval*, Butterworths, London (1971)
42. MINKER, J., WILSON, G. A. and ZIMMERMAN, B. H., 'An evaluation of query expansion by the addition of clustered terms for a document retrieval system', *Information Storage and Retrieval*, **8**, 329–348 (1972)
43. SALTON, G., 'Comment on "an evaluation of query expansion by the addition of clustered terms for a document retrieval system".' *Computing Reviews*, **14**, 232 (1973)
44. SCHULTZ, C. K., *H. P. Luhn: Pioneer of Information Science—Selected Works*, Macmillan, London (1968)
45. MARON, M. E. and KUHNS, J. L., 'On relevance, probabilistic indexing and information retrieval', *Journal of the ACM*, **7**, 216–244 (1960)
46. MARON, M. E., 'Automatic indexing: an experimental enquiry', *Journal of the ACM*, **8**, 404–417 (1961)
47. BATTY, C. D., 'Automatic generation of indexing languages', *Journal of Documentation*, **25**, 142–151 (1969)
48. SIMON, H. A., 'On a class of skew distributions', *Biometrika*, **42**, 425–440 (1955)
49. DOYLE, L. B., 'The microstatistics of text', *Information Storage and Retrieval*, **1**, 189–214 (1963)
50. SPARCK JONES, K., 'Index term weighting', *Information Storage and Retrieval*, **9**, 619–633 (1973)
51. STEVENS, M. E., *Automatic Indexing: A State of the Art Report*, Monograph 91, National Bureau of Standards, Washington (1965)
52. SPARCK JONES, K., *Automatic Indexing: A State of the Art Review*, review commissioned by the Office for Scientific and Technical Information, London (1974)
53. SALTON, G., *A Theory of Indexing*, Technical report No. TR74-203, Department of Computer Science, Cornell University, Ithaca, New York (1974)
54. BORKO, H., 'Toward a theory of indexing', *Information Processing and Management*, **13**, 355–365 (1977)
55. GHOSE, A. and DHAWLE, A. S., 'Problems of thesaurus construction', *Journal of the American Society for Information Science*, **28**, 211–217 (1977)

Three
AUTOMATIC
CLASSIFICATION

Introduction

In this chapter I shall attempt to present a coherent account of classification in such a way that the principles involved will be sufficiently understood for anyone wishing to use classification techniques in IR to do so without too much difficulty. The emphasis will be on their application in document clustering, although many of the ideas are applicable to pattern recognition, automatic medical diagnosis, and keyword clustering.

A formal definition of classification will not be attempted; for our purposes it is sufficient to think of classification as describing the process by which a classificatory system is constructed. The word 'classification' is also used to describe the result of such a process. Although indexing is often thought of (wrongly I think) as 'classification' we specifically exclude this meaning. A further distinction to be made is between 'classification' and 'diagnosis'. Everyday language is very ambiguous on this point:

'How would you classify (identify) this?'
'How are these best classified (grouped)?'

The first example refers to diagnosis whereas the second talks about classification proper. These distinctions have been made before in the literature by Kendall[1] and Jardine and Sibson[2].

In the context of information retrieval, a classification is required for a purpose. Here I follow Macnaughton-Smith[3] who states: 'All classifications, even the most general are carried out for some more or less explicit "special purpose" or set of purposes which should

36

influence the choice of [classification] method and the results obtained.' The purpose may be to group the documents in such a way that retrieval will be faster or alternatively it may be to construct a thesaurus automatically. Whatever the purpose the 'goodness' of the classification can finally only be measured by its performance during retrieval. In this way we can side-step the debate about 'natural' and 'best' classifications and leave it to the philosophers (see for example Hempel[4]).

There are two main areas of application of classification methods in IR:

(1) keyword clustering;
(2) document clustering.

The first area is very well dealt with in a recent book by Sparck Jones[5]. Document clustering, although recommended forcibly by Salton and his co-workers, has had very little impact. One possible reason is that the details of Salton's work on document clustering became submerged under the welter of experiments performed on the SMART system. Another is possibly that as the early enthusiasm for clustering waned, the realisation dawned that significant experiments in this area required quantities of expensive data and large amounts of computer time.

Good[6] and Fairthorne[7] were amongst the first to recommend that automatic classification might prove useful in document retrieval. A clear statement of what is implied by document clustering was made early on by R. M. Hayes[8]: 'We define the organisation as the grouping together of items (e.g. documents, representations of documents) which are then handled as a unit and lose, to that extent, their individual identities. In other words, classification of a document into a classification slot, to all intents and purposes identifies the document with that slot. Thereafter, it and other documents in the slot are treated as identical until they are examined individually. It would appear, therefore, that documents are grouped because they are in some sense related to each other; but more basically, they are grouped because they are likely to be *wanted* together, and logical relationship is the means of measuring this likelihood,' In the main people have achieved the 'logical organisation' in two different ways. Firstly through direct classification of the documents, and secondly via the intermediate calculation of a measure of closeness between documents. The first approach has proved theoretically to be intractable so that any experimental test results cannot be considered to be reliable. The second approach to classification is fairly well documented now, and above all, there are some forceful arguments recommending it in a particular form. It is this approach which is to be emphasised here.

The efficiency of document clustering has been emphasised by

37

Salton[9], he says: 'Clearly in practice it is not possible to match each analysed document with each analysed search request because the time consumed by such operation would be excessive. Various solutions have been proposed to reduce the number of needed comparisons between information items and requests. A particular promising one generates groups of related documents, using an automatic document matching procedure. A representative document *group vector* is then chosen for each document group, and a search request is initially checked against all the group vectors only. Thereafter, the request is checked against only those individual documents where group vectors show a high score with the request.' Salton believes that although document clustering saves time it necessarily reduces the effectiveness of a retrieval system. I believe a case has been made showing that on the contrary document clustering has *potential* for improving the effectiveness (Jardine and Van Rijsbergen[10]).

Measures of association

Some classification methods are based on a binary relationship between objects. On the basis of this relationship a classification method can construct a system of clusters. The relationship is described variously as 'similarity', 'association' and 'dissimilarity'. Ignoring dissimilarity for the moment as it will be defined mathematically later, the other two terms mean much the same except that 'association' will be reserved for the similarity between objects characterised by discrete-state attributes. The measure of similarity is designed to quantify the likeness between objects so that if one assumes it is possible to group objects in such a way that an object in a group is more like the other members of the group than it is like any object outside the group, then a cluster method enables such a group structure to be discovered.

Informally speaking, a measure of association increases as the number or proportion of shared attribute states increases. Numerous coefficients of association have been described in the literature, see for example Goodman and Kruskal[11,12], Kuhns[13], Cormack[14] and Sneath and Sokal[15]. Several authors have pointed out that the difference in retrieval performance achieved by different measures of association is insignificant, providing that these are appropriately normalised. Intuitively one would expect this since most measures incorporate the same information. Lerman[16] has investigated the mathematical relationship between many of the measures and has shown that many are monotone with respect to each other. It follows that a cluster method depending only on the rank-ordering of the association values would give identical clusterings for all these measures.

There are five commonly used measures of association in information retrieval. Since in information retrieval documents and requests are most commonly represented by term or keyword lists, I shall simplify matters by assuming that an object is represented by a set of keywords and that the counting measure | . | gives the size of the set. We can easily generalise to the case where the keywords have been weighted, by simply choosing an appropriate measure (in the measure-theoretic sense).

The simplest of all association measures is

$$|X \cap Y| \qquad \text{\textit{Simple matching coefficient}}$$

which is the number of shared index terms. This coefficient does not take into account the sizes of X and Y. The following coefficients which have been used in document retrieval take into account the information provided by the sizes of X and Y.

$$2 \frac{|X \cap Y|}{|X| + |Y|} \qquad \text{\textit{Dice's coefficient}}$$

$$\frac{|X \cap Y|}{|X \cup Y|} \qquad \text{\textit{Jaccard's coefficient}}$$

$$\frac{|X \cap Y|}{|X|^{1/2} \times |Y|^{1/2}} \qquad \text{\textit{Cosine coefficient}}$$

$$\frac{|X \cap Y|}{\min(|X|, |Y|)} \qquad \text{\textit{Overlap coefficient}}$$

These may all be considered to be normalised versions of the simple matching coefficient. Failure to normalise leads to counter intuitive results as the following example shows:

$$\text{If} \qquad S_1(X, Y) = |X \cap Y| \qquad S_2(X, Y) = \frac{2|X \cap Y|}{|X| + |Y|}$$

$$\text{then} \quad |X_1| = 1 \; |Y_1| = 1 \qquad |X_1 \cap Y_2| = 1 \Rightarrow S_1 = 1 \; S_2 = 1$$

$$|X_2| = 10 \; |Y_2| = 10 \qquad |X_2 \cap Y_2| = 1 \Rightarrow S_1 = 1 \; S_2 = 1/10$$

$S_1(X_1, Y_1) = S_1(X_2, Y_2)$ which is clearly absurd since X_1 and Y_1 are identical representatives whereas X_2 and Y_2 are radically different. The normalisation for S_2, scales it between 0 and 1, maximum similarity being indicated by 1.

Doyle[17] hinted at the importance of normalisation in an amusing way: 'One would regard the postulate "All documents are created equal" as being a reasonable foundation for a library description. Therefore one would like to count either documents or things which

39

pertain to documents, such as index tags, being careful of course to deal with the same number of index tags for each document. Obviously, if one decides to describe the library by counting the word tokens of the text as "of equal interest" one will find that documents contribute to the description in proportion to their size, and the postulate "Big documents are more important than little documents" is at odds with "All documents are created equal".'

I now return to the promised mathematical definition of dissimilarity. The reasons for preferring the 'dissimilarity' point of view are mainly technical and will not be elaborated here. Interested readers can consult Jardine and Sibson[2] on the subject, only note that any dissimilarity function can be transformed into a similarity function by a simple transformation of the form $s = (1 + d)^{-1}$ but the reverse is not always true.

If P is the set of objects to be clustered, a pairwise dissimilarity coefficient D is a function from $P \times P$ to the non-negative real numbers. D, in general, satisfies the following conditions

$D1$ $D(X, Y) \geqslant 0$ for all $X, Y \in P$

$D2$ $D(X, X) = 0$ for all $X \in P$

$D3$ $D(X, Y) = D(Y, X)$ for all $X, Y \in P$

Informally, a dissimilarity coefficient is a kind of 'distance' function. In fact many of the dissimilarity coefficients satisfy the triangle inequality:

$D4$ $D(X, Y) \leqslant D(X, Z) + D(Y, Z)$

which may be recognised as the theorem from Euclidean geometry which states that the sum of the lengths of two sides of a triangle is always greater than the length of the third side.

An example of a dissimilarity coefficient satisfying $D1 - D4$ is

$$\frac{|X \triangle Y|}{|X| + |Y|}$$

where $(X \triangle Y) = (X \cup Y) - (X \cap Y)$ is the symmetric difference of sets X and Y. It is simply related to Dice's coefficient by

$$1 - \frac{2|X \cap Y|}{|X| + |Y|} = \frac{|X \triangle Y|}{|X| + |Y|}$$

and is monotone with respect to Jaccard's coefficient subtracted from 1. To complete the picture I shall express this last DC in a different form. Instead of representing each document by a set of keywords we represent it by a binary string where the absence or presence of the ith keyword is indicated by a zero or one in the ith position respectively. In that case

$$\frac{\Sigma x_i(1 - y_i) + \Sigma y_i(1 - x_i)}{\Sigma x_i + \Sigma y_i}$$

where summation is over the total number of different keywords in the document collection.

Salton considered document representatives as binary vectors embedded in an n-dimensional Euclidean space, where n is the total number of index terms.

$$\frac{|X \cap Y|}{|X|^{1/2} |Y|^{1/2}}$$

can then be interpreted as the cosine of the angular separation of the two binary vectors X and Y. This readily generalises to the case where X and Y are arbitrary real vectors (i.e. weighted keyword lists) in which case we write

$$\frac{(X, Y)}{\|X\| \, \|Y\|}$$

where (X, Y) is the inner product and $\|.\|$ the length of a vector. If the space is Euclidean then for

$$X = (x_1, \ldots, x_n) \text{ and } Y = (y_1, \ldots, y_n)$$

we get

$$\frac{\sum_{i=1}^{n} x_i y_i}{\left(\sum_{i=1}^{n} x_i^2\right)^{1/2} \left(\sum_{i=1}^{n} y_i^2\right)^{1/2}}$$

Some authors have attempted to base a measure of association on a probabilistic model[18]. They measure the association between two objects by the extent to which their distributions deviate from stochastic independence. This way of measuring association will be of particular importance when in Chapter 6 I discuss how the association between index terms is to be used to improve retrieval effectiveness. There I use the *expected mutual information measure* to measure association. For two discrete probability distributions $P(x_i)$ and $P(x_j)$ it can be defined as follows,

$$I(x_i, x_j) = \sum_{x_i, x_j} P(x_i, x_j) \, \log \frac{P(x_i, x_j)}{P(x_i) P(x_j)}$$

When x_i and x_j are independent $P(x_i)P(x_j) = P(x_i, x_j)$ and so $I(x_i, x_j) = 0$. Also $I(x_i, x_j) = I(x_j, x_i)$ which shows that it is symmetric. It also has the

41

nice property of being invariant under one-to-one transformations of the co-ordinates. Other interesting properties of this measure may be found in Osteyee and Good[19]. Rajski[20] shows how $I(x_i, x_j)$ may be simply transformed into a distance function on discrete probability distributions. $I(x_i, x_j)$ is often interpreted as a measure of the statistical information contained in x_i about x_j (or vice versa). When we apply this function to measure the association between two index terms, say i and j, then x_i and x_j are binary variables. Thus $P(x_i = 1)$ will be the probability of occurrence of the term i and similarly $P(x_i = 0)$ will be the probability of its non-occurrence. The extent to which two index terms i and j are associated is then measured by $I(x_i, x_j)$ which measures the extent to which their distributions deviate from stochastic independence.

A function very similar to the expected mutual information measure was suggested by Jardine and Sibson[2] specifically to measure dissimilarity between two *classes* of objects. For example we may be able to discriminate two classes on the basis of their probability distributions over a simple two-point space $\{1, 0\}$. Thus let $P_1(1), P_1(0)$ and $P_2(1), P_2(0)$ be the probability distributions associated with class I and II respectively. Now on the basis of the difference between them we measure the dissimilarity between I and II by what Jardine and Sibson call the *Information Radius*, which is

$$uP_1(1) \ \log \ \frac{P_1(1)}{uP_1(1) + vP_2(1)} \ + \ vP_2(1) \ \log \ \frac{P_2(1)}{uP_1(1) + vP_2(1)} \ +$$

$$+ \ uP_1(0) \ \log \ \frac{P_1(0)}{uP_1(0) + vP_2(0)} \ + \ vP_2(0) \ \log \ \frac{P_2(0)}{uP_1(0) + vP_2(0)}$$

Here u and v are positive weights adding to unity. This function is readily generalised to multi-state, or indeed continuous distributions. It is also easy to show that under some interpretation the expected mutual information measure is a special case of the information radius. This fact will be of some importance in Chapter 6. To see it we write $P_1(.)$ and $P_2(.)$ as two conditional distributions $P(./w_1)$ and $P(./w_2)$. If we now interpret $u = P(w_1)$ and $v = P(w_2)$, that is the prior probability of the conditioning variable in $P(./w_i)$, then on substituting into the expression for the information radius and using the identities

$$P(x) = P(x/w_1) \, P(w_1) + P(x/w_2) P(w_2) \qquad x = 0, 1$$

$$P(x/w_i) = P(x, w_i) P(x) \qquad\qquad i = 1, 2$$

we recover the expected mutual information measure $I(x, w_i)$.

42

Classification methods

Let me start with a description of the kind of data for which classification methods are appropriate. The data consists of *objects* and their corresponding descriptions. The objects may be documents, keywords, hand written characters, or species (in the last case the objects themselves are classes as opposed to individuals). The descriptors come under various names depending on their structure:

(1) multi-state attributes (e.g. colour)
(2) binary-state (e.g. keywords)
(3) numerical (e.g. hardness scale, or weighted keywords)
(4) probability distributions.

The fourth category of descriptors is applicable when the objects are classes. For example, the leaf width of a species of plants may be described by a normal distribution of a certain mean and variance. It is in an attempt to summarise and simplify this kind of data that classification methods are used.

Some excellent surveys of classification methods now exist, to name but a few, Ball[21], Cormack[14] and Dorofeyuk[22]. In fact methods of classification are now so numerous, that Good[23] has found it necessary to give a classification of classification.

Sparck Jones[24] has provided a very clear intuitive break down of classification methods in terms of some general characteristics of the resulting classificatory system. In what follows the primitive notion of 'property' will mean feature of an object. I quote:

'(1) Relation between properties and classes
    (a) monothetic
    (b) polythetic
(2) Relation between objects and classes
    (a) exclusive
    (b) overlapping
(3) Relation between classes and classes
    (a) ordered
    (b) unordered'

The first category has been explored thoroughly by numerical taxonomists. An early statement of the distinction between monothetic and polythetic is given by Beckner[25]: 'A class is ordinarily defined by reference to a set of properties which are both necessary and sufficient (by stipulation) for membership in the class. It is possible, however, to define a group K in terms of a set G of properties $f_1, f_2, \ldots, f_n$ in a different manner. Suppose we have an aggregate of individuals (we shall not yet call them a class) such that

(1) each one possesses a large (but unspecified) number of the properties in G;

(2) each f in G is possessed by large numbers of these individuals; and

(3) no f in G is possessed by every individual in the aggregate.'

The first sentence of Beckner's statement refers to the classical Aristotelian definition of a class, which is now termed *monothetic*. The second part defines polythetic.

To illustrate the basic distinction consider the following example (*Figure 3.1*) of 8 individuals (1–8) and 8 properties (A–H). The possession of a property is indicated by a plus sign. The individuals 1–4 constitute a polythetic group each individual possessing three out of four of the properties A,B,C,D. The other 4 individuals can be split into two monothetic classes {5,6} and {7,8}. The distinction between monothetic and polythetic is a particularly easy one to make providing the properties are of a simple kind, e.g. binary-state attributes. When the properties are more complex the definitions are rather more difficult to apply, and in any case are rather arbitrary.

The distinction between overlapping and exclusive is important both from a theoretical and practical point of view. Many classification methods can be viewed as data-simplification methods. In the process of classification information is discarded so that the members of one class are indistinguishable. It is in an attempt to minimise the amount of information thrown away, or to put it differently, to have a classification which is in some sense 'closest' to the original data, that overlapping classes are allowed. Unfortunately this plays havoc with the

	A	B	C	D	E	F	G	H
1	+	+	+					
2	+	+		+				
3	+		+	+				
4		+	+	+				
5					+	+	+	
6					+	+	+	
7					+	+		+
8					+	+		+

Figure 3.1. An illustration of the difference between monothetic and polythetic

efficiency of implementation for a particular application. A compromise can be adopted in which the classification method generates overlapping classes in the first instance and is finally 'tidied up' to give exclusive classes.

An example of an ordered classification is a hierarchy. The classes are ordered by inclusion, i.e. the classes at one level are nested in the classes at the next level. To give a simple example of unordered classification is more difficult. Unordered classes generally crop up in automatic thesaurus construction. The classes sought for a thesaurus are those which satisfy certain homogeneity and isolation conditions but in general cannot be simply related to each other. (See for example the use and definition of clumps in Needham[26].) For certain applications ordering is irrelevant, whereas for others such as document clustering it is of vital importance. The ordering enables efficient search strategies to be devised.

The discussion about classification has been purposely vague up to this point. Although the break down scheme discussed gives some insight into classification methods, it is of little use when discussing any *particular* classification method. Like all categorisations it isolates some ideal types; but any particular instance will often fall between categories or be a member of a large proportion of categories.

Let me now be more specific about current (and past) approaches to classification, particularly in the context of information retrieval.

The cluster hypothesis

Before describing the battery of classification methods that are now used in information retrieval, I should like to discuss the underlying hypothesis for their use in document clustering. This hypothesis may be simply stated as follows: *closely associated documents tend to be relevant to the same requests.* I shall refer to this hypothesis as the *Cluster Hypothesis.*

A basic assumption in retrieval systems is that documents relevant to a request are separated from those which are not relevant, i.e. that the relevant documents are more like one another than they are like non-relevant documents. Whether this is true for a collection can be tested as follows. Compute the association between all pairs of documents:

(a) both of which are relevant to a request, and
(b) one of which is relevant and the other non-relevant.

Summing over a set of requests gives the relative distribution of

45

relevant–relevant (R–R) and relevant–non-relevant (R–N-R) associations of a collection. Plotting the relative frequency against strength of association for two hypothetical collections X and Y we might get distributions as shown in *Figure 3.2.*

From these it is apparent:

(a) that the separation for collection X is good while for Y it is poor; and

(b) that the strength of the association between relevant documents is greater for X than for Y.

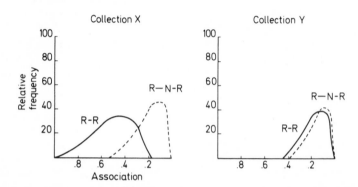

Figure 3.2. R–R is the distribution of relevant–relevant associations, and R–N-R is the distribution of relevant–non-relevant associations

It is this separation between the distributions that one attempts to exploit in document clustering. It is on the basis of this separation that I would claim that document clustering can lead to more effective retrieval than say a linear search. A linear search ignores the relationship that exists between documents. If the hypothesis is satisfied for a particular collection (some promising results have been published in Jardine and Van Rijsbergen[10], and Van Rijsbergen and Sparck Jones[27] for three test collections), then it is clear that structuring the collection in such a way that the closely associated documents appear in one class, will not only speed up the retrieval but may also make it more effective, since a class once found will tend to contain only relevant and no non-relevant documents.

I should add that these conclusions can only be verified, finally, by experimental work on a large number of collections. One reason for this is that although it may be possible to structure a document collection so that relevant documents are brought together there is no guarantee

46

that a search strategy will infallibly find the class of documents containing the relevant documents. It is a matter for experimentation whether one can design search strategies which will do the job. So far most experiments in document clustering have been moderately successful but by no means conclusive.

Note that the Cluster Hypothesis refers to given document descriptions. The object of making permanent or temporary changes to a description by such techniques as keyword classifications can therefore be expressed as an attempt to increase the distance between the two distributions R-R and R-N-R. That is, we want to make it more likely that we will retrieve relevant documents and less likely that we will retrieve non-relevant ones.

As can be seen from the above, the Cluster Hypothesis is a convenient way of expressing the aim of such operations as document clustering. Of course, it does not say anything about how the separation is to be exploited.

The use of clustering in information retrieval

There are a number of discussions in print now which cover the use of clustering in IR. The most important of these are by Litofsky[28], Crouch[29], Prywes and Smith[30] and Fritzche[31]. Rather than repeat their chronological treatment here, I shall instead try to isolate the essential features of the various cluster methods.

In choosing a cluster method for use in experimental IR, two, often conflicting, criteria have frequently been used. The first of these, and in my view the most important at this stage of the development of the subject, is the *theoretical soundness* of the method. By this I mean that the method should satisfy certain criteria of adequacy. To list some of the more important of these:

(1) the method produces a clustering which is unlikely to be altered drastically when further objects are incorporated, i.e. it is stable under growth;

(2) the method is stable in the sense that small errors in the description of the objects lead to small changes in the clustering;

(3) the method is independent of the initial ordering of the objects.

These conditions have been adapted from Jardine and Sibson[2]. The point is that any cluster method which does not satisfy these conditions is unlikely to produce any meaningful experimental results. Unfortunately not many cluster methods do satisfy these criteria, probably because algorithms implementing them tend to be less efficient than *ad hoc* clustering algorithms.

The second criterion for choice is the *efficiency* of the clustering process in terms of speed and storage requirements. In some experimental work this has been the overriding consideration. But it seems to me a little early in the day to insist on efficiency even before we know much about the behaviour of clustered files in terms of the effectiveness of retrieval (i.e. the ability to retrieve wanted and hold back unwanted documents). In any case, many of the 'good' theoretical methods (ones which are likely to produce meaningful experimental results) can be modified to increase the efficiency of their clustering process.

Efficiency is really a property of the algorithm implementing the cluster method. It is sometimes useful to distinguish the cluster method from its algorithm, but in the context of IR this distinction becomes slightly less than useful since many cluster methods are *defined* by their algorithm, so no explicit mathematical formulation exists.

In the main, two distinct approaches to clustering can be identified:

(1) the clustering is based on a measure of similarity between the objects to be clustered;
(2) the cluster method proceeds directly from the object descriptions.

The most obvious examples of the first approach are the *graph theoretic* methods which define clusters in terms of a graph derived from the measure of similarity. This approach is best explained with an example (see *Figure 3.3*). Consider a set of objects to be clustered. We compute a numerical value for each pair of objects indicating their similarity. A graph corresponding to this set of similarity values is obtained as follows. A threshold value is decided upon, and two objects are considered linked if their similarity value is above the threshold. The cluster definition is simply made in terms of the graphical representation.

A *string* is a connected sequence of objects from some starting point.

A *connected component* is a set of objects such that each object is connected to at least one other member of the set and the set is maximal with respect to this property.

A *maximal complete subgraph* is a subgraph such that each node is connected to every other node in the subgraph and the set is maximal with respect to this property, i.e. if one further node were included anywhere the completeness condition would be violated. An example of each is given in *Figure 3.4*. These methods have been used extensively in keyword clustering by Sparck Jones and Jackson[32], Augustson and Minker[33] and Vaswani and Cameron[34].

A large class of *hierarchic* cluster methods is based on the initial measurement of similarity. The most important of these is *single-link*

48

Objects: {1,2,3,4,5,6}

Similarity matrix:

	1	2	3	4	5	6
2	.6					
3	.6	.8				
4	.9	.7	.7			
5	.9	.6	.6	.9		
6	.5	.5	.5	.9	.5	

Threshold: .89

Graph:

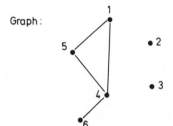

Figure 3.3. A similarity coefficient for 6 objects and the graph that can be derived from it by thresholding

which is the only one to have been extensively used in document retrieval. It satisfies all the criteria of adequacy mentioned above. In fact, Jardine and Sibson[2] have shown that under a certain number of reasonable conditions single-link is the *only* hierarchic method satisfying these important criteria. It will be discussed in some detail in the next section.

A further class of cluster methods based on measurement of similarity is the class of so-called 'clump' methods. They proceed by seeking sets which satisfy certain cohesion and isolation conditions defined in terms of the similarity measure. The computational difficulties of this approach have largely caused it to be abandoned. An attempt to generate a hierarchy of clumps was made by Van

49

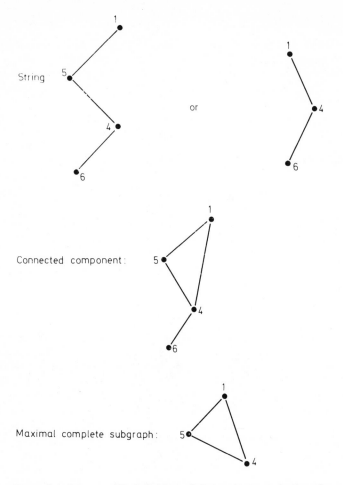

Figure 3.4. Some possible definitions of clusters in terms of subgraphs

Rijsbergen[35] but as expected, the cluster definition was so strict that very few sets could be found to satisfy it.

Efficiency has been the overriding consideration in the definition of the algorithmically defined cluster methods used in IR. For this reason most of these methods have tended to proceed directly from object description to final classification without an intermediate calculation of a similarity measure. Another distinguishing characteristic of these methods is that they do not seek an underlying structure in the data but attempt to impose a suitable structure on it. This is achieved by

50

restricting the number of clusters and by bounding the size of each cluster.

Rather than give a detailed account of all the heuristic algorithms, I shall instead discuss some of the main types and refer the reader to further developments by citing the appropriate authors. Before proceeding we need to define some of the concepts used in designing these algorithms.

The most important concept is that of *cluster representative* variously called cluster profile, classification vector, or centroid. It is simply an object which summarises and represents the objects in the cluster. Ideally it should be near to every object in the cluster in some average sense; hence the use of the term centroid. The similarity of the objects to the representative is measured by a *matching function* (sometimes called similarity or correlation function). The algorithms also use a number of *empirically* determined parameters such as:

(1) the number of clusters desired;
(2) a minimum and maximum size for each cluster;
(3) a threshold value on the matching function, below which an object will not be included in a cluster;
(4) the control of overlap between clusters;
(5) an arbitrarily chosen objective function which is optimised.

Almost all of the algorithms are iterative, i.e. the final classification is achieved by iteratively improving an intermediate classification. Although most algorithms have been defined only for one-level classification, they can obviously be extended to multi-level classification by the simple device of considering the clusters at one level as the objects to be classified at the next level.

Probably the most important of this kind of algorithm is Rocchio's clustering algorithm[36] which was developed on the SMART project. It operates in three stages. In the *first* stage it selects (by some criterion) a number of objects as cluster centres. The remaining objects are then assigned to the centres or to a 'rag-bag' cluster (for the misfits). On the basis of the initial assignment the cluster representatives are computed and all objects are once more assigned to the clusters. The assignment rules are explicitly defined in terms of thresholds on a matching function. The final clusters may overlap (i.e. an object may be assigned to more than one cluster). The *second* stage is essentially an iterative step to allow the various input parameters to be adjusted so that the resulting classification meets the prior specification of such things as cluster size, etc. more nearly. The *third* stage is for 'tidying up'. Unassigned objects are forcibly assigned, and overlap between clusters is reduced.

Most of these algorithms aim at reducing the number of passes that

51

have to be made of the file of object descriptions. There are a small number of clustering algorithms which only require one pass of the file of object descriptions. Hence the name 'Single-Pass Algorithm' for some of them. Basically they operate as follows:

(1) the object descriptions are processed serially;
(2) the first object becomes the cluster representative of the first cluster;
(3) each subsequent object is matched against all cluster representatives existing at its processing time;
(4) a given object is assigned to one cluster (or more if overlap is allowed) according to some condition on the matching function;
(5) when an object is assigned to a cluster the representative for that cluster is recomputed;
(6) if an object fails a certain test it becomes the cluster representative of a new cluster.

Once again the final classification is dependent on input parameters which can only be determined empirically (and which are likely to be different for different sets of objects) and must be specified in advance.

The simplest version of this kind of algorithm is probably one due to Hill[37]. Subsequently many variations have been produced mainly the result of changes in the assignment rules and definition of cluster representatives. (See for example, Rieber and Marathe[38], Johnson and Lafuente[39] and Etzweiler and Martin[40].)

Related to the single-pass approach is the algorithm of MacQueen[41] which starts with an arbitrary initial partition of the objects. Cluster representatives are computed for the members (sets) of the partition, and objects are reallocated to the nearest cluster representative.

A third type of algorithm is represented by the work of Dattola[42]. His algorithm is based on an earlier algorithm by Doyle. As in the case of MacQueen, it starts with an initial arbitrary partition and set of cluster representatives. The subsequent processing reallocates the objects, some ending up in a 'rag-bag' cluster (cf. Rocchio). After each reallocation the cluster representative is recomputed, but the *new* cluster representative will only replace the *old* one if the *new* representative turns out to be nearer in some sense to the objects in the *new* cluster than the *old* representative. Dattola's algorithm has been used extensively by Murray[43] for generating hierarchic classifications. Related to Dattola's approach is that due to Crouch[29]. Crouch spends more time obtaining the initial partition (he calls them categories) and the corresponding cluster representatives. The initial phase is termed the 'categorisation stage', which is followed by the 'classification stage'. The second stage proceeds to reallocate objects in the normal way. His work is of some interest because of the extensive comparisons he made between the algorithms of Rocchio, Rieber and Marathe, Bonner (see below) and his own.

One further algorithm that should be mentioned here is that due to Litofsky[28]. His algorithm is designed only to work for objects described by binary state attributes. It uses cluster representatives and matching functions in an entirely different way. The algorithm shuffles objects around in an attempt to minimise the average number of different attributes present in the members of each cluster. The clusters are characterised by sets of attribute values where each set is the set of attributes common to all members of the cluster. The final classification is a hierarchic one. (For further details about this approach see also Lefkovitz[44].)

Finally, the Bonner[45] algorithm should be mentioned. It is a hybrid of the graph–theoretic and heuristic approaches. The initial clusters are specified by graph–theoretic methods (based on an association measure), and then the objects are reallocated according to conditions on the matching function.

The major advantage of the algorithmically defined cluster methods is their speed: order $n \log n$ (where n is the number of objects to be clustered) compared with order n^2 for the methods based on association measures. However, they have disadvantages. The final classification depends on the order in which the objects are input to the cluster algorithm, i.e. it suffers from the defect of order dependence. In addition the effects of errors in the object descriptions are unpredictable.

One obvious omission from the list of cluster methods is the group of mathematically or statistically based methods such as Factor Analysis and Latent Class Analysis. Although both methods were originally used in IR (see Borko and Bernick[46], Baker[47]) they have now largely been superseded by the cluster methods described above.

The method of single-link avoids the disadvantages just mentioned. Its appropriateness for document clustering is discussed here.

Single-link

The dissimilarity coefficient is the basic input to a single-link clustering algorithm. The output is a hierarchy with associated numerical levels called a *dendrogram*. Frequently the hierarchy is represented by a tree structure such that each node represents a cluster. The two representations are shown side by side in *Figure 3.5* for the same set of objects {A,B,C,D,E}. The clusters are: {A,B,}, {C}, {D}, {E} at level L_1, {A,B}, {C,D,E} at level L_2, and {A,B,C,D,E} at level L_3. At each level of

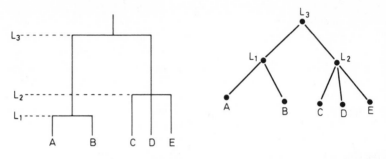

Figure 3.5. A dendrogram with corresponding tree

the hierarchy one can identify a set of classes, and as one moves up the hierarchy the classes at the lower levels are nested in the classes at the higher levels. A mathematical definition of a dendrogram exists, but is of little use, so will be omitted. Interested readers should consult Jardine and Sibson[2].

To give the reader a better feel for a single-link classification, here is a worked example (see *Figure 3.6*). A DC (dissimilarity coefficient) can be characterised by a set of graphs, one for each value taken by the DC. The different values taken by the DC in the example are $L = .1, .2, .3, .4$. The graph at each level is given by a set of vertices corresponding to the objects to be clustered, and any two vertices are linked if their dissimilarity is at most equal to the value of the level L. It should be clear that these graphs characterise the DC completely. Given the graphs and their interpretation a DC can be recovered, and vice versa. Graphs at values other than those taken by the DC are simply the same as at the next smallest value actually taken by the DC, for example, compare the graphs at $L = .15$ and $L = .1$.

It is now a simple matter to define single-link in terms of these graphs; at any level a single-link cluster is precisely the set of vertices of a connected component of the graph at that level. In the diagram I have enclosed each cluster with a dotted line. Note that whereas the graphs at any two distinct values taken by the DC will be different, this is not necessarily the case for the corresponding clusters at those levels. It may be that by increasing the level the links introduced between vertices do not change the total number of connected vertices in a component. For example the clusters at levels .3 and .4 are the same. The hierarchy is achieved by varying the level from the lowest possible value, increasing it through successive values of the DC until all objects are contained in one cluster. The reason for the name single-link is now apparent: for an object to belong to a cluster it needs to be linked to only one other member of the cluster.

54

Dissimilarity matrix:

2	.4			
3	.4	.2		
4	.3	.3	.3	
5	.1	.4	.4	.1
	1	2	3	4

Binary matrices :

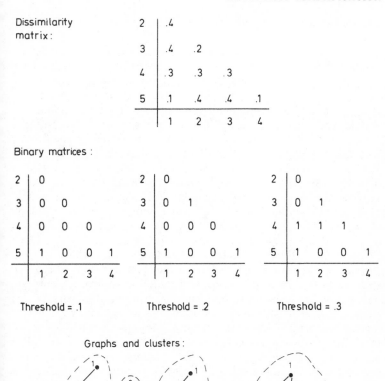

2	0			
3	0	0		
4	0	0	0	
5	1	0	0	1
	1	2	3	4

Threshold = .1

2	0			
3	0	1		
4	0	0	0	
5	1	0	0	1
	1	2	3	4

Threshold = .2

2	0			
3	0	1		
4	1	1	1	
5	1	0	0	1
	1	2	3	4

Threshold = .3

Graphs and clusters:

Figure 3.6. To show how single-link clusters may be derived from the dissimilarity coefficient by thresholding it

This description immediately leads to an *inefficient* algorithm for the generation of single-link classes. It was demonstrated in the example above. It simply consists of thresholding the DC at increasing levels of dissimilarity. The binary connection matrices are then calculated at each threshold level, from which the connected components can easily be extracted. This is the basis for many published single-link algorithms. From the point of view of IR, where one is trying to construct a *searchable* tree it is too inefficient (see Van Rijsbergen[48] for an appropriate implementation).

55

The appropriateness of stratified hierarchic cluster methods

There are many other hierarchic cluster methods, to name but a few: complete-link, average-link, etc. For a critique of these methods see Sibson[49]. My concern here is to indicate their appropriateness for document retrieval. It is as well to realise that the kind of retrieval intended is one in which the entire cluster is retrieved without any further subsequent processing of the documents in the cluster. This is in contrast with the methods proposed by Rocchio, Litofsky, and Crouch who use clustering purely to help limit the extent of a linear search.

Stratified systems of clusters are appropriate because the level of a cluster can be used in retrieval strategies as a parameter analogous to rank position or matching function threshold in a linear search. Retrieval of a cluster which is a good match for a request at a low level in the hierarchy tends to produce high precision* but low recall*; just as a cut-off at a low rank position in a linear search tends to yield high precision but low recall. Similarly, retrieval of a cluster which is a good match for a request at a high level in the hierarchy tends to produce high recall but low precision. *Hierarchic* systems of clusters are appropriate for three reasons. First, very efficient strategies can be devised to search a hierarchic clustering. Secondly, construction of a hierarchic system is much faster than construction of a non-hierarchic (that is, stratified but overlapping) system of clusters. Thirdly, the storage requirements for a hierarchic structure are considerably less than for a non-hierarchic structure, particularly during the classification phase.

Given that hierarchic methods are appropriate for document clustering the question arises: 'Which method?' The answer is that under certain conditions (made precise in Jardine and Sibson[2]) the only acceptable stratified hierarchic cluster method is single-link. Let me immediately qualify this by saying that it applies to a method which operates from a dissimilarity coefficient (or some equivalent variant), and does *not* take into account methods based directly on the object descriptions.

Single-link and the minimum spanning tree

The single-link tree (such as the one shown in *Figure 3.5*) is closely related to another kind of tree: the *minimum spanning tree,* or MST, also derived from a dissimilarity coefficient (Gower and Ross[50]). This

---

* See introduction for definition.

second tree is quite different from the first, the nodes instead of representing clusters represent the individual objects to be clustered. The MST is the tree of minimum length connecting the objects, where by 'length' I mean the sum of the weights of the connecting links in the tree. Similarly we can define a *maximum spanning tree* as one of maximum length. Whether we are interested in a minimum or maximum spanning tree depends entirely on the application we have in mind. For convenience we will concentrate on the minimum spanning tree since it derives naturally from a dissimilarity coefficient and is more common anyway. (In Chapter 6 we shall have cause to use a maximum spanning tree based on the expected mutual information measure). Given the minimum spanning tree then the single-link clusters are obtained by deleting links from the MST in order of decreasing length; the connected sets after each deletion are the single-link clusters. The order of deletion and the structure of the MST ensure that the clusters will be nested into a hierarchy.

The MST contains more information than the single-link hierarchy and only indirectly information about the single-link clusters. Thus, although we can derive the single-link hierarchy from it by a simple thresholding process, we cannot reverse this and uniquely derive the MST from the single-link hierarchy. It is interesting to consider in the light of this whether the MST would not be more suitable for document clustering than the single-link hierarchy. Unfortunately, it does not seem possible to update a spanning tree dynamically. To add a new object to a single-link hierarchy is relatively straightforward but to add one to an MST is much more complicated.

The representation of the single-link hierarchy through an MST has proved very useful in connecting single-link with other clustering techniques[51]. For example, Boulton and Wallace[52] have shown, using the MST representation, that under suitable assumptions the single-link hierarchy will minimise their information measure of classification. They see classification as a way of economically describing the original object descriptions, and the best classification is one which does it most economically in an information-theoretic sense. It is interesting that the MST has, independently of their work, been used to reduce storage when storing object descriptions, which amounts to a practical application of their result[53].

Implementation of classification methods

It is fairly difficult to talk about the implementation of an automatic classification method without at the same time referring to the file structure representing it inside the computer. Nevertheless there are a few remarks of importance which can be made.

Just as in many other computational problems, it is possible to trade core storage and computation time. In experimental IR, computation time is likely to be at a premium and a classification process can usually be speeded up by using extra storage.

One important decision to be made in any retrieval system concerns the organisation of storage. Usually part of the file structure will be kept in fast store and the rest on backing store. In experimental IR we are interested in a flexible system and getting experiments done quickly. Therefore, frequently much or all of a classification structure is kept in fast store although this would never be done in an operational system where the document collections are so much bigger.

Another good example of the difference in approach between experimental and operational implementations of a classification is in the permanence of the cluster representatives. In experiments we often want to vary the cluster representatives at search time. In fact we require that each cluster representative can be quickly specified and implemented at search time. Of course, were we to design an operational classification, the cluster representatives would be constructed once and for all at cluster time.

Probably one of the most important features of a classification implementation is that it should be able to deal with a changing and growing document collection. Adding documents to the classification should not be too difficult. For instance, it should not be necessary to take the document classification 'off the air' for lengthy periods to update it. So, we expect the classification to be designed in such a way that a new batch of documents can be readily inserted without reclassifying the entire set of both old and new documents.

Although many classification algorithms claim this feature, the claim is almost invariably not met. Because of the heuristic nature of many of the algorithms, the updated classification is not the same as it would have been if the increased set had been classified from scratch. In addition, many of the updating strategies mess up the classification to such an extent that it becomes necessary to throw away the classification after a series of updates and reclassify completely.

These comments tend to apply to the $n \log n$ classification methods. Unfortunately they are usually recommended over the n^2 methods for two reasons. Firstly because $n \log n$ is considerably less than n^2, and secondly because the time increases only as $\log n$ for the $n \log n$ methods but as n for the n^2 methods. On the face of it these are powerful arguments. However, I think they mislead. If we assume that the $n \log n$ methods cannot be updated without reclassifying each time and that the n^2 methods can (for example single-link), then the correct

58

comparison is between

$$\sum_{i=1}^{t} n_i \log n_i \qquad \text{and} \qquad N^2$$

where $n_1 < n_2 < \ldots < n_t = N$, and t is the number of updates. In the limit when n is a continuous variable and the sum becomes an integral we are better off with N^2. In the discrete case the comparison depends rather on the size of the updates $n_i - n_{i-1}$. So unless we can design an $n \log n$ dependence as extra documents are added, we may as well stick with the n^2 methods which satisfy the soundness conditions and preserve n^2 dependence during updating.

In any case if one is willing to forgo some of the theoretical adequacy conditions then it is possible to modify the n^2 methods to 'break the n^2 barrier'. One method is to sample from the document collection and construct a *core clustering* using an n^2 method on the sample of the documents. The remainder of the documents can then be fitted into the core clustering by a very fast assignment strategy, similar to a search strategy which has $\log n$ dependence. A second method is to initially do a *coarse* clustering of the document collection and then apply the finer classification method of the n^2 kind to each cluster in turn. So, if there are N documents and we divide into k coarse clusters by a method that has order N time dependence (e.g. Rieber and Marathe's method) then the total cluster time will be of order $N + \Sigma (N/k)^2$ which will be less than N^2.

Another comment to be made about $n \log n$ methods is that although they have this time dependence in theory, examination of a number of the algorithms implementing them shows that they actually have an n^2 dependence (e.g. Rocchio's algorithm). Furthermore, most $n \log n$ methods have only been tested on single-level classifications and it is doubtful whether they would be able to preserve their $n \log n$ dependence if they were used to generate hierarchic classifications (Senko[54]).

In experiments where we are often dealing with only a few thousand documents we may find that the proportionality constant in the $n \log n$ method is so large that the actual time taken for clustering is greater than that for an n^2 method. Croft[55] recently found this when he compared the efficiency of SNOB (Boulton and Wallace[56]), an $n \log n$ cluster method, with single-link. In fact it is possible to implement single-link in such a way that the generation of the similarity values is overlapped in real time with the cluster generation process.

The implementation of classification algorithms for use in IR is by necessity different from implementations in other fields such as for example numerical taxonomy. The major differences arise from differences in the scale and in the use to which a classification structure is to be put.

In the case of scale, the size of the problem in IR is invariably such that for cluster methods based on similarity matrices it becomes impossible to store the entire similarity matrix, let alone allow random access to its elements. If we are to have a reasonably useful cluster method based on similarity matrices we must be able to generate the similarity matrix in small sections, use each section to update the classification structure immediately after it has been generated and then throw it away. The importance of this fact was recognised by Needham[57]. Van Rijsbergen[48] has described an implementation of single-link which satisfies this requirement.

When a classification is to be used in IR, it affects the design of the algorithm to the extent that a classification will be represented by a file structure which is

(1) easily updated;
(2) easily searched; and
(3) reasonably compact.

Only (3) needs some further comment. It is inevitable that parts of the storage used to contain a classification will become redundant during an updating phase. This being so it is of some importance to be able to reuse this storage, and if the redundant storage becomes excessive to be able to process the file structure in such a way that it will subsequently reside in one contiguous part of core. This 'compactness' is particularly important during experiments in which the file structure is read into core before being accessed.

Conclusion

Let me briefly summarise the logical structure of this chapter. It started very generally with a descriptive look at automatic classification and its uses. It then discussed association measures which form the basis of an important class of classification methods. Next came a breakdown of classification methods. This was followed by a statement of the hypothesis underlying the use of automatic classification in document clustering. It went on to examine in some detail the use of classification methods in IR leading up to recommendation of single-link for document clustering. Finally we made some practical points about implementation.

This chapter ended on a rather practical note. We continue in this vein in the next chapter where we discuss file structures. These are important if we are to appreciate how it is that we can get dictionaries, document clustering, search strategies, and such like to work inside a computer.

Bibliographic remarks

In recent years a vast literature on automatic classification has been generated. One reason for this is that applications for these techniques have been found in such diverse fields as Biology, Pattern Recognition, and Information Retrieval. The best introduction to the field is still provided by Sneath and Sokal[15] (a much revised and supplemented version of their earlier book) which looks at automatic classification in the context of numerical taxonomy. Second to this I would recommend a collection of papers edited by Cole[58].

A book and a report on cluster analysis with a computational emphasis are Anderberg[59] and Wishart[60] respectively. Both give listings of Fortran programs for various cluster methods. Other books with a numerical taxonomy emphasis are Everitt[61], Hartigan[62] and Clifford and Stephenson[63]. A recent book with a strong statistical flavour is Van Ryzin[64].

Two papers worth singling out are Sibson[65] and Fisher and Van Ness[66]. The first gives a very lucid account of the foundations of cluster methods based on dissimilarity measures. The second does a detailed comparison of some of the more well-known cluster methods (including single-link) in terms of such conditions on the clusters as connectivity and convexity.

Much of the early work in document clustering was done on the SMART project. An excellent idea of its achievement in this area may be got by reading ISR-10 (Rocchio[36]), ISR-19 (Kerchner[67]), ISR-20 (Murray[43]), and Dattola[68]. Each has been predominantly concerned with document clustering.

There are a number of areas in IR where automatic classification is used which have not been touched on in this chapter. Probably the most important of these is the use of 'Fuzzy Sets' which is an approach to clustering pioneered by Zadeh[69]. Its relationship with the measurement of similarity is explicated in Zadeh[70]. More recently it has been applied in document clustering by Negoita[71], Chan[72] and Radecki[73].

One further interesting area of application of clustering techniques is in the clustering of citation graphs. A measure of closeness is defined between *journals* as a function of the frequency with which they cite one another. Groups of closely related journals can thus be isolated (Disiss[74]). Related to this is the work of Preparata and Chien[75] who study citation patterns between *documents* so that mutually cited documents can be stored as closely together as possible. The early work of Ivie[76] was similarly motivated in that he proposed to collect feedback information from users showing which pairs of documents were frequently found to be relevant to the same request. The frequency was then taken as proportional to the strength of association, and documents more closely associated were made more readily accessible than those less closely associated.

Finally, the reader may be interested in pursuing the use of cluster methods in pattern recognition since some of the ideas developed there are applicable to IR. Both Duda and Hart[77] and Watanabe[78] devote a chapter to clustering in the context of pattern recognition.

References

1. KENDALL, M. G., In *Multivariate Analysis* (Edited by P. R. Krishnaiah), Academic Press, London and New York, 165–184 (1966)
2. JARDINE, N. and SIBSON, R., *Mathematical Taxonomy*, Wiley, London and New York (1971)
3. MACNAUGHTON-SMITH, P., *Some Statistical and Other Numerical Techniques for Classifying Individuals,* Studies in the causes of delinquency and the treatment of offenders. Report No. 6, HMSO, London (1965)
4. HEMPEL, C. G., *Aspects of Scientific Explanation and Other Essays in the Philosophy of Science,* The Free Press, New York, 137–154 (1965)
5. SPARCK JONES, K., *Automatic Keyword Classification for Information Retrieval,* Butterworths, London (1971)
6. GOOD, I. J., *Speculations Concerning Information Retrieval,* Research Report PC-78, IBM Research Centre, Yorktown Heights, New York (1958)
7. FAIRTHORNE, R. A., 'The mathematics of classification'. *Towards Information Retrieval,* Butterworths, London, 1–10 (1961)
8. HAYES, R. M., 'Mathematical models in information retrieval'. In *Natural Language and the Computer* (Edited by P. L. Garvin), McGraw-Hill, New York, 287 (1963)
9. SALTON, G., *Automatic Information Organization and Retrieval,* McGraw-Hill, New York, 18 (1968)
10. JARDINE, N. and VAN RIJSBERGEN, C. J., 'The use of hierarchic clustering in information retrieval', *Information Storage and Retrieval,* 7, 217–240 (1971)
11. GOODMAN, L. and KRUSKAL, W., 'Measures of association for cross-classifications', *Journal of the American Statistical Association,* 49, 732–764 (1954)
12. GOODMAN, L. and KRUSKAL, W., 'Measures of association for cross-classification II: Further discussions and references', *Journal of the American Statistical Association,* 54, 123–163 (1959)
13. KUHNS, J. L., 'The continuum of coefficients of association'. In *Statistical Association Methods for Mechanised Documentation,* (Edited by Stevens *et al.*) National Bureau of Standards, Washington, 33–39 (1965)
14. CORMACK, R. M., 'A review of classification', *Journal of the Royal Statistical Society,* Series A, 134, 321–353 (1971)

15. SNEATH, P. H. A. and SOKAL, R. R., *Numerical Taxonomy: The Principles and Practice of Numerical Classification*, W. H. Freeman and Company, San Francisco (1973)
16. LERMAN, I. C., *Les Bases de la Classification Automatique*, Gauthier-Villars, Paris (1970)
17. DOYLE, L. B., 'The microstatistics of text', *Information Storage and Retrieval*, 1, 189–214 (1963)
18. MARON, M. E. and KUHNS, J. L., 'On relevance, probabilistic indexing and information retrieval', *Journal of the ACM*, 7, 216–244 (1960)
19. OSTEYEE, D. B. and GOOD, I. J., *Information, Weight of Evidence, the Singularity between Probability Measures and Signal Detection*, Springer Verlag, Berlin (1974)
20. RAJSKI, C., 'A metric space of discrete probability distributions', *Information and Control*, 4, 371–377 (1961)
21. BALL, G. H., 'Data-analysis in the social sciences: What about the details?', *Proceedings of the Fall Joint Computer Conference*, 27, 533–559 (1966)
22. DOROFEYUK, A. A., 'Automatic Classification Algorithms (Review)', *Automation and Remote Control*, 32, 1928–1958 (1971)
23. GOOD, I. J., 'Categorization of classification' In *Mathematics and Computer Science in Biology and Medicine*, HMSO, London, 115–125 (1965)
24. SPARCK JONES, K., 'Some thoughts on classification for retrieval', *Journal of Documentation*, 26, 89–101 (1970)
25. BECKNER, M., *The Biological Way of Thought*, Columbia University Press, New York, 22 (1959)
26. NEEDHAM, R. M., 'The application of digital computers to classification and grouping', Ph.D. Thesis, University of Cambridge (1961)
27. VAN RIJSBERGEN, C. J. and SPARCK JONES, K., 'A test for the separation of relevant and non-relevant documents in experimental retrieval collections', *Journal of Documentation*, 29, 251–257 (1973)
28. LITOFSKY, B., 'Utility of automatic classification systems for information storage and retrieval', Ph.D. Thesis, University of Pennsylvania (1969)
29. CROUCH, D., 'A clustering algorithm for large and dynamic document collections', Ph.D. Thesis, Southern Methodist University (1972)
30. PRYWES, N. S. and SMITH, D. P., 'Organization of Information', *Annual Review of Information Science and Technology*, 7, 103–158 (1972)
31. FRITZCHE, M., 'Automatic clustering techniques in information retrieval', Diplomarbeit, Institut für Informatik der Universität Stuttgart (1973)
32. SPARCK JONES, K. and JACKSON, D. M., 'The use of automatically-obtained keyword classifications for information retrieval', *Information Storage and Retrieval*, 5, 175–201 (1970)
33. AUGUSTSON, J. G. and MINKER, J., 'An analysis of some graph-theoretic cluster techniques', *Journal of the ACM*, 17, 571–588 (1970)
34. VASWANI, P. K. T. and CAMERON, J. B., *The National Physical Laboratory Experiments in Statistical Word Associations and their use in Document Indexing and Retrieval*, Publication 42, National Physical Laboratory, Division of Computer Science (1970)
35. VAN RIJSBERGEN, C. J., 'A clustering algorithm', *Computer Journal*, 13, 113–115 (1970)
36. ROCCHIO, J. J., 'Document retrieval systems–optimization and evaluation', Ph.D. Thesis, Harvard University. Report ISR-10 to National Science Foundation, Harvard Computation Laboratory (1966)
37. HILL, D. R., 'A vector clustering technique', In *Mechanised Information Storage, Retrieval and Dissemination*, (Edited by Samuelson), North-Holland, Amsterdam (1968)

63

38. RIEBER, S. and MARATHE, U. P., 'The single pass clustering method', In Report ISR-16 to the National Science Foundation, Cornell University, Department of Computer Science (1969)

39. JOHNSON, D. B. and LAFUENTE, J. M., 'A controlled single pass classification algorithm with application to multilevel clustering', In Report ISR-18 to the National Science Foundation and the National Library of Medicine (1970)

40. ETZWEILER, L. and MARTIN, C., 'Binary cluster division and its application to a modified single pass clustering algorithm', In Report No. ISR-21 to the National Library of Medicine (1972)

41. MacQUEEN, J., 'Some methods for classification and analysis of multivariate observations', In *Proceedings of the Fifth Berkeley Symposium on Mathematical Statistics and Probability, 1965,* University of California Press, 281–297 (1967)

42. DATTOLA, R. T., 'A fast algorithm for automatic classification', In Report ISR-14 to the National Science Foundation, Section V, Cornell University, Department of Computer Science (1968)

43. MURRAY, D. M., 'Document retrieval based on clustered files', Ph.D. Thesis, Cornell University, Report ISR-20 to National Science Foundation and to the National Library of Medicine (1972)

44. LEFKOVITZ, D., *File Structures for On-line Systems,* Spartan Books, New York (1969)

45. BONNER, R. E., 'On some clustering techniques', *IBM Journal of Research and Development,* 8, 22–32 (1964)

46. BORKO, H. and BERNICK, M., 'Automatic document classification', *Journal of the ACM,* 10, 151–162 (1963)

47. BAKER, F. B., 'Information retrieval based upon latent class analysis', *Journal of the ACM,* 9, 512–521 (1962)

48. VAN RIJSBERGEN, C. J., 'An algorithm for information structuring and retrieval', *The Computer Journal,* 14, 407–412 (1971)

49. SIBSON, R., 'Some observations of a paper by Lance and Williams', *The Computer Journal,* 14, 156–157 (1971)

50. GOWER, J. C. and ROSS, G. J. S., 'Minimum spanning trees and single-linkage cluster analysis', *Applied Statistics,* 18, 54–64 (1969)

51. ROHLF, J., 'Graphs implied by the Jardine–Sibson Overlapping clustering methods, B_k', *Journal of the American Statistical Association,* 69, 705–710 (1974)

52. BOULTON, D. M. and WALLACE, C. S., 'An information measure for single link classification', *The Computer Journal,* 18, 236–238 (1975)

53. KANG, A. N. C., LEE, R. C. T., CHANG, C.-L. and CHANG, S.-K., 'Storage reduction through minimal spanning trees and spanning forests', *IEEE Transactions on Computers,* C-26, 425–434 (1977)

54. SENKO, M. E., 'File organization and management information systems', *Annual Review of Information Science and Technology,* 4, 111–137 (1969)

55. CROFT, W. B., 'Document clustering', M.Sc. Thesis, Department of Computer Science, Monash University, Australia (1975)

56. BOULTON, D. M. and WALLACE, C. S., 'A program for numerical classification', *The Computer Journal,* 13, 63–69 (1970)

57. NEEDHAM, R. M., 'Problems of scale in automatic classification', In *Statistical Association methods for mechanised documentation* (Abstract) (Edited by M. E. Stevens *et al.*), National Bureau of Standards, Washington (1965)

58. COLE, A. J., *Numerical Taxonomy,* Academic Press, New York (1969)

59. ANDERBERG, M. R., *Cluster Analysis for Applications,* Academic Press, London and New York (1973)
60. WISHART, D., *FORTRAN II Program for 8 Methods of Cluster Analysis (CLUSTAN I)* Computer Contribution 38 State Geological Survey. The University of Kansas, Lawrence, Kansas, U.S.A. (1969)
61. EVERITT, B., *Cluster Analysis,* Heineman Educational Books, London (1974)
62. HARTIGAN, J. A., *Clustering Algorithms,* Wiley, New York and London (1975)
63. CLIFFORD, H. T. and STEPHENSON, W., *An Introduction to Numerical Classification,* Academic Press, New York (1975)
64. VAN RYZIN, J., *Classification and Clustering,* Academic Press, New York (1977)
65. SIBSON, R., 'Order invariant methods for data analysis', *Journal of the Royal Statistical Society,* Series B, **34**, No. 3, 311–349 (1972)
66. FISHER, L. and VAN NESS, J. W., 'Admissible clustering procedures', *Biometrika,* **58**, 91–104 (1971)
67. KERCHNER, M. D., 'Dynamic document processing in clustered collections', Ph.D. Thesis, Cornell University. Report ISR-19 to National Science Foundation and to the National Library of Medicine (1971)
68. DATTOLA, R. T., *Automatic classification in document retrieval systems,* Ph.d. Thesis, Cornell University (1973)
69. ZADEH, L. A., 'Fuzzy sets', *Information and Control,* **8**, 338–353 (1965)
70. ZADEH, L. A., 'Similarity relations and fuzzy orderings', *Information Sciences,* **3**, 177–200 (1971)
71. NEGOITA, C. V., 'On the application of the fuzzy sets separation theorem for automatic classification in information retrieval systems', *Information Sciences,* **5**, 279–286 (1973)
72. CHAN, F. K., 'Document classification through use of fuzzy relations and determination of significant features', M.Sc. Thesis, Department of Computer Science, University of Alberta, Canada (1973)
73. RADECKI, T., 'Mathematical model of time-effective information retrieval system based on the theory of fuzzy sets', *Information Processing and Management,* **13**, 109–116 (1977)
74. DISISS, 'Design of information systems in the social sciences. Clustering of journal titles according to citation data: preparatory work, design; data collection and preliminary analysis.' Bath, Bath University Library, Working Paper No. 11 (1973)
75. PREPARATA, F. F. and CHIEN, R. T., 'On clustering techniques of citation graphs', Report R-349, Co-ordinated Science Laboratory, University of Illinois, Urbana, Illinois (1967)
76. IVIE, E. L., 'Search procedures based on measures of relatedness between documents', Ph.D. Thesis, M.I.T., Report MAC-TR-29 (1966)
77. DUDA, R. O., and HART, P. E., *Pattern Classification and Scene Analysis,* Wiley, New York (1973)
78. WATANABE, S., *Knowing and Guessing,* Wiley, New York (1969)

Four

FILE STRUCTURES

Introduction

This chapter is mainly concerned with the way in which file structures are used in document retrieval. Most surveys of file structures address themselves to applications in data management which is reflected in the terminology used to describe the basic concepts. I shall (on the whole) follow Hsiao and Harary[1] whose terminology is perhaps slightly non-standard but emphasises the logical nature of file structures. A further advantage is that it enables me to bridge the gap between data management and document retrieval easily. A few other good references on file structures are Roberts[2], Bertziss[3], Dodd[4], and Climenson[5].

Logical or physical organisation and data independence

There is one important distinction that must be made at the outset when discussing file structures. And that is the difference between the *logical* and *physical* organisation of the data. On the whole a file structure will specify the logical structure of the data, that is the relationships that will exist between data items independently of the way in which these relationships may actually be realised within any computer. It is this logical aspect that we will concentrate on. The physical organisation is much more concerned with optimising the use of the storage medium when a particular logical structure is stored on, or in it. Typically for every unit of physical store there will be a number of units of the logical structure (probably records) to be stored in it. For example, if we were to store a tree structure on a magnetic disk the physical organisation would be concerned with the best way of

66

packing the nodes of the tree on the disk given the access characteristics of the disk.

The work on data bases has been very much concerned with a concept called *data independence*. The aim of this work is to enable programs to be written independently of the logical structure of the data they would interact with. The independence takes the following form, should the file structure overnight be changed from an inverted to a serial file the program should remain unaffected. This independence is achieved by interposing a *data model* between the user and the data base. The user sees the data model rather than the data base, and all his programs communicate with the model. The user therefore has no interest in the structure of the file.

There is a school of thought that says that applications in library automation and information retrieval should follow this path as well[6, 7]. And so it should. Unfortunately, there is still much debate about what a good data model should look like. Furthermore, operational implementations of some of the more advanced theoretical systems do not exist yet. So any suggestion that an IR system might be implemented through a data base package should still seem premature. Also, the scale of the problems in IR is such that efficient implementation of the application still demands close scrutiny of the file structure to be used.

Nevertheless, it is worth taking seriously the trend away from user knowledge of file structures, a trend that has been stimulated considerably by attempts to construct a theory of data[8, 9]. There are a number of proposals for dealing with data at an abstract level. The best known of these by now is the one put forward by Codd[8], which has become known as the relational model. In it data are described by n-tuples of attribute values. More formally if the data is described by *relations,* a relation on a set of *domains* $D_1, \ldots, D_n$ can be represented by a set of ordered n-tuples each of the form $(d_1, \ldots, d_n)$ where $d_i \in D_i$. As it is rather difficult to cope with general relations, various levels (three in fact) of normalisation have been introduced restricting the kind of relations allowed.

A second approach is the *hierarchical* approach. It is used in many existing data base systems. This approach works as one might expect: data is represented in the form of hierarchies. Although it is more restrictive than the relational approach it often seems to be the natural way to proceed. It can be argued that in many applications a hierarchic structure is a good approximation to the natural structure in the data, and that the resulting loss in precision of representation is worth the gain in efficiency and simplicity of representation.

The third approach is the *network* approach associated with the proposals by the Data Base Task Group of CODASYL. Here data items

67

are linked into a network in which any given link between two items exists because it satisfies some condition on the attributes of those items, for example, they share an attribute. It is more general than the hierarchic approach in the sense that a node can have any number of immediate superiors. It is also equivalent to the relational approach in descriptive power.

The whole field of data base structures is still very much in a state of flux. The advantages and disadvantages of each approach are discussed very thoroughly in Date[10], who also gives excellent annotated citations to the current literature. There is also a recent *Computing Survey*[11] which reviews the current state of the art. There have been some very early proponents of the relational approach in IR, as early as 1967 Maron[12] and Levien[13] discussed the design and implementation of an IR systems via relations, be it binary ones. Also, Prywes and Smith in their review chapter in the *Annual Review of Information Science and Technology* more recently recommended the DBTG proposals as ways of implementing IR systems[7].

Lurking in the background of any discussion of file structures nowadays is always the question whether data base technology will overtake all. Thus it may be that any application in the field of library automation and information retrieval will be implemented through the use of some appropriate data base package. This is certainly a possibility but not likely to happen in the near future. There are several reasons. One is that data base systems are *general* purpose systems whereas automated library and retrieval systems are *special* purpose. Normally one pays a price for generality and in this case it is still too great. Secondly, there now is a considerable investment in providing special purpose systems (for example, MARC)[14] and this is not written off very easily. Nevertheless a trend towards increasing use of data-base technology exists and is well illustrated by the increased prominence given to it in the *Annual Review of Information Science and Technology*.

A language for describing file structures

Like all subjects in computer science the terminology of file structures has evolved higgledy-piggledy without much concern for consistency, ambiguity, or whether it was possible to make the kind of distinctions that were important. It was only much later that the need for a well-defined, unambiguous language to describe file structures became apparent. In particular, there arose a need to communicate ideas about file structures without getting bogged down by hardware considerations.

This section will present a formal description of file structures. The framework described is important for the understanding of any file structure. The terminology is based on that introduced by Hsiao and Harary (but also see Hsiao[15] and Manola and Hsiao[16]). Their terminology has been modified and extended by Severance[17], a summary of this can be found in van Rijsbergen[18]. Jonkers[19] has formalised a different framework which provides an interesting contrast to the one described here.

Basic terminology

Given a set of 'attributes' A and a set of 'values' V, then a *record R* is a subset of the cartesian product $A \times V$ in which each attribute has one and only one value. Thus R is a set of ordered pairs of the form (an attribute, its value). For example, the record for a document which has been processed by an automatic content analysis algorithm would be

$$R = \{(K_1, x_1), (K_2, x_2), \ldots (K_m, x_m)\}$$

The K_i's are keywords functioning as attributes and the value x_i can be thought of as a numerical weight. Frequently documents are simply characterised by the absence or presence of keywords, in which case we write

$$R = \{K_{t_1}, K_{t_2}, \ldots, K_{t_i}\}$$

where K_{t_i} is present if $x_{t_i} = 1$ and is absent otherwise.

Records are collected into logical units called *files*. They enable one to refer to a set of records by name, the *file name*. The records within a file are often organised according to relationships between the records. This logical organisation has become known as a *file structure* (or data structure).

It is difficult in describing file structures to keep the logical features separate from the physical ones. The latter are characteristics forced upon us by the recording media (e.g. tape, disk). Some features can be defined abstractly (with little gain) but are more easily understood when illustrated concretely. One such feature is a *field*. In any implementation of a record, the attribute values are usually positional, that is the identity of an attribute is given by the position of its attribute value within the record. Therefore the data within a record is registered sequentially and has a definite beginning and end. The record is said to be divided into *fields* and the nth field carries the nth attribute value. Pictorially we have an example of a record with associated fields in *Figure 4.1*.

69

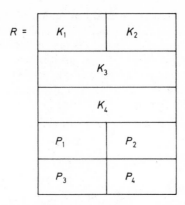

Figure 4.1. An example of a record with associated fields

The fields are not necessarily constant in length. To find the value of the attribute K_4, we first find the address of the record R (which is actually the address of the start of the record) and read the data in the 4th field.

In the same picture I have also shown some fields labelled P_i. They are addresses of other records, and are commonly called *pointers*. Now we have extended the definition of a record to a set of attribute-value pairs *and* pointers. Each pointer is usually associated with a particular attribute-value pair. For example, (see *Figure 4.2*) pointers could be used to link all records for which the value x_1 (of attribute K_1) is a, similarly for x_2 equal to b, etc.

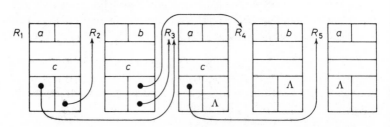

Figure 4.2. A demonstration of the use of pointers to link records

To indicate that a record is the last record pointed to in a list of records we use the *null pointer* Λ. The pointer associated with attribute K in record R will be called a *K-pointer*. An attribute (keyword) that is used in this way to organise a file is called a *key*.

70

To unify the discussion of file structures we need some further concepts. Following Hsiao and Harary again, we define a *list L* of records with respect to a keyword *K*, or more briefly a *K-list* as a set of records containing *K* such that;

(1) the *K*-pointers are distinct;
(2) each non-null *K*-pointer in *L* gives the address of a record within *L*;
(3) there is a unique record in *L* not pointed to by any record containing *K*; it is called the *beginning* of the list; and
(4) there is a unique record in *L* containing the null *K*-pointer; it is the *end* of the list.

(Hsiao and Harary state condition (2) slightly differently so that no two *K*-lists have a record in common; this only appears to complicate things.)

From our previous example:

$$K_1\text{-list} : R_1, R_3, R_5$$

$$K_2\text{-list} : R_2, R_4$$

$$K_4\text{-list} : R_1, R_2, R_3$$

Finally, we need the definition of a *directory* of a file. Let *F* be a file whose records contain just *m* different keywords $K_1, K_2, \ldots, K_m$. Let n_i be the number of records containing the keyword K_i, and h_i be the number of K_i-lists in *F*. Furthermore, we denote by a_{ij} the beginning address of the *j*th K_i-list. Then the *directory* is the set of sequences

$$(K_i, n_i, h_i, a_{i1}, a_{i2}, \ldots a_{ih_i}) \quad i = 1, 2, \ldots m$$

We are now in a position to give a unified treatment of sequential files, inverted files, index-sequential files and multi-list files.

Sequential files

A sequential file is the most primitive of all file structures. It has *no* directory and *no* linking pointers. The records are generally organised in lexicographic order on the value of some key. In other words, a particular attribute is chosen whose value will determine the order of the records. Sometimes when the attribute value is constant for a large number of records a second key is chosen to give an order when the first key fails to discriminate.

The implementation of this file structure requires the use of a sorting routine.

71

Its main advantages are:

(1) it is easy to implement;
(2) it provides fast access to the next record using lexicographic order.

Its disadvantages:

(1) it is difficult to update — inserting a new record may require moving a large proportion of the file;
(2) random access is extremely slow.

Sometimes a file is considered to be sequentially organised despite the fact that it is *not* ordered according to any key. Perhaps the date of acquisition is considered to be the key value, the newest entries are added to the end of the file and therefore pose no difficulty to updating.

Inverted files

The importance of this file structure will become more apparent when Boolean Searches are discussed in the next chapter. For the moment we limit ourselves to describing its structure.

An *inverted file* is a file structure in which every list contains only one record. Remember that a list is defined with respect to a keyword K, so every K-list contains only one record. This implies that the directory will be such that $n_i = h_i$ for all i, that is, the number of records containing K_i will equal the number of K_i-lists. So the directory will have an address for each record containing K_i. For document retrieval this means that given a keyword we can immediately locate the addresses of all the documents containing that keyword. For the previous example let us assume that a non-blank entry in the field corresponding to an attribute indicates the presence of a keyword and a blank entry its absence. Then the directory will point to the file in the way shown in *Figure 4.3*. The definition of an inverted file does *not* require that the addresses in the directory are in any order. However, to facilitate operations such as conjunction ('and') and disjunction ('or') on any two inverted lists, the addresses are normally kept in record number order. This means that 'and' and 'or' operations can be performed with one pass through both lists. The penalty we pay is of course that the inverted file becomes slower to update.

Index-sequential files

An index-sequential file is an inverted file in which for every keyword K_i, we have $n_i = h_i = 1$ and $a_{11} < a_{21} \ldots < a_{m1}$. This situation can only

72

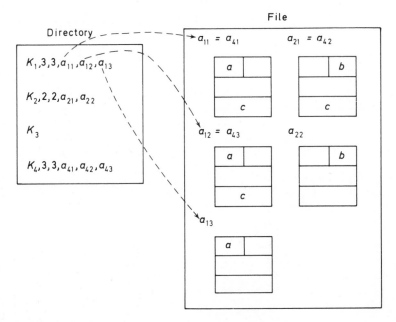

Figure 4.3. An inverted file

arise if each record has just one unique keyword, or one unique attribute-value. In practice therefore, this set of records may be ordered sequentially by a key. Each key value appears in the directory with the associated address of its record. An obvious interpretation of a key of this kind would be the record number. In our example none of the attributes would do the job except the record number. Diagrammatically the index-sequential file would therefore appear as shown in *Figure 4.4*. I have deliberately written R_i instead of K_i to emphasise the nature of the key.

In the literature an index-sequential file is usually thought of as a sequential file with a hierarchy of indices. This does not contradict the previous definition, it merely describes the way in which the directory is implemented. It is not surprising therefore that the indexes ('index' = 'directory' here) are often oriented to the characteristics of the storage medium. For example (see *Figure 4.5*) there might be three levels of indexing: track, cylinder and master. Each entry in the track index will contain enough information to locate the start of the track, and the key of the last record in the track, which is also normally the highest value on that track. There is a track index for each cylinder. Each entry in the cylinder index gives the last record on each cylinder

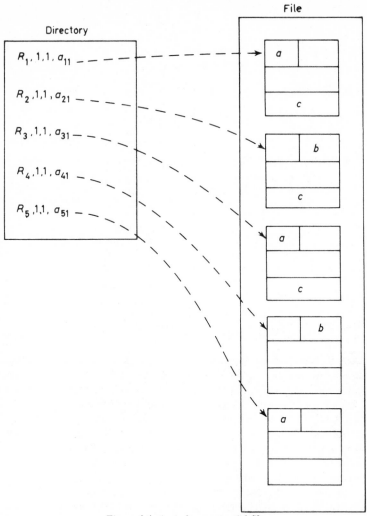

Figure 4.4. An index-sequential file

and the address of the track index for that cylinder. If the cylinder index itself is stored on tracks, then the master index will give the highest key referenced for each track of the cylinder index and the starting address of that track.

No mention has been made of the possibility of overflow during an updating process. Normally provision is made in the directory to

74

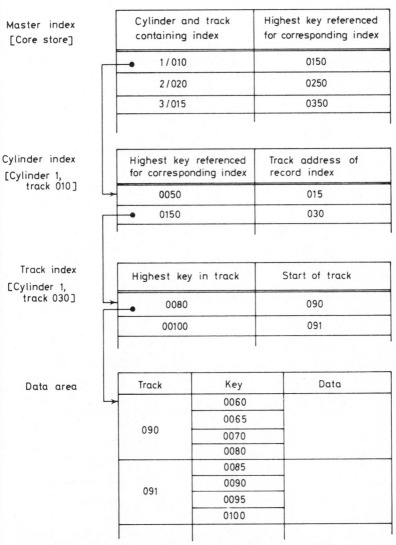

Figure 4.5. An example of an implementation of an index-sequential file (Adapted from D. R. Judd, The Use of Files, *Macdonald and Elsevier, London and New York, 1973, page 46)*

75

administer an overflow area. This of course increases the number of book-keeping entries in each entry of the index.

Multi-lists

A multi-list is really only a slightly modified inverted file. There is one list per keyword, i.e. $h_i = 1$. The records containing a particular keyword K_i are chained together to form the K_i-list and the start of the K_i-list is given in the directory, as illustrated in *Figure 4.6*. Since there

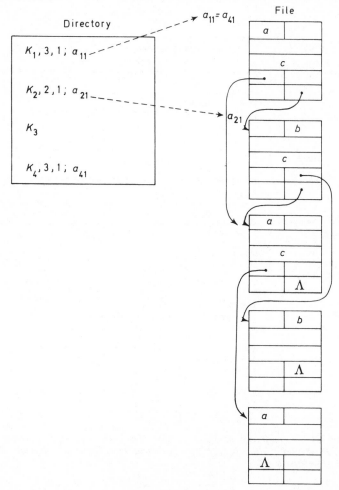

Figure 4.6. A multi-list

76

is no K_3-list the field reserved for its pointer could well have been omitted. So could any blank pointer field, so long as no ambiguity arises as to which pointer belongs to which keyword. One way of ensuring this, particularly if the data values (attribute-values) are fixed format, is to have the pointer not pointing to the beginning of the record but pointing to the location of the next pointer in the chain.

The multi-list is designed to overcome the difficulties of updating an inverted file. The addresses in the directory of an inverted file are normally kept in record-number order. But, when the time comes to add a new record to the file, this sequence must be maintained, and inserting the new address can be expensive. No such problem arises with the multi-list, we update the appropriate K-lists by simply chaining in the new record. The penalty we pay for this is of course the increase in search time. This is in fact typical of many of the file structures. Inherent in their design is a trade-off between search time and update time.

Cellular multi-lists

A further modification of the multi-list is inspired by the fact that many storage media are divided into *pages,* which can be retrieved one at a time. A K-list may cross several page boundaries which means that several pages may have to be accessed to retrieve one record. A modified multi-list structure which avoids this is called a *cellular multi-list.* The K-lists are limited so that they will not cross the page (cell) boundaries.

At this point the full power of the notation introduced before comes into play. The directory for a cellular multi-list will be the set of sequences

$$(K_i, n_i, h_i, a_{i1}, \ldots, a_{ih_i}) \quad i = 1, 2, \ldots, m$$

where the h_i have been picked to ensure that a K_i-list does not cross a page boundary. In an implementation, just as in the implementation of an index-sequential file, further information will be stored with each address to enable the right page to be located for each key value.

Ring structures

A *ring* is simply a linear list that closes upon itself. In terms of the definition of a K-list, the beginning and end of the list are the same record. This data-structure is particularly useful to show classification of data.

77

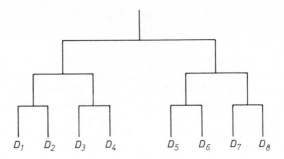

Figure 4.7. A dendrogram

Let us suppose that a set of documents

$$\{D_1, D_2, D_3, D_4, D_5, D_6, D_7, D_8\}$$

has been classified into four groups, that is

$$\{(D_1, D_2), (D_3, D_4), (D_5, D_6), (D_7, D_8)\}$$

Furthermore these have themselves been classified into two groups,

$$\{((D_1, D_2), (D_3, D_4)), ((D_5, D_6), (D_7, D_8))\}$$

The dendrogram for this structure would be that given in *Figure 4.7*. To represent this in storage by means of ring structures is now a simple matter (see *Figure 4.8*).

The D_i indicates a description (representation) of a document. Notice how the rings at a lower level are contained in those at a higher

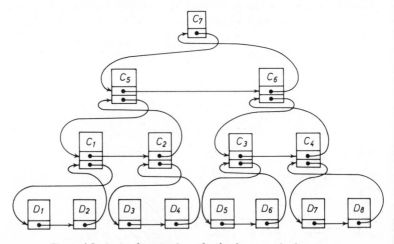

Figure 4.8. An implementation of a dendrogram via ring structures

78

level. The field marked C_i normally contains some identifying information with respect to the ring it subsumes. For example, C_1 in some way identifies the class of documents $\{D_1, D_2\}$.

Were we to group documents according to the keywords they shared, then for each keyword we would have a group of documents, namely, those which had that keyword in common. C_i would then be the field containing the keyword uniting that particular group. The rings would of course overlap (*Figure 4.9*), as in this example:

$$D_1 = \{K_1, K_2\}$$

$$D_2 = \{K_2, K_3\}$$

$$D_3 = \{K_1, K_4\}$$

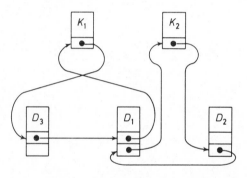

Figure 4.9. Two overlapping rings

The usefulness of this kind of structure will become more apparent when we discuss searching of classifications. If each ring has associated with it a record which contains identifying information for its members, then, a search strategy searching a structure such as this will first look at C_i (or K_i in the second example) to determine whether to proceed or abandon the search.

Threaded lists

In this section an elementary knowledge of list processing will be assumed. Readers who are unfamiliar with this topic should consult the little book by Foster[20].

A simple list representation of the classification

$$((D_1, D_2), (D_3, D_4)), ((D_5, D_6), (D_7, D_8))$$

79

is given in *Figure 4.10*. Each sublist in this structure has associated with it a record containing *only* two pointers. (We can assume that D_i is really a pointer to document D_i.) The function of the pointers should be clear from the diagram. The main thing to note, however, is that the record associated with a list does *not* contain any identifying information.

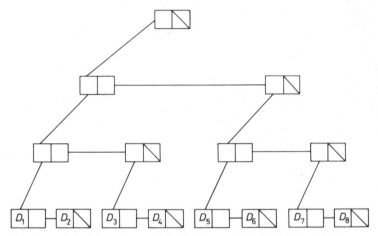

Figure 4.10. A list structure implementation of a hierarchic classification

A modification of the implementation of a list structure like this which makes it resemble a set of ring structures is to make the right hand pointer of the *last* element of a sublist point back to the head of the sublist. Each sublist has become effectively a ring structure. We now have what is commonly called a *threaded list* (see *Figure 4.11*). The representation I have given is a slight oversimplification in that we need to flag which elements are data elements (giving access to the documents D_i) and which elements are just pointer elements. The major advantage associated with a threaded list is that it can be traversed without the aid of a stack. Normally when traversing a conventional list structure the return addresses are stacked, whereas in the threaded list they have been incorporated in the data structure.

One disadvantage associated with the use of list and ring structures for representing classifications is that they can only be entered at the 'top'. An additional index giving entry to the structure at each of the data elements increases the update speed considerably.

Another modification of the simple list representation has been studied extensively by Stanfel[21, 22] and Patt[23]. The individual elements

80

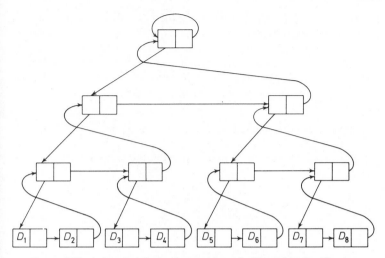

Figure 4.11. A threaded list implementation of a hierarchic classification

(or cells) of the list structure are modified to incorporate one extra field, so that instead of each element looking like this

$$\boxed{\ P_1\ |\ P_2\ }$$ it now looks like this $$\boxed{\ S\ |\ P_1\ |\ P_2\ }$$

where the P_i's are pointers and S is a symbol. Otherwise no essential change has been made to the simple representation. This structure has become known as the *Doubly Chained Tree*. Its properties have mainly been investigated for storing variable length keys, where each key is made up by selecting symbols from a finite (usually small) alphabet. For example, let $\{A,B,C\}$ be the set of key symbols and let R_1, R_2, R_3, R_4, R_5 be five records to be stored. Let us assign keys made of the 3 symbols, to the records as follows:

$$\begin{array}{ll} AAA & R_1 \\ AB & R_2 \\ AC & R_3 \\ BB & R_4 \\ BC & R_5 \end{array}$$

An example of a doubly chained tree containing the keys and giving

81

access to the records is given in *Figure 4.12*. The topmost element contains no symbol, it merely functions as the start of the structure. Given an arbitrary key its presence or absence is detected by matching it against keys in the structure. Matching proceeds level by level, once a matching symbol has been found at one level, the P_1 pointer is followed to the set of *alternative* symbols at the next level down. The matching will terminate either:

(1) when the key is exhausted, that is, no more key symbols are left to match; or
(2) when no matching symbol is found at the current level.

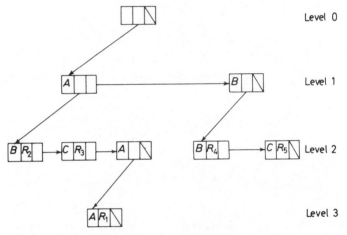

Figure 4.12. An example of a doubly chained tree

For case (1) we have:

(a) the key is present if the P_1 pointer in the same cell as the last matching symbol now points to a record;
(b) P_1 points to a further symbol, that is, the key 'falls short' and is therefore not in the structure.

For case (2), we also have that the key is not in the structure, but now there is a mismatch.

Stanfel and Patt have concentrated on generating search trees with minimum expected search time, and preserving this property despite updating. For the detailed mathematics demonstrating that this is possible the reader is referred to their cited work.

82

Trees

Although computer scientists have adopted trees as file structures, their properties were originally investigated by mathematicians. In fact a substantial part of the *Theory of Graphs* is devoted to the study of trees. Excellent books on the mathematical aspects of trees (and graphs) have been written by Berge[24], Harary *et al.*,[25] and Ore[26]. Harary's book also contains a useful glossary of concepts in graph theory. In addition Bertziss[3] and Knuth[27] discuss topics in graph theory with applications in information processing.

There are numerous definitions of *trees*. I have chosen a particularly simple one from Berge. If we think of a *graph* as a set of *nodes* (or points or vertices) and a set of *lines* (or edges) such that each line connects exactly two nodes, then a *tree* is defined to be a finite connected graph with no cycles, and possessing at least two nodes. To define a cycle we first define a chain. We represent the line u_k joining two nodes x and y by $u_k = [x,y]$. A *chain* is a *sequence* of lines, in which each line u_k has one node in common with the preceding line u_{k-1}, and the other vertex in common with the succeeding line u_{k+1}. An example of a chain is $[a,x_1]$, $[x_1,x_2]$, $[x_2,x_3]$, $[x_3,b]$. A *cycle* is a finite chain which begins at a node and terminates at the same node (i.e. in the example $a = b$).

Berge gives the following theorem showing many equivalent characterisations of trees.

Theorem. Let H be a graph with at least n nodes, where $n > 1$; any one of the following equivalent properties characterises a tree.

(1) H is connected and does not possess any cycles.
(2) H contains no cycles and has $n - 1$ lines.
(3) H is connected and has $n - 1$ lines.
(4) H is connected but loses this property if any line is deleted.
(5) Every pair of nodes is connected by one and only one chain.

One thing to be noticed in the discussion so far is that no mention has been made of a *direction* associated with a line. In most applications in computer science (and IR) one node is singled out as special. This node is normally called the *root* of the tree, and every other node in the tree can only be reached by starting at the root and proceeding along a chain of lines until the node sought is reached. Implicitly therefore, a direction is associated with each line. In fact, when one comes to represent a tree inside a computer by a list structure, often the addresses are stored in a way which allows movement in only one direction. It is convenient to think of a tree as a *directed* graph with a reserved node as the root of the tree. Of course, if one has a root then each path (directed chain) starting at the root will eventually terminate at a particular node from which no further branches emerge. These nodes are called the *terminal* nodes of the tree.

By now it is perhaps apparent that when we were talking about ring structures and threaded lists in some of our examples we were really demonstrating how to implement a tree structure. The dendrogram in *Figure 4.7* can easily be represented as a tree (*Figure 4.13*). The documents are stored at the terminal nodes and each node represents a class (cluster) of documents. A search for a particular set of documents would be initiated at the root and would proceed along the arrows until the required class was found.

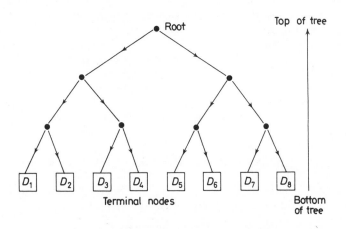

Figure 4.13. A tree representation of a dendrogram

Another example of a tree structure is the directory associated with an index-sequential file. It was described as a hierarchy of indexes, but could equally well have been described as a tree structure.

The use of tree structures in computer science dates back to the early 1950s when it was realised that the so-called *binary search* could readily be represented by a *binary* tree. A binary tree is one in which each node (except the terminal nodes) has exactly two branches leaving it. A binary search is an efficient method for detecting the presence or absence of a key value among a set of keys. It presupposes that the keys have been sorted. It proceeds by successive division of the set, at each division discarding half the current set as not containing the sought key. When the set contains N sorted keys the search time is of order $\log_2 N$. Furthermore, after some thought one can see how this process can be simply represented by a binary tree.

Unfortunately, in many applications one wants the ability to *insert* a key which has been found to be absent. If the keys are stored sequentially then the time taken by the insertion operation may be of order N. If one, however, *stores* the keys in a binary tree this lengthy insert time may be overcome, both search and insert time will be of order $\log_2 N$. The keys are stored at the nodes, at each node a left branch will lead to 'smaller' keys, a right branch will lead to 'greater' keys. A search terminating on a terminal node will indicate that the key is not present and will need to be inserted.

The structure of the tree as it grows is largely dependent on the order in which new keys are presented. Search time may become unnecessarily long because of the lop-sidedness of the tree. Fortunately, it can be shown (Knuth[28]) that random insertions do not change the expected $\log_2 N$ time dependence of the tree search. Nevertheless, methods are available to prevent the possibility of *degenerate trees*. These are trees in which the keys are stored in such a way that the expected search time is far from optimal. For example, if the keys were to arrive for insertion already ordered then the tree to be built would simply be as shown in *Figure 4.14*.

It would take us too far afield for me to explain the techniques for avoiding degenerate trees. Essentially, the binary tree is maintained in such a way that at any node the subtree on the left branch has approximately as many levels as the subtree on the right branch. Hence the name *balanced* tree for such a tree. The search paths in a balanced tree will never be more than 45 per cent longer than the optimum. The expected search and insert times are still of order $\log N$. For further details the reader is recommended to consult Knuth[28].

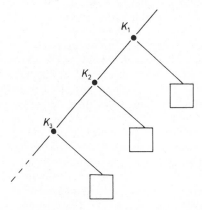

Figure 4.14. An example of a degenerate tree

So far we have assumed that each key was equally likely as a search argument. If one has data giving the probability that the search argument is K_i (a key already in the tree), and the probability that the search argument lies between K_i and K_{i+1}, then again techniques are known for reordering the tree to optimise the expected search time. Essentially one makes sure that the more frequently accessed keys have the shortest search paths from the root. One well-known technique used when only the *second* set of probabilities is known, and the others assigned the value zero, is the Hu-Tucker algorithm. Again the interested reader may consult Knuth.

At this point it is probably a good idea to point out that these efficiency considerations are largely irrelevant when it comes to representing a document classification by a tree structure. The situation in document retrieval is different in the following aspects:

(1) we do not have a useful *linear* ordering on the documents;
(2) a search request normally does not seek the absence or presence of a document.

In fact, what we do have is that documents are more or less similar to each other, and a request seeks documents which in some way best match the request. A tree structure representing a document classification is therefore chosen so that similar documents may be close together. Therefore to rearrange a tree structure to satisfy some 'balancedness' criterion is out of the question. The search efficiency is achieved by bringing together documents which are likely to be required together.

This is not to say that the above efficiency considerations are unimportant in the general context of IR. Many operations, such as the searching of a dictionary, and using a suffix stripping algorithm can be made very efficient by appropriately structuring the binary tree.

The discussion so far has been limited to *binary* trees. In many applications this two-way split is inappropriate. The natural way to represent document classifications is by a general tree structure, where there is no restriction on the number of branches leaving a node. Another example is the directory of an index sequential file which is normally represented by an *m*-way tree, where *m* is the number of branches leaving a node.

Finally, more comments are in order about the manipulation of tree structures in mass storage devices. Up to now we have assumed that to follow a set of pointers poses no particular problems with regard to retrieval speed. Unfortunately, present random access devices are sufficiently slow for it to be impossible to allow an access for, say, each node in a tree. There are ways of partitioning trees in such a way that the number of disk accesses during a tree search can be reduced.

Essentially, it involves storing a number of nodes together in one 'page' of disk storage. During a disk access this page is brought into fast memory, is then searched, and the next page to be accessed is determined.

Scatter storage or hash addressing

One file structure which does not relate very well to the ones mentioned before is known as *Scatter Storage*. The technique by which the file structure is implemented is often called *Hash Addressing*. Its underlying principle is appealingly simple. Given that we may access the data through a number of keys K_i, then the address of the data in store is located through a key transformation function f which when applied to K_i evaluates to give the address of the associated data. We are assuming here that with each key is associated only one data item. Also for convenience we will assume that each record (data and key) fits into one location, whose address is in the image space of f. The addresses given by the application of f to the keys K_i are called the *hash addresses* and f is called a *hashing function*. Ideally f should be such that it spreads the hash addresses uniformly over the available storage. Of course this would be achieved if the function were one-to-one. Unfortunately this cannot be so because the range of possible key values is usually considerably larger than the range of the available storage addresses. Therefore, given any hashing function we have to contend with the fact that two distinct keys K_i and K_j are likely to map to the same address $f(K_i)$ $(=f(K_j))$. Before I explain some of the ways of dealing with this I shall give a few examples of hashing functions.

Let us assume that the available storage is of size 2^m then three simple transformations are as follows:

(1) if K_i is the key, then take the square of its binary representation and select m bits from the middle of the result;

(2) cut the binary representation of K_i into pieces each of m bits and add these together. Now select the m least significant bits of the sum as the hash address;

(3) divide the integer corresponding to K_i by the length of the available store 2^m and use the remainder as the hash address.

Each of these methods has disadvantages. For example, the last one may give the same address rather frequently if there are patterns in the keys. Before using a particular method the reader is advised to consult the now extensive literature on the subject, e.g. Morris[29], or Lum *et al.*[30].

As mentioned before there is the problem of collisions, that is, when two distinct keys hash to the same address. The first point to be made about this problem is that it destroys some of the simplicity of hashing. Initially it may have been thought that the key need not be stored with the data at the hash address. Unfortunately this is not so. No matter what method we use to resolve collisions we still need to store the key with the data so that at search time when a key is hashed we can distinguish its data from the data associated with keys which have hashed to the same address.

There are a number of strategies for dealing with collisions. Essentially they fall into two classes, those which use pointers to link together collided keys and those which do not. Let us first look at the ones which do not use pointers. These have a mechanism for searching the store, starting at the address where the collision occurred, for an empty storage location if a record needs to be inserted, or, for a matching key value at retrieval time. The simplest of these advances from the hash address each time moving along a fixed number of locations, say s, until an empty location or the matching key value is found. The collision strategy thus traces out a well defined sequence of locations. This method of dealing with collisions is called the *linear* method. The tendency with this method is to store collided records as closely to the initial hash address as possible. This leads to an undesirable effect called *primary clustering*. In this context all this means is that the records tend to concentrate in groups or bunch-up. It destroys the uniform nature of the hashing function. To be more precise, it is desirable that hash addresses are equally likely, however, the first empty location at the end of a collision sequence increases in likelihood in proportion to the number of records in the collision sequence. To see this one needs only to realise that a key hashed to *any* location in the sequence will have its record stored at the end of the sequence. Therefore big groups of records tend to grow even bigger. This phenomenon is aggravated by a small step size s when seeking an empty location. Sometimes $s = 1$ is used in which case the collision strategy is known as the *open addressing technique*. Primary clustering is also worse when the hash table (available storage) is relatively full.

Variations in the linear method which avoid primary clustering involve making the step size a variable. One way is to set s equal to $ai + bi^2$ on the ith step. Another is to invoke a random number generator which calculates the step size afresh each time. These last two collision handling methods are called the *quadratic* and *random* method respectively. Although they avoid primary clustering they are nevertheless subject to *secondary* clustering, which is caused by keys hashing to the same address *and* following the same sequence in search

88

FILE STRUCTURES

of an empty location. Even this can be avoided, see for example Bell
and Kaman[31].

The second class of collision handling methods involves extra storage
space which is used to chain together collided records. When a collision
occurs at a hash address it may be because it is the head of a chain of
records which have all hashed to that address, or it may be that a record
is stored there which belongs to a chain starting at some other address.
In both cases a free location is needed which in the first case is simply
linked in and stores the new record, in the second case the intermediate
chain element is moved to the free location and the new record is
stored at its own hash address thus starting a new chain (a one-element
chain so far). A variation on this method is to use a two-level store. At
the first level we have a hash table, at the second level we have a *bump*
table which contains all the collided records. At a hash address in the
hash table we will find either, a record if no collisions have taken place
at that address, or, a pointer to a chain of records which collided at that
address. This latter chaining method has the advantage that records
need never be moved once they have been entered in the bump table.
The storage overhead is larger since records are put in the bump table
before the hash table is full.

For both classes of collision strategies one needs to be careful about
deletions. For the linear, quadratic etc. collision handling strategies we
must ensure that when we delete a record at an address we do not make
records which collided at that address unreachable. Similarly with the
chaining method we must ensure that a deleted record does not leave a
gap in the chain, that is, after deletion the chain must be reconnected.

The advantages of hashing are several. Firstly it is simple. Secondly
its insertion and search strategies are identical. Insertion is merely a
failed search. If K_i is the hashed key, then if a search of the collision
sequence fails to turn up a match in K_i, its record is simply inserted at
the end of the sequence at the next free location. Thirdly, the search
time is independent of the number of keys to be inserted.

The application of hashing in IR has tended to be in the area of table
construction and look-up procedures. An obvious application is when
constructing the set of conflation classes during text processing. In
Chapter 2, I gave an example of a document representative as simply a
list of class names, each name standing for a set of equivalent words.
During a retrieval operation, a query will first be converted into a list of
class names. To do this each significant word needs to be looked up in a
dictionary which gives the name of the class to which it belongs. Clearly
there is a case for hashing. We simply apply the hashing function to the
word and find the name of the conflation class to which it belongs at
the hash address. A similar example is given in great detail by Murray[32].

89

Finally, let me recommend two very readable discussions on hashing, one is in Page and Wilson[33], the other is in Knuth's third volume[28].

Clustered files

It is now common practice to refer to a file processed by a clustering algorithm as a clustered file, and to refer to the resulting structure as a file structure. For example Salton[34] (p. 288) lists a clustered file as an alternative organisation to inverted, serial, chained files, etc. Although it may be convenient terminologically, it does disguise the real status of cluster methods. Cluster methods (or automatic classification methods) are more profitably discussed at the level of abstraction at which relations are discussed in connection with data bases, that is, in a thoroughly data independent way. In other words, selecting an appropriate cluster method and implementing it are two separate problems. Unfortunately not all users of clustering techniques see it this way, and so the current scene is rather confused. One factor contributing to the confusion is that clustering techniques have been used at a very low level of implementation of system software, for example, to reduce the number of page exceptions in a virtual memory. Therefore, those who use clustering merely to increase retrieval efficiency (in terms of storage and speed) will tend to see a classification structure as a file structure, whereas those who see clustering as a means of discovering (or summarising) some inherent structure in the data will look upon the same structure as a description of the data. Of course, this description may be used to achieve more efficient retrieval (and in IR more effective retrieval in terms of say precision and recall). Furthermore, if one looks carefully at some of the implementations of cluster methods one discovers that the classificatory system is represented inside the computer by one of the more conventional file structures.

Bibliographic remarks

There is now a vast literature on file structures although there are very few survey articles. Where possible I shall point to some of the more detailed discussions which emphasise an application in IR. Of course the chapter on file organisation in the *Annual Review* is a good source of references as well. Chapter 7 of Salton's latest book contains a useful introduction to file organisation techniques[34].

A general article on data structures of a more philosophical nature well worth reading is Mealey[35].

A description of the use of a *sequential* file in an on-line environment may be found in Negus and Hall[36]. The effectiveness and efficiency of an *inverted* file has been extensively compared with a file structure based on clustering by Murray[37]. Ein-Dor[38] has done a comprehensive comparison between an *inverted* file and a *tree structured* file. It is hard to find a discussion of an *index-sequential* file which makes special reference to the needs of document retrieval. Index-sequential organisation is now considered to be basic software which can be used to implement a variety of other file organisations. Nevertheless it is worth studying some of the aspects of its implementation. For this I recommed the paper by McDonell and Montgomery[39] who give a detailed description of an implementation for a mini-computer. *Multi-lists* and *cellular multi-lists* are fairly well covered by Lefkovitz[40]. *Ring structures* have been very popular in CAD and have been written up by Gray[41]. Extensive use was made of a modified *threaded list* by Van Rijsbergen[42] in his cluster-based retrieval experiments. The *doubly chained tree* has been adequately dealt with by Stanfel[21, 22] and Patt[23].

Work on tree structures in IR goes back a long way as illustrated by the early papers by Salton[43] and Sussenguth[44]. Trees have always attracted much attention in computer science, mainly for the ability to reduce expected search times in data retrieval. One of the earliest papers on this topic is by Windley[45] but the most extensive discussion is still to be found in Knuth[28] where not only methods of construction are discussed but also techniques of reorganisation.

More recently a special kind of tree, called a *trie*, has attracted attention. This is a tree structure which has records stored at its terminal nodes, and discriminators at the internal nodes. A discriminator at a node is made up from the attributes of the records dominated by that node. Or as Knuth puts it: 'A trie is essentially a *M*-ary tree whose nodes are *M*-place vectors with components corresponding to digits or characters. Each node on level l represents the set of all keys that begin with a certain sequence of l characters; the node specifies an *M*-way branch depending on the $(l + 1)$st character.' Tries were invented by Fredkins[46], further considered by Sussenguth[44], and more recently studied by Burkhard[47], Rivest[48], and Bentley[49]. The use of tries in data retrieval where one is interested in either a match or mismatch is very similar to the construction of hierarchic document classification, where each node of the tree representing the hierarchy is also associated with a 'discriminator' used to direct the search for relevant documents (see for example *Figure 5.3* in Chapter 5).

The use of hashing in document retrieval is dealt with in Higgins and Smith[50], and Chou[51].

It has become fashionable to refer to document collections which have been clustered as *clustered files*. I have gone to some pains to avoid the use of this terminology because of the conceptual difference that exists between a structure which is inherent in the data and can be discovered by clustering, and an organisation of the data to facilitate its manipulation inside a computer. Unfortunately this distinction becomes somewhat blurred when clustering techniques are used to generate a *physical* organisation of data. For example, the work by Bell *et al.*[52] is of this nature. Furthermore, it has recently become popular to cluster records simply to improve the efficiency of retrieval. Buckhard and Keller[53] base the design of a file structure on maximal complete subgraphs (or cliques). Hatfield and Gerald[54] have designed a paging algorithm for a virtual memory store based on clustering. Simon and Guiho[55] look at methods for preserving 'clusters' in the data when it is mapped onto a physical storage device.

Some of the work that has been largely ignored in this chapter, but which is nevertheless of importance when considering the implementation of a file structure, is concerned directly with the physical organisation of a storage device in terms of block sizes, etc. Unfortunately, general statements about this are rather hard to make because the organisation tends to depend on the hardware characteristics of the device and computer. Representative of work in this area is the paper by Lum *et al.*[56].

References

1. HSIAO, D. and HARARY, F., 'A formal system for information retrieval from files', *Communications of the ACM*, **13**, 67–73 (1970)
2. ROBERTS, D. C., 'File organization techniques', *Advances in Computers*, **12**, 115–174 (1972)
3. BERTZISS, A. T., *Data Structures: Theory and Practice*, Academic Press, London and New York (1971)
4. DODD, G. G., 'Elements of data management systems', *Computing Surveys*, **1**, 117–133 (1969)
5. CLIMENSON, W. D., 'File organization and search techniques', *Annual Review of Information Science and Technology*, **1**, 107–135 (1966)
6. WARHEIT, I. A., 'File organization of library records', *Journal of Library Automation*, **2**, 20–30 (1969)
7. PRYWES, N. S. and SMITH, D. P., 'Organization of information', *Annual Review of Information Science and Technology*, **7**, 103–158 (1972) Technology, 7, 103 158 (1972)
8. CODD, E. F., 'A relational model of data for large shared data banks', *Communications of the ACM*, **13**, 377–387 (1970)

9. SENKO, M. E., 'Information systems: records, relations, sets, entities, and things', *Information Systems*, 1, 3–13 (1975)

10. DATE, C. J., *An Introduction to Data Base Systems*, Addison-Wesley, Reading, Mass. (1975)

11. SIBLEY, E. H., 'Special Issue: Data base management systems', *Computing Surveys*, 8, No. 1 (1976)

12. MARON, M. E., 'Relational data file I: Design philosophy', In: *Information Retrieval* (Edited by Schecter 6), 211–223 (1967)

13. LEVIEN, R., 'Relational data file II: Implementation', In: *Information Retrieval* (Edited by Schecter 6), 225–241 (1967)

14. HAYES, R. M. and BECKER, J., *Handbook of Data Processing for Libraries*, Melville Publishing Co., Los Angeles, California (1974)

15. HSIAO, D., 'A generalized record organization', *IEEE Transactions on Computers*, C-20, 1490–1495 (1971)

16. MANOLA, F. and HSIAO, D. K., 'A model for keyword based file structures and access', *NRL Memorandum Report 2544*, Naval Research Laboratory, Washington D.C. (1973)

17. SEVERANCE, D. G., 'A parametric model of alternative file structures', *Information Systems*, 1, 51–55 (1975)

18. VAN RIJSBERGEN, C. J., 'File organization in library automation and information retrieval', *Journal of Documentation*, 32, 294–317 (1976)

19. JONKERS, H. L., 'A straightforward and flexible design method for complex data base management systems', *Information Storage and Retrieval*, 9, 401–415 (1973)

20. FOSTER, J. M., *List Processing*, Macdonald, London; and American Elsevier Inc., New York (1967)

21. STANFEL, L. E., 'Practical aspect of doubly chained trees for retrieval', *Journal of the ACM*, 19, 425–436 (1972)

22. STANFEL, L. E., 'Optimal trees for a class of information retrieval problems', *Information Storage and Retrieval*, 9, 43–59 (1973)

23. PATT, Y. N., 'Minimum search tree structure for data partitioned into pages', *IEEE Transactions on Computers*, C-21, 961–967 (1972)

24. BERGE, C., *The Theory of Graphs and its Applications*, Methuen, London (1966)

25. HARARY, F., NORMAN, R. Z. and CARTWRIGHT, D., *Structural Models: An Introduction to the Theory of Directed Graphs*, Wiley, New York (1966)

26. ORE, O., *Graphs and their Uses*, Random House, New York (1963)

27. KNUTH, D. E., *The Art of Computer Programming*, Vol. 1, *Fundamental Algorithms*, Addison-Wesley, Reading, Massachusetts (1968)

28. KNUTH, D. E., *The Art of Computer Programming*, Vol. 3, *Sorting and Searching*, Addison-Wesley, Reading, Massachusetts (1973)

29. MORRIS, R., 'Scatter storage techniques', *Communications of the ACM*, 11, 35–38 (1968)

30. LUM, V. Y., YUEN, P. S. T. and DODD, M., 'Key-to-address transform techniques: a fundamental performance study on large existing formatted files', *Communications of the ACM*, 14, 228–239 (1971)

31. BELL, J. R. and KAMAN, C. H., 'The linear quotient hash code', *Communications of the ACM*, 13, 675-677 (1970)

32. MURRAY, D. M., 'A scatter storage scheme for dictionary lookups'. *In*: Report ISR-16 to the National Science Foundation, Section II, Cornell University, Department of Computer Science (1969)

33. PAGE, E. S. and WILSON, L. B., *Information Representation and Manipulation in a Computer*, Cambridge University Press, Cambridge (1973)

93

FILE STRUCTURES

34. SALTON, G., *Dynamic Information and Library Processing*, Prentice-Hall, Englewood Cliffs, N.J. (1975)
35. MEALEY, G. H., 'Another look at data', *Proceedings AFIP Fall Joint Computer Conference*, 525–534 (1967)
36. NEGUS, A. E. and HALL, J. L., 'Towards an effective on-line reference retrieval system', Library Memo CLM-LM2/71, U.K. Atomic Energy Authority, Research Group (1971)
37. MURRAY, D. M., 'Document retrieval based on clustered files', Ph.D. Thesis, Cornell University Report ISR-20 to National Science Foundation and to the National Library of Medicine (1972)
38. EIN-DOR, P., 'The comparative efficiency of two dictionary structures for document retrieval, *Infor Journal*, **12**, 87–108 (1974)
39. McDONELL, K.J. and MONTGOMERY, A. Y., 'The design of indexed sequential files', *The Australian Computer Journal*, **5**, 115–126 (1973)
40. LEFKOVITZ, D., *File Structures for On-line Systems*, Spartan Books, New York (1969)
41. GRAY, J. C., 'Compound data structure for computer aided design: a survey', *Proceedings ACM National Meeting*, 355–365 (1967)
42. VAN RIJSBERGEN, C. J., 'An algorithm for information structuring and retrieval', *Computer Journal*, **14**, 407–412 (1971)
43. SALTON, G., Manipulation of trees in information retrieval', *Communications of the ACM*, **5**, 103–114 (1962)
44. SUSSENGUTH, E. H., 'Use of tree structures for processing files', *Communications of the ACM*, **6**, 272–279 (1963)
45. WINDLEY, P. F., 'Trees, forests and rearranging', *Computer Journal*, **3**, 84–88 (1960)
46. FREDKIN, E., 'Trie memory', *Communications of the ACM*, **3**, 490–499 (1960)
47. BURKHARD, W.A., 'Partial match queries and file designs', *Proceedings of the International Conference on Very Large Data Bases*, 523–525 (1975)
48. RIVEST, R., *Analysis of Associative Retrieval Algorithms*, Ph.D. Thesis, Stanford University, Computer Science (1974)
49. BENTLEY, J. L., 'Multidimensional binary search trees used for associative searching', *Communications of the ACM*, **13**, 675–677 (1975)
50. HIGGINS, L. D. and SMITH, F. J., 'Disc access algorithms', *Computer Journal*, **14**, 249–253 (1971)
51. CHOU, C. K., 'Algorithms for hash coding and document classification', Ph.D. Thesis, University of Illinois (1972)
52. BELL, C. J., ALDRED, B. K. and ROGERS, T. W., 'Adaptability to change in large data base information retrieval systems', Report No. UKSC-0027, UK Scientific Centre, IBM United Kingdom Limited, Neville Road, Peterlee, County Durham, U.K. (1972)
53. BURKHARD, W. A. and KELLER, R. M., 'Some approaches to best-match file searching', *Communications of the ACM*, **16**, 230–236 (1973)
54. HATFIELD, D. J. and GERALD, J., 'Program restructuring for virtual memory', *IBM Systems Journal*, **10**, 168–192 (1971)
55. SIMON, J. C. and GUIHO, G., 'On algorithms preserving neighbourhood to file and retrieve information in a memory', *International Journal Computer Information Sciences*, **1**, 3–15 (CR 23923) (1972)
56. LUM, V. Y., LING, H. and SENKO, M. E., 'Analysis of a complex data management access method by simulation modelling', *Proceedings AFIP Fall Joint Computer Conference*, 211–222 (1970)

Five

SEARCH STRATEGIES

Introduction

So far very little has been said about the actual process by which the required information is located. In the case of document retrieval the information is the subset of documents which are deemed to be relevant to the query. In Chapter 4, occasional reference was made to search efficiency, and the appropriateness of a file structure for searching. The kind of search that is of interest, is *not* the usual kind where the result of the search is clear cut, either yes, the item is present, or no, the item is absent. Good discussions of these may be found in Knuth[1] and Salton[2]. They are of considerable importance when dictionaries need to be set-up or consulted during text processing. However, we are more interested in search strategies in which the documents retrieved may be more or less relevant to the request.

All search strategies are based on comparison between the query and the stored documents. Sometimes this comparison is only achieved indirectly when the query is compared with clusters (or more precisely with the profiles representing the clusters).

The distinctions made between different kinds of search strategies can sometimes be understood by looking at the query language, that is the language in which the information need is expressed. The nature of the query language often dictates the nature of the search strategy. For example, a query language which allows search statements to be expressed in terms of logical combinations of keywords normally dictates a Boolean search. This is a search which achieves its results by logical (rather than numerical) comparisons of the query with the documents. However, I shall not examine query languages but instead capture the differences by talking about the search mechanisms.

Boolean search

A Boolean search strategy retrieves those documents which are 'true'

95

for the query. This formulation only makes sense if the queries are expressed in terms of index terms (or keywords) and combined by the usual logical connectives AND, OR, and NOT. For example, if the query $Q = (K_1 \text{ AND } K_2) \text{ OR } (K_3 \text{ AND } (\text{NOT } K_4))$ then the Boolean search will retrieve all documents indexed by K_1 and K_2, as well as all documents indexed by K_3 which are *not* indexed by K_4.

Some systems which operate by means of Boolean searches allow the user to narrow or broaden the search by giving the user access to a structured dictionary which for any given keyword stores related keywords which may be more general or more precise. For example, in the tree structure in *Figure 5.1*, the keyword K_1^1 is contained in the more general keyword K_1^0, but it can also be split up into 4 more precise keywords K_1^2, K_2^2, K_3^2, and K_4^2. Therefore, if one has an interactive system the search can easily be reformulated using some of these related terms.

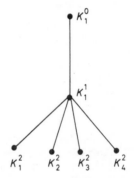

Figure 5.1. A set of hierarchically related keywords

An obvious way to implement the Boolean search is through the inverted file. We store a list for each keyword in the vocabulary, and in each list put the addresses (or numbers) of the documents containing that particular keyword. To satisfy a query we now perform the set operations, corresponding to the logical connectives, on the K_i-lists. For example, if

$$K_1\text{–list} : D_1, D_2, D_3, D_4$$

$$K_2\text{–list} : D_1, D_2$$

$$K_3\text{–list} : D_1, D_2, D_3$$

$$K_4\text{–list} : D_1$$

and $Q = (K_1 \text{ AND } K_2) \text{ OR } (K_3 \text{ AND } (\text{NOT } K_4))$

then to satisfy the $(K_1$ AND $K_2)$ part we *intersect* the K_1 and K_2 lists, to satisfy the $(K_3$ AND (NOT $K_4))$ part we *subtract* the K_4 list from the K_3 list. The OR is satisfied by now taking the *union* of the two sets of documents obtained for the parts. The result is the set $\{D_1, D_2, D_3\}$ which satisfies the query and each cocument in it is 'true' for the query.

A slight modification of the full Boolean search is one which only allows AND logic but takes account of the actual *number* of terms the query has in common with a document. This number has become known as the *co-ordination level*. The search strategy is often called *simple matching*. Because at any level we can have more than one document, the documents are said to be *partially* ranked by the co-ordination levels.

For the same example as before with the query $Q = K_1$ AND K_2 AND K_3 we obtain the following ranking:

Co-ordination level

3	D_1, D_2
2	D_3
1	D_4

In fact, simple matching may be viewed as using a primitive matching function. For each document D we calculate $|D \cap Q|$, that is the size of the overlap between D and Q, each represented as a set of keywords. This is the *simple matching coefficient* mentioned in Chapter 3.

Matching functions

Many of the more sophisticated search strategies are implemented by means of a *matching function*. This is a function similar to an association measure, but differing in that a matching function measures the association between a query and a document or cluster profile, whereas an association measure is applied to objects of the same kind. Mathematically the two functions have the same properties; they only differ in their interpretations.

There are many examples of matching functions in the literature. Perhaps the simplest is the one associated with the simple matching search strategy.

If M is the matching function, D the set of keywords representing the document, and Q the set representing the query, then:

$$M = \frac{2|D \cap Q|}{|D| + |Q|}$$

is another example of a matching function. It is of course the same as Dice's coefficient of Chapter 3.

A popular one used by the SMART project, which they call cosine correlation, assumes that the document and query are represented as numerical vectors in t-space, that is $Q = (q_1, q_2, \ldots, q_t)$ and $D = (d_1, d_2, \ldots, d_t)$ where q_i and d_i are numerical weights associated with the keyword i. The cosine correlation is now simply

$$r = \frac{\sum\limits_{i=1}^{t} q_i d_i}{\left(\sum\limits_{i=1}^{t} (q_i)^2 \sum\limits_{i=1}^{t} (d_i)^2 \right)^{\frac{1}{2}}}$$

or, in the notation for a vector space with a Euclidean norm,

$$r = \frac{(Q, D)}{||Q|| \, ||D||} = \text{cosine } \theta$$

where θ is the angle between vectors Q and D.

Serial search

Although serial searches are acknowledged to be slow, they are frequently still used as parts of larger systems. They also provide a convenient demonstration of the use of matching functions.

Suppose there are N documents D_i in the system, then the serial search proceeds by calculating N values $M(Q, D_i)$ for $i = 1$ to N. In other words the matching function is evaluated at each document for the same query Q. On the basis of the values $M(Q, D_i)$ the set of documents to be retrieved is determined. There are two ways of doing this:

(1) the matching function is given a suitable threshold, retrieving the documents above the threshold and discarding the ones below. If T is the threshold, then the retrieved set B is the set $\{D_i | M(Q, D_i) > T\}$;

(2) the documents are ranked in increasing order of matching function value. A rank position R is chosen as cut-off and all documents below the rank are retrieved so that $B = \{D_i | r(i) < R\}$ where $r(i)$ is the rank position assigned to D_i. The hope in each case is that the relevant documents are contained in the retrieved set.

The main difficulty with this kind of search strategy is the specification of the threshold or cut-off. It will always be arbitrary since there is no way of telling in advance what value for each query will produce the best retrieval.

Cluster representatives

Before we can sensibly talk about search strategies applied to clustered document collections, we need to say a little about the methods used to represent clusters. Whereas in a serial search we need to be able to match queries with each document in the file, in a search of a clustered file we need to be able to match queries with clusters. For this purpose clusters are represented by some kind of profile (a much overworked word), which here will be called a *cluster representative*. It attempts to summarise and characterise the cluster of documents.

A cluster representative should be such that an incoming query will be *diagnosed* into the cluster containing the documents *relevant* to the query. In other words we expect the cluster representative to discriminate the relevant from the non-relevant documents when matched against any query. This is a tall order, and unfortunately there is no theory enabling one to select the right kind of cluster representative. One can only proceed experimentally. There are a number of 'reasonable' ways of characterising clusters; it then remains a matter for experimental test to decide which of these is the most effective.

Let me first give an example of a very primitive cluster representative. If we assume that the clusters are derived from a cluster method based on a dissimilarity measure, then we can represent each cluster at some level of dissimilarity by a graph (see *Figure 5.2*). Here

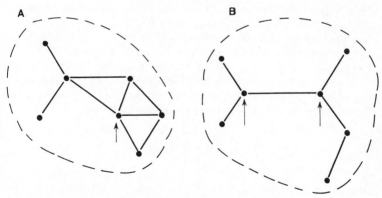

Figure 5.2. Examples of maximally linked documents as cluster representatives

99

A and **B** are two clusters. The nodes represent documents and the line between any two nodes indicates that their corresponding documents are less dissimilar than some specified level of dissimilarity. Now, one way of representing a cluster is to select a *typical* member from the cluster. A simple way of doing this is to find that document which is linked to the maximum number of other documents in the cluster. A suitable name for this kind of cluster representative is the *maximally linked document.* In the clusters **A** and **B** illustrated there are pointers to the candidates. As one would expect in some cases the representative is not unique. For example, in cluster **B** we have two candidates. To deal with this, one either makes an arbitrary choice or one maintains a list of cluster representatives for that cluster. The motivation leading to this particular choice of cluster representative is given in some detail in Van Rijsbergen[3] but need not concern us here.

Let us now look at other ways of representing clusters. We seek a method of representation which in some way 'averages' the descriptions of the members of the clusters. The method that immediately springs to mind is one in which one calculates the centroid (or centre of gravity) of the cluster. If $\{D_1, D_2, \ldots, D_n\}$ are the documents in the cluster and each D_i is represented by a numerical vector $(d_1, d_2, \ldots, d_t)$ then the centroid C of the cluster is given by

$$C = \frac{1}{n} \sum_{i=1}^{n} \frac{D_i}{||D_i||}$$

where $||D_i||$ is usually the Euclidean norm, i.e.

$$||D_i|| = \sqrt{d_1^2 + d_2^2 + \ldots + d_t^2}$$

More often than not the documents are not represented by numerical vectors but by binary vectors (or equivalently, sets of keywords). In that case we can still use a centroid type of cluster representative but the normalisation is replaced with a process which thresholds the components of the sum ΣD_i. To be more precise, let D_i now be a binary vector, such that a 1 in the jth position indicates the presence of the jth keyword in the document and a 0 indicates the contrary. The cluster representative is now derived from the sum vector

$$S = \sum_{i=1}^{n} D_i$$

(remember n is the number of documents in the cluster) by the following procedure. Let $C = (c_1, c_2, \ldots c_t)$ be the cluster representative and $[D_i]_j$ the jth component of the binary vector D_i, then two methods are:

$$(1) \quad c_j = \begin{cases} 1 \text{ if } \sum_{i=1}^{n} [D_i]_j > 1 \\ 0 \text{ otherwise} \end{cases}$$

or

$$(2) \quad c_j = \begin{cases} 1 \text{ if } \sum_{i=1}^{n} [D_i]_j > \log_2 n \\ 0 \text{ otherwise} \end{cases}$$

So, finally we obtain as a cluster representative a binary vector C. In both cases the intuition is that keywords occurring only once in the cluster should be ignored. In the second case we also normalise out the size n of the cluster.

There is some evidence to show that both these methods of representation are effective when used in conjunction with appropriate search strategies (see, for example, Van Rijsbergen[4] and Murray[5]). Obviously there are further variations on obtaining cluster representatives but as in the case of association measures it seems unlikely that retrieval effectiveness will change very much by varying the cluster representatives. It is more likely that the way the data in the cluster representative is used by the search strategy will have a larger effect.

There is another theoretical way of looking at the construction of cluster representatives and that is through the notion of a *maximal predictor* for a cluster[6]. Given that, as before, the documents D_i in a cluster are binary vectors then a binary cluster representative for this cluster is a predictor in the sense that each component (c_i) predicts the most likely value of that attribute in the member documents. It is maximal if its correct predictions are as numerous as possible. If one assumes that each member of a cluster of documents $D_1, \ldots, D_n$ is equally likely then the expected total number of *incorrect* predicted properties (or simply the expected total number of mismatches between cluster representative and member documents since everything in binary) is,

$$\sum_{i=1}^{n} \sum_{j=1}^{t} ([D_i]_j - c_j)^2$$

101

This can be rewritten as

$$\sum_{i=1}^{n} \sum_{j=1}^{t} ([D_i]_j - D._j)^2 + n \sum_{j=1}^{t} (D._j - c_j) \qquad (*)$$

where

$$D._j = \frac{1}{n} \sum_{i=1}^{n} [D_i]_j$$

The expression (*) will be minimised, thus maximising the number of correct predictions, when $C = (c_1, \ldots, c_t)$ is chosen in such a way that

$$\sum_{j=1}^{t} (D._j - c_j)^2$$

is a minimum. This is achieved by

$$(3) \qquad c_j = \begin{cases} 1 & \text{if } D._j > \frac{1}{2} \\ 0 & \text{otherwise} \end{cases}$$

So in other words a keyword will be assigned to a cluster representative if it occurs in more than half the member documents. This treats errors of prediction caused by absence or presence of keywords on an equal basis. Croft[7] has shown that it is more reasonable to differentiate the two types of error in IR applications. He showed that to predict falsely 0 ($c_j = 0$) is more costly than to predict falsely a 1 ($c_j = 1$). Under this assumption the value of ½ appearing in (3) is replaced by a constant less than ½, its exact value being related to the relative importance attached to the two types of prediction error.

Although the main reason for constructing these cluster representatives is to lead a search strategy to *relevant* documents, it should be clear that they can also be used to guide a search to documents meeting some condition on the matching function. For example, we may want to retrieve all documents D_i which match Q better than T, i.e.

$$\{D_i | M(Q, D_i) > T\}$$

For more details about the evaluation of cluster representative (3) for this purpose the reader should consult the work of Yu *et al.*[8, 9].

One major objection to most work on cluster representatives is that it treats the distribution of keywords in clusters as independent. This is not very realistic. Unfortunately, there does not appear to be any work to remedy the situation except that of Ardnaudov and Govorun[10].

Finally, it should be noted that cluster methods which proceed directly from document descriptions to the classification without first computing the intermediate dissimilarity coefficient, will need to make a choice of cluster representative *ab initio*. These cluster representatives are then 'improved' as the algorithm, adjusting the classification according to some objective function, steps through its iterations.

Cluster-based retrieval

Cluster-based retrieval has as its foundation the *cluster hypothesis*, which states that closely associated documents tend to be relevant to the same requests. Clustering picks out closely associated documents and groups them together into one cluster. In Chapter 3, I discussed many ways of doing this, here I shall ignore the actual mechanism of generating the classification and concentrate on how it may be searched with the aim of retrieving relevant documents.

Suppose we have a hierarchic classification of documents then a simple search strategy goes as follows (refer to *Figure 5.3* for details). The search starts at the root of the tree, node 0 in the example. It proceeds by evaluating a matching function at the nodes immediately descendant from node 0, in the example the nodes 1 and 2. This pattern repeats itself down the tree. The search is directed by a *decision rule,* which on the basis of comparing the values of a matching function at each stage decides which node to expand further. Also, it is necessary to have a *stopping rule* which terminates the search and forces a retrieval. In *Figure 5.3* the decision rule is: expand the node

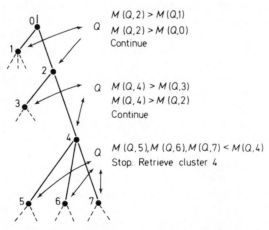

$M(Q,2) > M(Q,1)$
$M(Q,2) > M(Q,0)$
Continue

$M(Q,4) > M(Q,3)$
$M(Q,4) > M(Q,2)$
Continue

$M(Q,5), M(Q,6), M(Q,7) < M(Q,4)$
Stop. Retrieve cluster 4

Figure 5.3. A search tree and the appropriate values of a matching function illustrating the action of a decision rule and a stopping rule

103

corresponding to the maximum value of the matching function achieved within a filial set. The stopping rule is: stop if the current maximum is less than the previous maximum. A few remarks about this strategy are in order:

(1) we assume that effective retrieval can be achieved by finding just one cluster;

(2) we assume that each cluster can be adequately represented by a cluster representative for the purpose of locating the cluster containing the relevant documents;

(3) if the maximum of the matching function is not unique some special action, such as a look-ahead, will need to be taken;

(4) the search always terminates and will retrieve at least one document.

An immediate generalisation of this search is to allow the search to proceed down more than one branch of the tree so as to allow retrieval of more than one cluster. By necessity the decision rule and stopping rule will be slightly more complicated. The main difference being that provision must be made for *back-tracking*. This will occur when the search strategy estimates (based on the current value of the matching function) that further progress down a branch is a waste of time, at which point it may or may not retrieve the current cluster. The search then returns (back-tracks) to a previous branching point and takes an alternative branch down the tree.

The above strategies may be described as *top-down* searches. A *bottom-up* search is one which enters the tree at one of its terminal nodes, and proceeds in an upward direction towards the root of the tree. In this way it will pass through a sequence of nested clusters of increasing size. A decision rule is not required; we only need a stopping rule which could be simply a cut-off. A typical search would seek the largest cluster containing the document represented by the starting node and not exceeding the cut-off in size. Once this cluster is found, the set of documents in it is retrieved. To initiate the search in response to a request it is necessary to know in advance one terminal node appropriate for that request. It is not unusual to find that a user will already know of a document relevant to his request and is seeking other documents similar to it. This 'source' document can thus be used to initiate a bottom-up search. For a systematic evaluation of bottom-up searches in terms of efficiency and effectiveness see Croft[7].

If we now abandon the idea of having a multi-level clustering and accept a single-level clustering, we end up with the approach to document clustering which Salton and his co-workers have worked on extensively. The appropriate cluster method is typified by Rocchio's algorithm described in Chapter 3. The search strategy is in part a serial

search. It proceeds by first finding the best (or nearest) cluste
then looking within these. The second stage is achieved by doing
search of the documents in the selected cluster(s). The ou
frequently a ranking of the documents so retrieved.

Interactive search formulation

A user confronted with an automatic retrieval system is unlikely to be
able to express his information need in one go. He is more likely to
want to indulge in a trial-and-error process in which he formulates his
query in the light of what the system can tell him about his query. The
kind of information that he is likely to want to use for the
reformulation of his query is:

(1) the frequency of occurrence in the data base of his search terms;
(2) the number of documents likely to be retrieved by his query;
(3) alternative and related terms to be the ones used in his search;
(4) a small sample of the citations likely to be retrieved; and
(5) the terms used to index the citations in (4).

All this can be conveniently provided to a user during his search session
by an interactive retrieval system. If he discovers that one of his search
terms occurs very frequently he may wish to make it more specific by
consulting a hierarchic dictionary which will tell him what his options
are. Similarly, if his query is likely to retrieve too many documents he
can make it more specific.

The sample of citations and their indexing will give him some idea of
what kind of documents are likely to be retrieved and thus some idea of
how effective his search terms have been in expressing his information
need. He may modify his query in the light of this sample retrieval. This
process in which the user modifies his query based on actual search
results could be described as a form of *feedback*.

Examples, both operational and experimental, of systems providing
mechanisms of this kind are MEDLINE[11] and MEDUSA[12] both based
on the MEDLARS system. Another interesting sophisticated experimental system is that described by Oddy[13].

We now look at a mathematical approach to the use of feedback
where the system *automatically* modifies the query.

Feedback

The word feedback is normally used to describe the mechanism by
which a system can improve its performance on a task by taking

105

account of past performance. In other words a simple input-output system feeds back the information from the output so that this may be used to improve the performance on the next input. The notion of feedback is well established in biological and automatic control systems. It has been popularised by Norbert Wiener in his book *Cybernetics*. In information retrieval it has been used with considerable effect.

Consider now a retrieval strategy that has been implemented by means of a matching function M. Furthermore, let us suppose that both the query Q and document representatives D are t-dimensional vectors with real components where t is the number of index terms. Because it is my purpose to explain feedback I will consider its applications to a serial search only.

It is the aim of every retrieval strategy to retrieve the relevant documents A and withhold the non-relevant documents $\overline{A}$. Unfortunately relevance is defined with respect to the user's *semantic* interpretation of his query. From the point of view of the retrieval system his formulation of it may not be ideal. An ideal formulation would be one which retrieved only the relevant documents. In the case of a serial search the system will retrieve all D for which $M(Q, D) > T$ and not retrieve any D for which $M(Q, D) \leqslant T$, where T is a specified threshold. It so happens that in the case where M is the cosine correlation function, i.e.

$$M(Q, D) = \frac{(Q, D)}{||Q|| \, ||D||} = \frac{1}{||Q|| \, ||D||} \times (q_1 d_1 + q_2 d_2 \ldots q_t d_t),$$

the decision procedure

$$M(Q, D) - T > 0$$

corresponds to a linear discriminant function used to linearly separate two sets A and $\overline{A}$ in R^t. Nilsson[14] has discussed in great detail how functions such as this may be 'trained' by modifying the weights q_i to discriminate correctly between two categories. Let us suppose for the moment that A and $\overline{A}$ are known in advance, then the correct query formulation Q_0 would be one for which

$$M(Q_0, D) > T \qquad \text{whenever } D \in A$$

and

$$M(Q_0, D) \leqslant T \qquad \text{whenever } D \in \overline{A}$$

The interesting thing is that starting with any Q we can adjust it iteratively using feedback information so that it will converge to Q_0. There is a theorem (Nilsson[14], page 81) which states that providing Q_0

exists there is an iterative procedure which will ensure that Q will converge to Q_0 in a *finite* number of steps.

The iterative procedure is called the *fixed-increment error correction* procedure.

It goes as follows:

$$Q_i = Q_{i-1} + cD \qquad \text{if} \qquad M(Q_{i-1}, D) - T \leqslant 0$$
$$\text{and} \quad D \in A$$

$$Q_i = Q_{i-1} - cD \qquad \text{if} \qquad M(Q_{i-1}, D) - T > 0$$
$$\text{and} \quad D \in \overline{A}$$

and no change made to Q_{i-1} if it diagnoses correctly. c is the correction increment, its value is arbitrary and is therefore usually set to unity. In practice it may be necessary to cycle through the set of documents several times before the correct set of weights are achieved, namely those which will separate A and $\overline{A}$ linearly (this is always providing a solution exists).

The situation in actual retrieval is not as simple. We do not know the sets A and $\overline{A}$ in advance, in fact A is the set we hope to retrieve. However, given a query formulation Q and the documents retrieved by it we can ask the user to tell the system which of the documents retrieved were relevant and which were not. The system can then automatically modify Q so that at least it will be able to diagnose correctly those documents that the user has seen. The assumption is that this will improve retrieval on the next run by virtue of the fact that its performance is better on a sample.

Once again this is not the whole story. It is often difficult to fix the threshold T in advance so that instead documents are ranked in decreasing matching value on output. It is now more difficult to define what is meant by an ideal query formulation. Rocchio[15] in his thesis defined the *optimal* query Q_0 as one which maximised:

$$\Phi = \frac{1}{|A|} \sum_{D \in A} M(Q, D) - \frac{1}{|\overline{A}|} \sum_{D \in \overline{A}} M(Q, D)$$

If M is taken to be the cosine function $(Q, D)/\|Q\| \, \|D\|$ then it is easy to show that Φ is maximised by

$$Q_0 = c \left(\frac{1}{|A|} \sum_{D \in A} \frac{D}{\|D\|} - \frac{1}{|\overline{A}|} \sum_{D \in \overline{A}} \frac{D}{\|D\|} \right)$$

where c is an arbitrary proportionality constant.

107

If the summations instead of being over A and $\bar{A}$ are now made over $A \cap B_i$ and $\bar{A} \cap B_i$ where B_i is the set of retrieved documents on the ith iteration, then we have a query formulation which is optimal for B_i a subset of the document collection. By analogy to the linear classifier used before we now add this vector to the query formulation on the ith step to get:

$$Q_{i+1} = w_1 Q_i + w_2 \left[\frac{1}{|A \cap B_i|} \sum_{D \epsilon A \cap B_i} \frac{D}{||D||} - \frac{1}{|\bar{A} \cap B_i|} \sum_{D \epsilon \bar{A} \cap B_i} \frac{D}{||D||} \right]$$

where w_1 and w_2 are weighting coefficients. Salton[2] in fact used a slightly modified version. The most important difference being that there is an option to generate Q_{i+1} from Q_i, or Q, the original query. The effect of all these adjustments may be summarised by saying that the query is automatically modified so that index terms in relevant retrieved documents are given more weight (promoted) and index terms in non-relevant documents are given less weight (demoted).

Experiments have shown that relevance feedback can be very effective. Unfortunately the extent of the effectiveness is rather difficult to gauge, since it is rather difficult to separate the contribution to increased retrieval effectiveness produced when individual documents move up in rank from the contribution produced when *new* documents are retrieved. The latter of course is what the user most cares about.

Finally a few comments about the technique of relevance feedback in general. It appears to me that its implementation on an operational basis may be more problematic. It is not clear how users are to assess the relevance, or non-relevance of a document from such scanty evidence as citations. In an operational system it is easy to arrange for abstracts to be output but it is likely that a user will need to browse through the retrieved documents themselves to determine their relevance after which he is probably in a much better position to restate his query *himself.*

Bibliographic remarks

The book by Lancaster and Fayen[16] contains details of many operational on-line systems. Barraclough[17] has written an interesting survey article about on-line searching. Discussions on search strategies are usually found embedded in more general papers on information retrieval. There are, however, a few specialist references worth mentioning.

A now classic paper on the limitations of a Boolean search is Verhoeff *et al.*[18]. Miller[19] has tried to get away from a simple Boolean search by introducing a form of weighting although maintaining essentially a Boolean search. Angione[20] discusses the equivalence of Boolean and weighted searching. Rickman[21] has described a way of introducing automatic feedback into a Boolean search. Goffman[22] has investigated an interesting search strategy based on the idea that the relevance of a document to a query is conditional on the relevance of other documents to that query. In an early paper by Hyvarinen[23] one will find an information-theoretic definition of the 'typical member' cluster representative. Negoita[24] gives a theoretical discussion of a bottom-up search strategy in the context of cluster-based retrieval. Much of the early work on relevance feedback done on the SMART project has now been reprinted in Salton[25]. Two other independent pieces of work on feedback are Stanfel[26] and Bono[27].

References

1. KNUTH, D. E., *The Art of Computer Programming*, Vol. 3, *Sorting and Searching*, Addison-Wesley, Reading, Massachusetts (1973)
2. SALTON, G., *Automatic Information Organization and Retrieval*, McGraw-Hill, New York (1968)
3. VAN RIJSBERGEN, C. J., 'The best-match problem in document retrieval', *Communications of the ACM*, 17, 648-649 (1974)
4. VAN RIJSBERGEN, C. J., 'Further experiments with hierarchic clustering in document retrieval', *Information Storage and Retrieval*, 10, 1–14 (1974)
5. MURRAY, D. M., 'Document retrieval based on clustered files', Ph.D. Thesis, Cornell University Report ISR-20 to National Science Foundation and to the National Library of Medicine (1972)
6. GOWER, J. C., 'Maximal predictive classification', *Biometrics*, 30, 643–654 (1974)
7. CROFT, W. B., *Organizing and Searching Large Files of Document Descriptions*, Ph.D. Thesis, University of Cambridge (in preparation)
8. YU, C. T. and LUK, W. S., 'Analysis of effectiveness of retrieval in clustered files', *Journal of the ACM*, 24, 607–622 (1977)
9. YU, C. T., LUK, W. S. and SIU, M. K., 'On the estimation of the number of desired records with respect to a given query' (in preparation)
10. ARNAUDOV, D. D. and GOVORUN, N. N., *Some Aspects of the File Organization and Retrieval Strategy in Large Databases*, Joint Institute for Nuclear Research, Dubna (1977)
11. Medline Reference Manual, Medlars Management Section, Bibliographic Services Division, National Library of Medicine
12. BARRACLOUGH, E. D., MEDLARS on-line search formulation and indexing, *Technical Report Series*, No. 34, Computing Laboratory, University of Newcastle upon Tyne

13. ODDY, R. N., 'Information retrieval through man-machine dialogue', *Journal of Documentation*, **33**, 1–14 (1977)
14. NILSSON, N. J., *Learning Machines – Foundations of Trainable Pattern Classifying Systems*, McGraw-Hill, New York (1965)
15. ROCCHIO, J. J., 'Document retrieval systems – Optimization and evaluation', Ph.D. Thesis, Harvard University, Report ISR-10 to National Science Foundation, Harvard Computation Laboratory (1966)
16. LANCASTER, F. W. and FAYEN, E. G., *Information Retrieval On-line*, Melville Publishing Co., Los Angeles, California (1973)
17. BARRACLOUGH, E. D., 'On-line searching in information retrieval', *Journal of Documentation*, **33**, 220–238 (1977)
18. VERHOEFF, J., GOFFMAN, W. and BELZER, J., 'Inefficiency of the use of boolean functions for information retrieval systems', *Communications of the ACM*, **4**, 557–558, 594 (1961)
19. MILLER, W. L., 'A probabilistic search strategy for MEDLARS', *Journal of Documentation*, **27**, 254–266 (1971)
20. ANGIONE, P. V., 'On the equivalence of Boolean and weighted searching based on the convertibility of query forms', *Journal of the American Society for Information Science*, **26**, 112–124 (1975)
21. RICKMAN, J. T., 'Design consideration for a Boolean search system with automatic relevance feedback processing', *Proceedings of the ACM 1972 Annual Conference*, 478–481 (1972)
22. GOFFMAN, W., 'An indirect method of information retrieval', *Information Storage and Retrieval*, **4**, 361–373 (1969)
23. HYVARINEN, L., 'Classification of qualitative data', *BIT, Nordisk Tidskrift för Informationsbehandling*, **2**, 83–89 (1962)
24. NEGOITA, C. V., 'On the decision process in information retrieval', *Studii si cercetari de documentare*, **15**, 269–281 (1973)
25. SALTON, G., *The SMART Retrieval System – Experiment in Automatic Document Processing*, Prentice-Hall, Englewood Cliffs, New Jersey (1971)
26. STANFEL, L. E., 'Sequential adaptation of retrieval systems based on user inputs', *Information Storage and Retrieval*, **7**, 69–78 (1971)
27. BONO, P. R., 'Adaptive procedures for automatic document retrieval', Ph.D. Thesis, University of Michigan (1972)

Six

PROBABILISTIC RETRIEVAL

Introduction

So far in this book we have made very little use of probability theory in modelling any subsystem in IR. The reason for this is simply that the bulk of the work in IR is non-probabilistic, and it is only recently that some significant headway has been made with probabilistic methods[1,2,3]. The history of the use of probabilistic methods goes back as far as the early sixties but for some reason the early ideas never took hold. In this chapter I shall be describing methods of retrieval, i.e. searching and stopping rules, based on probabilistic considerations. In Chapter 2 I dealt with automatic indexing based on a probabilistic model of the distribution of word tokens *within* a document (text); here I will be concerned with the distribution of index terms over the set of documents making up a collection or file. I shall be relying heavily on the familiar assumption that the distribution of index terms throughout the collection, or within some subset of it, will tell us something about the likely relevance of any given document.

Perhaps it is as well to warn the reader that some of the material in this chapter is rather mathematical. However, I believe that the framework of retrieval discussed in this chapter is both elegant and potentially extremely powerful*. Although the work on it has been rather recent and thus some may feel that it should stand the test of time, I think it probably represents the most important break-through in IR in the last few years. Therefore I unashamedly make this chapter theoretical, since the theory must be thoroughly understood if any further progress is to be made. There are a number of equivalent ways

---

* This was recognised by Maron in his: 'The Logic Behind a Probabilistic Interpretation' as early as 1964[4].

of presenting the basic theory; I have chosen to present it in such a way that connections with other fields such as pattern recognition are easily made. I shall have more to say about other formulations in the Bibliographic Remarks at the end of the chapter.

The fundamental mathematical tool for this chapter is Bayes' Theorem: most of the equations derive directly from it. Although the underlying mathematics may at first look a little complicated the interpretation is rather simple. So, let me try and immediately give some interpretation of what is to follow.

Remember that the basic instrument we have for trying to separate the relevant from the non-relevant documents is a matching function, whether it be that we are in a clustered environment or an unstructured one. The reasons for picking any particular matching function have never been made explicit, in fact mostly they are based on intuitive argument in conjunction with Ockham's Razor. Now in this chapter I shall attempt to use simple probability theory to tell us what a matching function should look like and how it should be used. The arguments are mainly theoretical but in my view fairly conclusive. The only remaining doubt is about the acceptability of the assumptions, which I shall try and bring out as I go along. The data used to fix such a matching function are derived from the knowledge of the distribution of the index terms throughout the collection or some subset of it. If it is defined on some subset of documents then this subset can be defined by a variety of techniques: sampling, clustering, or trial retrieval. The data thus gathered are used to set the values of certain parameters associated with the matching function. Clearly, should the data contain relevance information then the process of defining the matching function can be iterated by some feedback mechanism similar to the one due to Rocchio described in the previous chapter. In this way the parameters of the matching function can be 'learnt'. It is on matching functions derived from relevance information that we shall concentrate.

It will be assumed in the sequel that the documents are described by binary state attributes, that is, absence or presence of index terms. This is not a restriction on the theory, in principle the extension to arbitrary attributes can be worked out, although it is not clear that this would be worth doing[5].

Estimation or calculation of relevance

When we search a document collection, we attempt to retrieve relevant documents without retrieving non-relevant ones. Since we have no oracle which will tell us without fail which documents are relevant and which are non-relevant we must use imperfect knowledge to guess for any given document whether it is relevant or non-relevant. Without going into the philosophical paradoxes associated with relevance, I shall assume that we can only guess at relevance through summary data about the document and its relationships with other documents. This is not an unreasonable assumption particularly if one believes that the only way relevance can ultimately be decided is for the user to read the full text. Therefore, a sensible way of computing our guess is to try and estimate for any document its probability of relevance

$$P_Q \text{ (relevance/document)}$$

where the Q is meant to emphasise that it is for a specific query. It is not clear at all what kind of probability this is (see Good[6] for a delightful summary of different kinds), but if we are to make sense of it with a computer and the primitive data we have, it must surely be one based on frequency counts. Thus our probability of relevance is a statistical notion rather than a semantic one, but I believe that the degree of relevance computed on the basis of statistical analysis will tend to be very similar to one arrived at on semantic grounds. Just as a matching function attaches a numerical score to each document and will vary from document to document so will the probability, for some it will be greater than for others and of course it will depend on the query. The variation between queries will be ignored for now, it only becomes important at the evaluation stage. So we will assume only one query has been submitted to the system and we are concerned with

$$P \text{ (relevance/document)}$$

Let us now assume (following Robertson[7]) that:

(I) The *relevance* of a document to a request is independent of other documents in the collection.

With this assumption we can now state a principle, in terms of probability of relevance, which shows that probabilistic information can be used in an optimal manner in retrieval. Robertson attributes this principle to W. S. Cooper although Maron in 1964 already claimed its optimality[4].

The probability ranking principle. If a reference retrieval system's response to each request is a ranking of the documents in the collection in order of decreasing probability of relevance to the user who submitted the request, where the probabilities are estimated as accurately as possible on the basis of whatever data have been made available to the system for this purpose, the overall effectiveness of

113

the system to its user will be the best that is obtainable on the basis of those data.

Of course this principle raises many questions as to the acceptability of the assumptions. For example, the Cluster Hypothesis, that closely associated documents tend to be relevant to the same requests, explicitly assumes the contrary of assumption (I). Goffman[8] too, in his work has gone to some pains to make an explicit assumption of dependence. I quote: 'Thus, if a document x has been assessed as relevant to a query s, the relevance of the other documents in the file X may be affected since the value of the information conveyed by these documents may either increase or decrease as a result of the information conveyed by the document x.' Then there is the question of the way in which overall effectiveness is to be measured. Robertson in his paper shows the probability ranking principle to hold if we measure effectiveness in terms of Recall and Fallout. The principle also follows simply from the theory in this chapter. But this is not the place to argue out these research questions, however, I do think it reasonable to adopt the principle as one upon which to construct a probabilistic retrieval model. One word of warning, the probability ranking principle can only be shown to be true for *one* query. It does not say that the performance over a range of queries will be optimised, to establish a result of this kind one would have to be specific about how one would average the performance across queries.

The probability ranking principle assumes that we can calculate P(relevance/document), not only that, it assumes that we can do it accurately. Now this is an extremely troublesome assumption and it will occupy us some more further on. The problem is simply that we do not know which are the relevant documents, nor do we know how many there are so we have no way of calculating P(relevance/document). But we can, by trial retrieval, guess at P(relevance/document) and hopefully improve our guess by iteration. To simplify matters in the subsequent discussion I shall assume that the statistics relating to the relevant and non-relevant documents are available and I shall use them to build up the pertinent equations. However, at all times the reader should be aware of the fact that in any practical situation the relevance information must be guessed at (or estimated).

So returning now to the immediate problem which is to calculate, or estimate, P(relevance/document). For this we use Bayes' Theorem, which relates the posterior probability of relevance to the prior probability of relevance and the likelihood of relevance after observing a document. Before we plunge into a formal expression of this I must introduce some symbols which will make things a little easier as we go along.

Basic probabilistic model*

Since we are assuming that each document is described by the presence/absence of index terms any document can be represented by a binary vector,

$$x = (x_1, x_2, \ldots, x_n)$$

where $x_i = 0$ or 1 indicates absence or presence of the ith index term. We also assume that there are two mutually exclusive events,

w_1 = document is relevant
w_2 = document is non-relevant

So in terms of these symbols what we wish to calculate for each document is $P(w_1/x)$ and perhaps $P(w_2/x)$ so that we may decide which is relevant and which is non-relevant. This is a slight change in objective from simply producing a ranking, we also wish the theory to tell us how to cut off the ranking. Therefore we formulate the problem as a decision problem. Of course we cannot estimate $P(w_i/x)$ directly so we must find a way of estimating it in terms of quantities we do know something about. Bayes' Theorem tells us that for discrete distributions

$$P(w_i/x) = \frac{P(x/w_i)P(w_i)}{P(x)} \qquad i = 1, 2$$

Here $P(w_i)$ is the *prior* probability of relevance ($i = 1$) or non-relevance ($i = 2$), $P(x/w_i)$ is proportional to what is commonly known as the *likelihood* of relevance or non-relevance given x; in the continuous case this would be a density function and we would write $p(x/w_i)$. Finally,

$$P(x) = \sum_{i=1}^{2} P(x/w_i)P(w_i),$$

which is the probability of observing x on a random basis given that it may be either relevant or non-relevant. Again this would be written as a density function $p(x)$ in the continuous case. Although $P(x)$ (or $p(x)$) will mostly appear as a normalising factor (i.e. ensuring that $P(w_1/x) + P(w_2/x) = 1$) it is in some ways the function we know most about, it does not require a knowledge of relevance for it to be specified. Before I discuss how we go about estimating the right hand side of Bayes' Theorem I will show how the decision for or against relevance is made.

---

* The theory that follows is at first rather abstract, the reader is asked to bear with it, since we soon return to the nuts and bolts of retrieval.

The decision rule we use is in fact well known as Bayes' Decision Rule. It is

$$[P(w_1/x) > P(w_2/x) \rightarrow x \text{ is relevant, } x \text{ is non-relevant}] * \qquad \text{D1}$$

The expression D1 is a short hand notation for the following: compare $P(w_1/x)$ with $P(w_2/x)$ if the first is greater than the second then decide that x is relevant otherwise decide x is non-relevant. The case $P(w_1/x) = P(w_2/x)$ is arbitrarily dealt with by deciding non-relevance. The basis for the rule D1 is simply that it minimises the *average* probability of error, the error of assigning a relevant document as non-relevant or vice versa. To see this note that for any x the probability of error is

$$P(\text{error}/x) = \begin{cases} P(w_1/x) & \text{if we decide } w_2 \\ P(w_2/x) & \text{if we decide } w_1 \end{cases}$$

In other words once we have decided one way (e.g. relevant) then the probability of having made an error is clearly given by the probability of the opposite way being the case (e.g. non-relevant). So to make this error as small as possible for any given x we must always pick that w_i for which $P(w_i/x)$ is largest and by implication for which the probability of error is the smallest. To minimise the *average* probability of error we must minimise

$$P(\text{error}) = \sum_x P(\text{error}/x)P(x)$$

This sum will be minimised by making $P(\text{error}/x)$ as small as possible for each x since $P(\text{error}/x)$ and $P(x)$ are always positive. This is accomplished by the decision rule D1 which now stands as justified.

Of course average error is not the only sensible quantity worth minimising. If we associate with each type of error a *cost* we can derive a decision rule which will minimise the overall *risk*. The overall risk is an average of the conditional risks $R(w_i/x)$ which itself in turn is defined in terms of a cost function l_{ij}. More specifically l_{ij} is the loss incurred for deciding w_i when w_j is the case. Now the associated *expected* loss when deciding w_i is called the *conditional risk* and is given by

$$R(w_i/x) = l_{i1}P(w_1/x) + l_{i2}P(w_2/x) \qquad i = 1,2$$

The *overall* risk is a sum in the same way that the average probability of error was, $R(w_i/x)$ now playing the role of $P(w_i/x)$. The overall risk is minimised by

$$[R(w_1/x) < R(w_2/x) \rightarrow x \text{ is relevant, } x \text{ is non-relevant}] \qquad \text{D2}$$

* The meaning of $[E \rightarrow p,q]$ is that if E is true then decide p, otherwise decide q.

116

D1 and D2 can be shown to be equivalent under certain conditions. First we rewrite D1, using Bayes' Theorem, in a form in which it will be used subsequently, viz.

$$[P(x/w_1)P(w_1) > P(x/w_2)P(w_2) \rightarrow x \text{ is relevant}, x \text{ is non-relevant}] \quad D3$$

Notice that $P(x)$ has disappeared from the equation since it does not affect the outcome of the decision. Now, using the definition of $R(w_i/x)$ it is easy to show that

$$[R(w_1/x) < R(w_2/x)] \equiv$$
$$[(l_{21} - l_{11})P(x/w_1)P(w_1) > (l_{12} - l_{22})P(x/w_2)P(w_2)]$$

When a special loss function is chosen, namely,

$$l_{ij} = \begin{cases} 0 & i = j \\ 1 & i \neq j \end{cases}$$

which implies that no loss is assigned to a correct decision (quite reasonable) and unit loss to any error (not so reasonable), then we have

$$[R(w_1/x) < R(w_2/x)] \equiv [P(x/w_1)P(w_1) > P(x/w_2)P(w_2)]$$

which shows the equivalence of D2 and D3, and hence of D1 and D2 under a binary loss function.

This completes the derivation of the decision rule to be used to decide relevance or non-relevance, or to put it differently to retrieve or not to retrieve. So far no constraints have been put on the form of $P(x/w_i)$, therefore the decision rule is quite general. I have set up the problem as one of deciding between two classes thereby ignoring the problem of ranking for the moment. One reason for this is that the analysis is simpler, the other is that I want the analysis to say as much as possible about the cut-off value. When ranking, the cut-off value is usually left to the user; within the model so far one can still rank, but the cut-off value will have an interpretation in terms of prior probabilities and cost functions. The optimality of the probability ranking principle follows immediately from the optimality of the decision rule at any cut-off. I shall now go on to be more precise about the exact form of the probability functions in the decision rule.

Form of retrieval function

The previous section was rather abstract and left the connection of the various probabilities with IR rather open. Although it is reasonable for us to want to calculate P(relevance/document) it is not at all clear as to how this should be done or whether the inversion through Bayes'

117

Theorem is the best way of getting at it. Nevertheless we will proceed assuming that $P(x/w_i)$ is the appropriate function to estimate. This function is of course a joint probability function and the interaction between the components of x may be arbitrarily complex. To derive a workable decision rule a simplifying assumption about $P(x/w_i)$ will have to be made. The conventional mathematically convenient way of simplifying $P(x/w_i)$ is to assume the component variables x_i of x to be *stochastically independent.* Technically this amounts to making the major assumption

$$P(x/w_i) = P(x_1/w_i)P(x_2/w_i) \ \ldots \ P(x_n/w_i) \qquad \text{A1}$$

Later I shall show how this stringent assumption may be relaxed. We also for the moment ignore the fact that assuming independence conditional on both w_1 and w_2 separately has implications about the dependence conditional on $w_1 \lor w_2$.

Let us now take the simplified form of $P(x/w_i)$ and work out what the decision rule will look like. First we define some variables

$$p_i = \text{Prob}\ (x_i = 1/w_1)$$

$$q_i = \text{Prob}\ (x_i = 1/w_2)$$

In words $p_i(q_i)$ is the probability that if the document is relevant (non-relevant) that the ith index term will be present. The corresponding probabilities for absence are calculated by subtracting from 1, i.e. $1 - p_i = \text{Prob}\ (x_i = 0/w_1)$. The likelihood functions which enter into D3 will now look as follows

$$P(x/w_1) = \prod_{i=1}^{n} p_i^{x_i}(1-p_i)^{1-x_i}$$

$$P(x/w_2) = \prod_{i=1}^{n} q_i^{x_i}(1-q_i)^{1-x_i}$$

To appreciate how these expressions work the reader should check that $P((0,1,1,0,0,1)/w_1) = (1-p_1)p_2p_3(1-p_4)(1-p_5)p_6$. Substituting for $P(x/w_i)$ in D3 and taking logs, the decision rule will be transformed into a *linear* discriminant function.

$$g(x) = \sum_{i=1}^{n} (a_ix_i + b_i(1-x_i)) + e$$

$$= \sum_{i=1}^{n} c_ix_i + C$$

where the constants a_i, b_i and e are obvious.

$$c_i = \log \frac{p_i(1-q_i)}{q_i(1-p_i)}$$

and

$$C = \sum_{i=1}^{n} \log \frac{1-p_i}{1-q_i} + \log \frac{P(w_1)}{P(w_2)} + \log \frac{l_{21} - l_{11}}{l_{12} - l_{22}}$$

The importance of writing it this way, apart from its simplicity, is that for each document x to calculate $g(x)$ we simply add the coefficients c_i for those index terms that are present, i.e. for those c_i for which $x_i = 1$. The c_i are often looked up as weights; Robertson and Sparck Jones[1] call c_i a *relevance weight*, and Salton calls $\exp(c_i)$ the *term relevance*. I shall simply refer to it as a coefficient or a weight. Hence the name *weighting function* for $g(x)$.

The constant C which has been assumed the same for all documents x will of course vary from query to query, but it can be interpreted as the cut-off applied to the retrieval function. The only part that can be varied with respect to a given query is the cost function, and it is this variation which will allow us to retrieve more or less documents. To see this let us assume that $l_{11} = l_{22} = 0$ and that we have some choice in setting the ratio l_{21}/l_{11} by picking a value for the relative importance we attach to missing a relevant document compared with retrieving a non-relevant one. In this way we can generate a ranking, each rank position corresponding to a different ratio l_{21}/l_{12}.

Let us now turn to the other part of $g(x)$, namely, c_i and let us try and interpret it in terms of the conventional 'contingency' table.

	Relevant	Non-relevant	
$x_i = 1$	r	$n - r$	n
$x_i = 0$	$R - r$	$N - n - R + r$	$N - n$
	R	$N - R$	N

There will be one such table for each index term; I have shown it for the index term i although the subscript i has not been used in the cells. If we have *complete* information about the relevant and non-relevant documents in the collection then we can estimate p_i by r/R and q_i by $(n - r)/(N - R)$. Therefore $g(x)$ can be rewritten as follows:

$$g(x) = \sum_{i=1}^{n} x_i \log \frac{r/(R - r)}{(n - r)/(N - n - R + r)} + C$$

This is in fact the weighting formula F4 used by Robertson and Sparck Jones[1] in their so called retrospective experiments. For later

119

convenience let us set

$$K_i(N,r,n,R) = \log \frac{r/(R-r)}{(n-r)/(N-n-R+r)}$$

There are a number of ways of looking at K_i. The most interesting interpretation of K_i is to say that it measures the extent to which the ith term can discriminate between the relevant and non-relevant documents.

Typically the 'weight' $K_i(N,r,n,R)$ is estimated from a contingency table in which N is not the total number of documents in the system but instead is some subset specifically chosen to enable K_i to be estimated. Later I will use the above interpretation of K_i to motivate another function similar to K_i to measure the discrimination power of an index term.

The index terms are not independent

Although it may be mathematically convenient to assume that the index terms are independent it by no means follows that it is realistic to do so. The objection to independence is not new, in 1964 J. H. Williams[9] expressed it this way: 'The assumption of independence of words in a document is usually made as a matter of mathematical convenience. Without the assumption, many of the subsequent mathematical relations could not be expressed. With it, many of *the conclusions should be accepted with extreme caution.*' It is only because the mathematics become rather intractable if dependence is assumed that people are quick to assume independence. But, 'dependence is the norm rather than the contrary' to quote the famous probability theorist De Finetti[10]. Therefore the correct procedure is to assume dependence and allow the analysis to simplify to the independent case should the latter be true. When speaking of dependence here we mean *stochastic* dependence; it is not intended as logical dependence although this may imply stochastic dependence. For IR data, stochastic dependence is simply measured by a correlation function or in some other equivalent way. The assumption of dependence could be crucial when we are trying to estimate P(relevance/document) in terms of $P(x/w_i)$ since the accuracy with which this latter probability is estimated will no doubt affect the retrieval performance. So our immediate task is to make use of dependence (correlation) between index terms to improve our estimate of $P(x/w_i)$ on which our decision rule rests.

120

In general the dependence can be arbitrarily complex as the following identity illustrates,

$$P(x) = P(x_1)P(x_2/x_1)P(x_3/x_1,x_2) \ \ldots \ P(x_n/x_1,x_2, \ldots, x_{n-1})$$

Therefore, to capture all dependence data we would need to condition each variable in turn on a steadily increasing set of other variables. Although in principle this may be possible, it is likely to be computationally inefficient, and impossible in some instances where there is insufficient data to calculate the high order dependencies. Instead we adopt a method of approximation to estimate $P(x)$ which captures the significant dependence information. Intuitively this may be described as one which looks at each factor in the bove expansion and selects from the conditioning variables one particular variable which accounts for most of the dependence relation. In other words we seek a product approximation of the form

$$P_t(x) = \prod_{i=1}^{n} P(x_{m_i}/x_{m_{j(i)}}) \qquad\qquad 0 \leqslant j(i) < i \qquad\qquad \text{A2}$$

where $(m_1, m_2, \ldots, m_n)$ is a permutation of the integers $1, 2, \ldots, n$ and $j(.)$ is a function mapping i into integers less than i, and $P(x_i/x_{m_0})$ is $P(x_i)$. An example for a six component vector $x = (x_1, \ldots, x_6)$ might be

$$P_t(x) = P(x_1)P(x_2/x_1)P(x_3/x_2)P(x_4/x_2)P(x_5/x_2)P(x_6/x_5)$$

Notice how similar the A2 assumption is to the independence assumption A1, the only difference being that in A2 each factor has a conditioning variable associated with it. In the example the permutation $(m_1, m_2, \ldots, m_6)$ is $(1, 2, \ldots, 6)$ which is just the natural order, of course the reason for writing the expansion for $P_t(x)$ the way I did in A2 is to show that a permutation of $(1, 2, \ldots, 6)$ must be sought that gives a *good* approximation. Once this permutation has been found the variables could be relabelled so as to have the natural order again.

The permutation and the function $j(.)$ together define a *dependence tree* and the corresponding $P_t(x)$ is called a probability distribution of (first-order) tree dependence. The tree corresponding to our six variable example is shown in *Figure 6.1*. The tree shows which variable appears either side of the conditioning stroke in $P(./.)$. Although I have chosen to write the function $P_t(x)$ the way I did with x_1 as the unconditioned variable, and hence the root of the tree, and all others consistently conditioned each on its parent node, in fact any one of the nodes of the tree could be singled out as the root as long as the conditioning is done consistently with respect to the new root node. (In *Figure 6.1* the 'direction' of conditioning is marked by the direction associated with

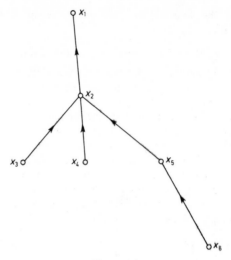

Figure 6.1.

an edge.) The resulting $P_t(x)$ will be the same as can easily be shown by using the fact that

$$P(x_{m_i}/x_{m_{j(i)}}) = P(x_{m_{j(i)}}/x_{m_i})P(x_{m_i})/P(x_{m_{j(i)}})$$

Applying this to the link between the root node x_1 and its immediate descendant x_2 in the example will shift the root to x_2 and change the expansion to

$$P_t(x_1, x_2, \ldots \ x_6) = P(x_2)P(x_1/x_2)P(x_3/x_2)P(x_4/x_2)P(x_5/x_2)P(x_6/x_5)$$

Of course to satisfy the rule about relabelling we would exchange the names '1' and '2'. All expansions transformed in this way are equivalent in terms of goodness of approximation to $P(x)$. It is therefore the *tree* which represents the class of equivalent expansions. Clearly there are a large number of possible dependence trees, the approximation problem we have is to find the *best* one; which amounts to finding the best permutation and mapping $j(.)$.

   In what follows I shall assume that the relabelling has been done and that $x_{m_i} = x_i$.

Selecting the best dependence trees

Our problem now is to find a probability function of the form $P_t(x)$ on a set of documents which is the best approximation to the true joint
122

probability function $P(x)$, and of course a better approximation than the one afforded by making assumption A1*. The set on which the approximation is defined can be arbitrary, it might be the entire collection, the relevant documents (w_1), or the non-relevant documents (w_2). For the moment I shall leave the set unspecified, all three are important. However, when constructing a decision rule similar to D4 we shall have to approximate $P(x/w_1)$ and $P(x/w_2)$.

The goodness of the approximation is measured by a well known function (see, for example, Kullback[12]); if $P(x)$ and $P_a(x)$ are two discrete probability distributions then

$$I(P,P_a) = \sum_x P(x) \log \frac{P(x)}{P_a(x)}$$

is a measure of the extent to which $P_a(x)$ approximates $P(x)$. In terms of this function we want to find a distribution of tree dependence $P_t(x)$ such that $I(P,P_t)$ is a minimum. Or to put it differently to find the dependence tree among all dependence trees which will make $I(P,P_t)$ as small as possible.

If the extent to which two index terms i and j deviate from independence is measured by the *expected mutual information measure* (EMIM) (see Chapter 3, p. 41).

$$I(x_i, x_j) = \sum_{x_i, x_j} P(x_i, x_j) \log \frac{P(x_i, x_j)}{P(x_i)P(x_j)}$$

then the best approximation $P_t(x)$, in the sense of minimising $I(P,P_t)$, is given by the maximum spanning tree (MST) (see Chapter 3, p. 56) on the variables $x_1, x_2, \ldots, x_n$. The spanning tree is derived from the graph whose nodes are the index terms $1, 2, \ldots, n$, and whose edges are weighted with $I(x_i, x_j)$. The MST is simply the tree spanning the nodes for which the total weight

$$\sum_{i=1}^{n} I(x_i, x_{j(i)})$$

is a maximum. This is a highly condensed statement of how the dependence tree is arrived at, unfortunately a fuller statement would be rather technical. A detailed proof of the optimisation procedure can be found in Chow and Liu[13]. Here we are mainly interested in the application of the tree structure.

One way of looking at the MST is that it incorporates the most significant of the dependencies between the variables subject to the global constraint that the sum of them should be a maximum. For

* That this is indeed the case is shown by Ku and Kullback[11].

example, in *Figure 6.1* the links between the variables (nodes, x_1, ..., x_6 have been put in just because the sum

$$I(x_1, x_2) + I(x_2, x_3) + I(x_2, x_4) + I(x_2, x_5) + I(x_5, x_6)$$

is a maximum. Any other sum will be less than or equal to this sum. Note that it does *not* mean that any individual weight associated with an edge in the tree will be greater than one not in the tree, although this will mostly be the case.

Once the dependence tree has been found the approximating distribution can be written down immediately in the form A2. From this I can derive a discriminant function just as I did in the independent case.

$$t_i = \text{Prob } (x_i = 1/x_{j(i)} = 1)$$

$$r_i = \text{Prob } (x_i = 1/x_{j(i)} = 0) \text{ and } r_1 = \text{Prob } (x_1 = 1)$$

$$P(x_i/x_{j(i)}) = [t_i^{x_i}(1-t_i)^{1-x_i}]^{x_{j(i)}} [r_i^{x_i}(1-r_i)^{1-x_i}]^{1-x_{j(i)}}$$

then

$$\log P(x) = \sum_{i=1}^{n} [x_i \log r_i + (1-x_i) \log (1-r_i)] +$$

$$+ \sum_{i=1}^{n} \left[x_{j(i)} \log \frac{1-t_i}{1-r_i} + x_i x_{j(i)} \log \frac{t_i(1-r_i)}{(1-t_i)r_i} \right] + \text{constant}$$

This is a *non-linear* weighting function which will simplify to the one derived from A1 when the variables are assumed to be independent, that is, when $t_i = r_i$. The constant has the same interpretation in terms of prior probabilities and loss function. The complete decision function is of course

$$g(x) = \log P(x/w_1) - \log P(x/w_2)$$

which now involves the calculation (or estimation) of twice as many parameters as in the linear case. It is only the sum involving $x_{j(i)}$ which make this weighting function different from the linear one, and it is this part which enables a retrieval strategy to take into account the fact that x_i depends on $x_{j(i)}$. When using the weighting function a document containing $x_{j(i)}$, or both x_i and $x_{j(i)}$, will receive a contribution from that part of the weighting function.

It is easier to see how $g(x)$ combines different weights for different terms if one looks at the weights contributed to $g(x)$ for a given document x for different settings of a pair of variables $x_i, x_{j(i)}$. When $x_i = 1$ and $x_{j(i)} = 0$ the weight contributed is

$$\log \frac{\text{Prob}(x_i = 1/(x_{j(i)} = 0)\wedge w_1)}{\text{Prob}(x_i = 1/(x_{j(i)} = 0)\wedge w_2)}$$

and similarly for the other three settings of x_i and $x_{j(i)}$.

This shows how simple the non-linear weighting function really is. For example, given a document in which i occurs but $j(i)$ does not, then the weight contributed to $g(x)$ is based on the ratio of two probabilities. The first is the probability of occurrence of i in the set of relevant documents given that $j(i)$ does not occur, the second is the analogous probability computed on the non-relevant documents. On the basis of this ratio we decide how much evidence there is for assigning x to the relevant or non-relevant documents. It is important to remember at this point that the evidence for making the assignment is usually based on an *estimate* of the pair of probabilities.

Estimation of parameters

The use of a weighting function of the kind derived above in actual retrieval requires the estimation of pertinent parameters. I shall here deal with the estimation of t_i and r_i for the non-linear case, obviously the linear case will follow by analogy. To show what is involved let me give an example of the estimation process using simple maximum likelihood estimates. The basis for our estimates is the following 2-by-2 table.

	$x_i = 1$	$x_i = 0$	
$x_{j(i)} = 1$	[1]	[2]	[7]
$x_{j(i)} = 0$	[3]	[4]	[8]
	[5]	[6]	[9]

Here I have adopted a labelling scheme for the cells in which [x] means the number of occurrences in the cell labelled x. Ignoring for the moment the nature of the set on which this table is based; our estimates might be as follows:

$$P(x_i = 1/x_{j(i)} = 1) = t_i \sim \frac{[1]}{[7]}$$

$$P(x_i = 1/x_{j(i)} = 0) = r_i \sim \frac{[3]}{[8]}$$

125

In general we would have two tables of this kind when setting up our function $g(x)$, one for estimating the parameters associated with $P(x/w_1)$ and one for $P(x/w_2)$. In the limit we would have complete knowledge of which documents in the collection were relevant and which were not. Were we to calculate the estimates for this limiting case, this would only be useful in showing what the upper bound to our retrieval would be under this *particular model*. More realistically, we would have a sample of documents, probably small (not necessarily random), for which the relevance status of each document was known. This small set would then be the source data for any 2-by-2 tables we might wish to construct. The estimates therefore would be biased in an unavoidable way.

The estimates shown above are examples of *point estimates*. There are a number of ways of arriving at an appropriate rule for point estimation. Unfortunately the best form of estimation rule is still an open problem[14]. In fact some statisticians believe that point estimation should not be attempted at all[15]. However in the context of IR it is hard to see how one can avoid making point estimates. One major objection to any point estimation rule is that in deriving it some 'arbitrary' assumptions are made. Fortunately in IR there is some chance of justifying these assumptions by pointing to experimental data gathered from retrieval systems, thereby removing some of the arbitrariness.

Two basic assumptions made in deriving any estimation rule through Bayesian decision theory are:

(1) the form of the prior distribution on the parameter space, i.e. in our case the assumed probability distribution on the possible values of the binomial parameter; and
(2) the form of the loss function used to measure the error made in estimating the parameter.

Once these two assumptions are made explicit by defining the form of the distribution and loss function, then, together with *Bayes' Principle* which seeks to minimise the posterior conditional expected loss given the observations, we can derive a number of different estimation rules. The statistical literature is not much help when deciding which rule is to be preferred. For details the reader should consult Van Rijsbergen[2] where further references to the statistical literature are given. The important rules of estimating a proportion p all come in the form

$$\hat{p} = \frac{x + a}{n + a + b}$$

where x is the number of successes in n trials, and a and b are parameters dictated by the particular combination of prior and loss function. Thus we have a whole class of estimation rules. For example when $a=b=0$ we have the usual estimate x/n, and when $a=b=\frac{1}{2}$ we have a rule attributed to Sir Harold Jeffreys by Good[16]. This latter rule is in fact the rule used by Robertson and Sparck Jones[1] in their estimates. Each setting of a and b can be justified in terms of the reasonableness of the resulting prior distribution. Since what is found reasonable by one man is not necessarily so for another, the ultimate choice must rest on performance in an experimental test. Fortunately in IR we are in a unique position to do this kind of test.

One important reason for having estimation rules different from the simple x/n, is that this is rather unrealistic for small samples. Consider the case of one sample ($n = 1$) and the trial result $x = 0$ (or $x = 1$) which would result in the estimate for p as $p = 0$ (or $p = 1$). This is clearly ridiculous, since in most cases we would already know with high probability that $0 < p < 1$. To overcome this difficulty we might try and incorporate this prior knowledge in a distribution on the possible values of the parameter we are trying to estimate. Once we have accepted the feasibility of this and have specified the way in which estimation error is to be measured, Bayes' Principle (or some other principle) will usually lead to a rule different from x/n.

This is really as much as I wish to say about estimation rules, and therefore I shall not push the technical discussion on these points any further; the interested reader should consult the readily accessible statistical literature.

Recapitulation

At this point I should like to summarise the formal argument thus far so that we may reduce it to simple English. One reason for doing this now is that so far I have stuck closely to what one might call a 'respectable' theoretical development. But as in most applied subjects, in IR when it comes to implementing or using a theory one is forced by either inefficiency or inadequate data to diverge from the strict theoretical model. Naturally one tries to diverge as little as possible, but it is of the essence of research that heuristic modifications to a theory are made so as to fit the real data more closely. One obvious consequence is that it may lead to a better new theory.

The first point to make then, is that, we have been trying to estimate P(relevance/document), that is, the probability of relevance for a given document. Although I can easily write the preceding sentence it is not at all clear that it will be meaningful. Relevance in itself is a difficult notion, that the *probability* of relevance means something can be

127

objected to on the same grounds that one might object to the probability of Newton's Second Law of Motion being the case. Some would argue that the probability is either one or zero depending on whether it is true or false. Similarly one could argue for relevance. The second point is that the probability P(relevance/document) can be got at by considering the inverse probability $P(x$/relevance), thus relating the two through Bayes' Theorem. It is not that I am questioning the use of Bayes' Theorem when applied to probabilities, which is forced upon us anyhow if we want to use probability theory consistently, no, what I am questioning is that $P(x$/relevance) means something in IR and hence can lead us to P(relevance/x). I think that we have to assume that it does, and realise that this assumption will enable us to connect P(relevance/x) with the distributional information about index terms.

To approach the problem in this way would be useless unless one believed that for many index terms the distribution over the relevant documents is different from that over the non-relevant documents. If we assumed the contrary, that is $P(x$/relevance) = $P(x$/non-relevance) then the P(relevance/document) would be the same as the prior probability P(relevance), constant for all documents and hence incapable of discriminating them which is of no use in retrieval. So really we are assuming that there is indirect information available through the joint distribution of index terms over the two sets which will enable us to discriminate them. Once we have accepted this view of things then we are also committed to the formalism derived above. The commitment is that we must guess at P(relevance/document) as accurately as we can, or equivalently guess at P(document/relevance) and P(relevance), through the distributional knowledge we have of the attributes (e.g. index terms) of the document.

The elaboration in terms of ranking rather than just discrimination is trivial: the cut-off set by the constant in $g(x)$ is gradually relaxed thereby increasing the number of documents retrieved (or assigned to the relevant category). The result that the ranking is optimal follows from the fact that at each cut-off value we minimise the overall risk. This optimality should be treated with some caution since it assumes that we have got the form of the $P(x/w_i)$'s right and that our estimation rule is the best possible. Neither of these are likely to be realised in practice.

If one is prepared to let the user set the cut-off *after* retrieval has taken place then the need for a theory about cut-off disappears. The implication is that instead of working with the ratio

$$\frac{P(x/\text{relevance})}{P(x/\text{non-relevance})}$$

we work with the ratio

$$\frac{P(x/\text{relevance})}{P(x)}$$

In the latter case we do not see the retrieval problem as one of discriminating between relevant and non-relevant documents, instead we merely wish to compute the $P(\text{relevance}/x)$ for each document x and present the user with documents in decreasing order of this probability. Whichever way we look at it we still require the estimation of two joint probability functions.

The decision rules derived above are couched in terms of $P(x/w_i)$. Therefore one would suppose that the estimation of these probabilities is crucial to the retrieval performance, and of course the fact that they can only be estimated is one explanation for the sub-optimality of the performance. To facilitate the estimation one makes assumptions about the form of $P(x/w_i)$. An obvious one is to assume stochastic independence for the components of x. But in general I think this is unrealistic because it is in the nature of information retrieval that index terms will be related to one another. To quote an early paper of Maron's on this point: 'To do this [enlarge upon a request] one would need to program a computing machine to make a statistical analysis of index terms so that the machine will "know" which terms are most closely associated with one another and can indicate *the most probable direction* in which a given request should be enlarged' [Maron's italics] [4]. Therefore a more realistic approach is to assume some sort of dependence between the terms when estimating $P(x/w_1)$ and $P(x/w_2)$ (or $P(x)$).

I will now proceed to discuss ways of using this probabilistic model of retrieval and at the same time discuss some of the practical problems that arise. At first I will hardly modify the model at all. But then I will discuss a way of using it which does not necessarily accord strictly with the assumptions upon which it was built in the first place. Naturally the justification for any of this will lie in the province of experimental tests of which many still remain to be done [17]. But first I shall explain a minor modification arising from the need to reduce the dimensionality of our problem.

The curse of dimensionality

In deriving the decision rules I assumed that a document is represented by an n-dimensional vector where n is the size of the index term vocabulary. Typically n would be very large, and so the dimension of the (binary) document vectors is always likely to be greater than the number of samples used to estimate the parameters in the decision function. That this will lead to problems has been pointed out repeatedly in the pattern recognition literature. Although the analysis of the problem in pattern recognition applies to IR as well, the solutions are not directly applicable. In pattern recognition the problem is: given the number of samples that have been used to 'train' the decision function (our weighting function), is there an optimum number of measurements that can be made of an unknown pattern so that the average probability of correct assignment can be maximised? In our case how many index terms can we legitimately use to decide on relevance. Hughes[18] shows that for a very general probabilistic structure the number of measurements is surprisingly small even though reasonably sized samples are used to 'train' the decision function.

Ideally one would like to be able to choose a (small) subset of index terms to which the weighting function $g(.)$ would be restricted thereby maximising the average probability of correct assignment. In pattern recognition there are complicated techniques for doing just that for the equivalent problem. In information retrieval we are fortunate in that there is a natural way in which the dimensionality of the problem can be reduced. We accept that the query terms are a fair guide to the best features to be used in the application of $g(.)$ to decide between relevance and non-relevance. Therefore rather than computing the weighting function for all possible terms we restrict $g(.)$ to the terms specified in the query and possibly their close associates. This would be as if during the retrieval process all documents are projected from a high dimensional space into a subspace spanned by a small number of terms.

Computational details

I now turn to some of the more practical details of computing $g(x)$ for each x when the variables x_i are assumed to be stochastically dependent. The main aim of this section will be to demonstrate that the computations involved are feasible. The clearest way of doing this is to discuss the calculation of each 'object' EMIM, MST, and $g(.)$ separately and in that order.

1. Calculation of EMIM

The calculation of the expected mutual information measure can be simplified. Then EMIM itself can be approximated to reduce the computation time even further. We take the simplification first.

130

When computing $I(x_i, x_j)$ for the purpose of constructing an MST we need only to know the rank ordering of the $I(x_i, x_j)$'s. The absolute values do not matter. Therefore if we use simple maximum likelihood estimates for the probabilities based on the data contained in the following table (using the same notation as on p. 125).

	$x_i = 1$	$x_i = 0$	
$x_j = 1$	[1]	[2]	[7]
$x_i = 0$	[3]	[4]	[8]
	[5]	[6]	[9]

then $I(x_i, x_j)$ will be strictly monotone with

$$[1] \ \log \ \frac{[1]}{[5] \ [7]} + [2] \ \log \ \frac{[2]}{[6] \ [7]} + [3] \ \log \ \frac{[3]}{[5] \ [8]}$$

$$+ [4] \ \log \ \frac{[4]}{[6] \ [8]}$$

This is an extremely simple formulation of EMIM and easy to compute. Consider the case when it is $P(x)$ we are trying to calculate. The MST is then based on co-occurrence data derived from the entire collection. Once we have this (i.e. [1]) and know the number of documents ([9]) in the file then any inverted file will contain the rest of the frequency data needed to fill in the counts in the other cells. That is from [5] and [7] given by the inverted file we can deduce [2] [3] [4] [6] and [8].

The problem of what to do with zero entries in one of the cells 1 to 4 is taken care of by letting $0 \log 0 = 0$. The marginals cannot be zero since we are only concerned with terms that occur at least once in the documents.

Next we discuss the possibility of approximation. Maron and Kuhns[19] in their early work used

$$d(x_i, x_j) = P(x_i = 1, x_j = 1) - P(x_i = 1) P(x_j = 1) \qquad (*)$$

to measure the deviation from independence for any two index terms i and j. Apart from the log this is essentially the first term of the EMIM expansion. An MST (dependence tree) constructed on the basis of (*) clearly would not lead to an optimal approximation of $P(x/w_i)$ but the fit might be good enough and certainly the corresponding tree can be

131

calculated more efficiently based on (*) than one based on the full EMIM. Similarly Ivie[20] used

$$\log \frac{P(x_i = 1, x_j = 1)}{P(x_i = 1) P(x_j = 1)}$$

as a measure of association. No doubt there are other ways of approximating the EMIM which are easier to compute, but whether they can be used to find a dependence tree leading to good approximation of the joint probability function must remain a matter for experimental test.

2. Calculation of MST

There are numerous published algorithms for generating an MST from pairwise association measures, the most efficient probably being the recent one due to Whitney[21]. The time dependence of his algorithm is $O(n^2)$ where n is the number of index terms to be fitted into the tree. This is not a barrier to its use on large data sets, for it is easy to partition the data by some coarse clustering technique as recommended on p. 59, after which the *total* spanning tree can be generated by applying the MST algorithm to each cluster of index terms in turn. This will reduce the time dependence from $O(n^2)$ to $O(k^2)$ where $k \ll n$.

It is along these lines that Bentley and Friedman[22] have shown that by exploiting the geometry of the space in which the index terms are points the computation time for generating the MST can be shown to be almost always $O(n \log n)$. Moreover if one is prepared to accept a spanning tree which is *almost* an MST then a computation time of $O(n \log n)$ is guaranteed.

One major inefficiency in generating the MST is of course due to the fact that all $n(n-1)/2$ associations are computed whereas only a small number are in fact significant in the sense that they are non-zero and could therefore be chosen for a weight of an edge in the spanning tree. However, a high proportion are zero and could safely be omitted. Unfortunately the only way we can ignore them is to first compute them. Croft[23] in a recent design for the single-link algorithm has discovered a way of ignoring associations without first computing them. It does however presuppose that a file and its inverted form are available, so that if this is not so some computation time would need to be invested in the inversion. It may be that a similar algorithm could be devised for computing an MST.

3. Calculation of $g(x)$

It must be emphasised that in the non-linear case the estimation of the parameters for $g(x)$ will ideally involve a different MST for each of $P(x/w_1)$ and $P(x/w_2)$. Of course one only has complete information about the distribution of index terms in the relevant/non-relevant sets in an experimental situation. The calculation of $g(x)$ using complete information may be of interest when deriving upper bounds for retrieval effectiveness under the model as for example was done for the independent case in Robertson and Sparck Jones[1]. In an operational situation where no relevant documents are known in advance, the technique of relevance feedback would have to be used to estimate the parameters repeatedly so that the performance may converge to the upper bound. That in theory the convergence will take place is guaranteed by the convergence theorem for the linear case at least as discussed on p. 106 in Chapter 5. The limitations mentioned there also apply here.

There is a choice of how one would implement the model for $g(x)$ depending on whether one is interested in setting the cut-off *a priori* or *a posteriori*. In the former case one is faced with trying to build an MST for the index terms occurring in the relevant documents and one for the ones occurring in the non-relevant documents. Since one must do this from sample information the dependence trees could be far from optimal. One heuristic way of meeting the situation is to construct a dependence tree for the *whole* collection. The *structure* of this tree is then assumed to be the structure for the two dependence trees based on the relevant and non-relevant documents. $P(x/w_1)$ and $P(x/x_2)$ are then calculated by computing the conditional probabilities for the connected nodes dictated by the one dependence tree. How good this particular approximation is can only be demonstrated by experimental test.

If one assumes that the cut-off is set *a posteriori* then we can rank the documents according to $P(w_1/x)$ and leave the user to decide when he has seen enough. In other words we use the form

$$P(w_1/x) = \frac{P(x/w_1)P(w_1)}{P(x)}$$

to calculate (estimate) the probability of relevance for each document x. Now here we only need to estimate for $P(x/w_1)$, since to calculate $P(x)$ we simply use the spanning tree for the entire collection without considering relevance information at all. This second approach has some advantages (ignoring the absence of an explicit mention of cut-off), one being that if dependence is assumed on the entire collection then this is consistent with assuming *independence* on the relevant documents,

133

which from a computational point of view would simplify things enormously. Although independence on w_1 is unlikely it nevertheless may be forced upon us by the fact that we can never get enough information by sampling or trial retrieval to measure the extent of the dependence.

An alternative way of using the dependence tree (Association Hypothesis)

Some of the arguments advanced in the previous section can be construed as implying that the only dependence tree we have enough information to construct is the one on the entire document collection. Let us pursue this line of argument a little further. To construct a dependence tree for index terms without using relevance information is similar to constructing an index term classification. In Chapter 3 I pointed out the relationship between the MST and single-link, which shows that the one is not very different from the other. This leads directly to the idea that perhaps the dependence tree could be used in the same way as one would a term clustering.

The basic idea underlying term clustering was explained in Chapter 2. This could be summarised by saying that based on term clustering various strategies for term *deletion* and *addition* can be implemented. Forgetting about 'deletion' for the moment, it is clear how the dependence tree might be used to add in terms to, or expand, the query. The reason for doing this was neatly put by Maron in 1964: 'How can one increase the probability of retrieving a class of documents that includes relevant material not otherwise selected? One obvious method suggests itself: namely, to enlarge the initial request by using additional index terms which have a similar or related meaning to those of the given request'[4]. The assumption here is that 'related meaning' can be discovered through statistical association. Therefore I suggest that given a query, which is an *incomplete* specification of the information need and hence the relevant documents, we use the document collection (through the dependence tree) to tell us what other terms not already in the query may be useful in retrieving relevant documents. Thus I am claiming that index terms directly related (i.e. connected) to a query term in the dependence tree are likely to be useful in retrieval. In a sense I have reformulated the hypothesis on which term clustering is based (see p. 31). Let me state it formally now, and call it the *Association Hypothesis*:

> If an index term is good at discriminating relevant from non-relevant documents then any closely associated index term is also likely to be good at this.

134

The way we interpret this hypothesis is that a term in the query used by a user is likely to be there because it is a good discriminator and hence we are interested in its close associates. The hypothesis does not specify the way in which association between index terms is to be measured although in this chapter I have made a case for using EMIM. Neither does it specify a measure of 'discrimination', this I consider in the next section. The Association Hypothesis in some ways is a *dual* to the Cluster Hypothesis (p. 45) and can be tested in the same way.

Discrimination power of an index term

On p. 120 I defined

$$K_i(N, r, n, R) = \log \frac{r/(R - r)}{(n - r)/(N - n - R + r)}$$

and in fact there made the comment that it was a measure of the power of term i to discriminate between relevant and non-relevant documents. The weights in the weighting function derived from the independence assumption A1 are exactly these K_i's. Now if we forget for the moment that these weights are a consequence of a particular model and instead consider the notion of discrimination power of an index term on its own merits. Certainly this is not a novel thing to do, Salton in some of his work has sought effective ways of measuring the 'discrimination value' of index terms[24]. It seems reasonable to attach to any index term that enters into the retrieval process a weight related to its discrimination power. K_i as a measure of this power is slightly awkward in that it becomes undefined when the argument of the log function becomes zero. We therefore seek a more 'robust' function for measuring discrimination power. The function I am about to recommend for this purpose is indeed more robust, has an interesting interpretation, and enables me to derive a general result of considerable interest in the next section. However it must be emphasised that it is only an example of a function which enables some sense to be made of the notion 'discrimination power' in this and the next section. It should therefore not be considered unique although it is my opinion that any alternative way of measuring discrimination power in this context would come very close to the measure I suggest here.

Instead of K_i I suggest using the *information radius*, defined in Chapter 3 on p. 42, as a measure of the discrimination power of an index term. It is a close cousin of the expected mutual information measure a relationship that will come in useful later on. Using u and v as positive weights such as $u + v = 1$ and the usual notation for the probability functions we can write the information radius as follows:

$$uP(x_i = 1/w_1) \log \frac{P(x_i = 1/w_1)}{uP(x_i = 1/w_1) + vP(x_i = 1/w_2)} +$$

$$+ vP(x_i = 1/w_2) \log \frac{P(x_i = 1/w_2)}{uP(x_i = 1/w_1) + vP(x_i = 1/w_2)} +$$

$$+ uP(x_i = 0/w_1) \log \frac{P(x_i = 0/w_1)}{uP(x_i = 0/w_1) + vP(x_i = 0/w_2)} +$$

$$+ vP(x_i = 0/w_2) \log \frac{P(x_i = 0/w_2)}{uP(x_i = 0/w_i) + vP(x_i = 0/w_2)}$$

The interesting interpretation of the information radius that I referred to above is illustrated most easily in terms of continuous probability functions. Instead of using the densities $p(./w_1)$ and $p(./w_2)$ I shall use the corresponding probability measure μ_1 and μ_2. First we define the average of two directed divergencies[25],

$$R(\mu_1, \mu_2/v) = uI(\mu_1/v) + vI(\mu_2/v)$$

where $I(\mu_i/v)$ measures the expectation on μ_i of the information in favour of rejecting v for μ_i given by making an observation; it may be regarded as the information gained from being told to reject v in favour of μ_i. Now the information radius is the minimum

$$\inf R(\mu_1, \mu_2/v)$$

thereby removing the arbitrary v. In fact it turns out that the minimum is achieved when

$$v = u\mu_1 + v\mu_2$$

that is, an average of the two distributions to be discriminated. If we now adopt u and v as the prior probabilities then v is in fact given by the density

$$p(x) = p(x/w_1)P(w_1) + p(x/w_2)P(w_2)$$

defined over the entire collection without regard to relevance. Now of this distribution we are reasonably sure, the distribution μ_1 and μ_2 we are only guessing at; therefore it is reasonable when measuring the difference between μ_1 and μ_2 that v should incorporate as much of the information that is available. The information radius does just this.

There is one technical problem associated with the use of the information radius, or any other 'discrimination measure' based on all four cells of the contingency table, which is rather difficult to resolve. As a measure of discrimination power it does not distinguish between

136

the different contributions made to the measure by the different cells. So, for example, an index term might be a good discriminator because it occurs frequently in the non-relevant documents and infrequently in the relevant documents. Therefore, to weight an index term proportional to the discrimination measure whenever it is present in a document is exactly the wrong thing to do. It follows that the data contained in the contingency table must be used when deciding on a weighting scheme.

Discrimination gain hypothesis

In the derivation above I have made the assumption of independence or dependence in a straightforward way. I have assumed either independence on both w_1 and w_2, or dependence. But, as implied earlier, this is not the only way of making these assumptions. Robertson and Sparck Jones[1] make the point that assuming independence on the relevant *and* non-relevant documents can imply dependence on the total set of documents. To see this consider two index terms i and j, and

$$P(x_i, x_j) = P(x_i, x_j/w_1)P(w_1) + P(x_i, x_i/w_2)P(w_2)$$

$$P(x_i)P(x_j) = [P(x_i/w_1)P(w_1) + P(x_i/w_2)P(w_2)]$$
$$[P(x_j/w_1)P(w_1) + P(x_j/w_2)P(w_2)]$$

If we assume *conditional* independence on both w_1 and w_2 then

$$P(x_i, x_j) = P(x_i/w_1)P(x_j/w_1)P(w_1) + P(x_i/w_2)P(x_j/w_2)P(w_2)$$

For *unconditional* independence as well, we must have

$$P(x_i, x_j) = P(x_i)P(x_j)$$

This will only happen when $P(w_1) = 0$ or $P(w_2) = 0$, or $P(x_i/w_1) = P(x_i/w_2)$, or $P(x_j/w_1) = P(x_j/w_2)$, or in words, when at least one of the index terms is useless at discriminating relevant from non-relevant documents. In general therefore conditional *in*dependence will imply unconditional *de*pendence. Now let us assume that the index terms are indeed conditionally independent then we get the following remarkable results.

Kendall and Stuart[26] define a partial correlation coefficient for any two distributions by

$$\rho(X, Y/W) = \frac{\rho(X, Y) - \rho(X, W)\rho(Y, W)}{(1 - \rho(X, W)^2)^{\frac{1}{2}}(1 - \rho(Y, W)^2)^{\frac{1}{2}}}$$

where $\rho(.,./W)$ and $\rho(.,.)$ are the conditional and ordinary correlation coefficients respectively. Now if X and Y are conditionally independent then

$$\rho(X, Y/W) = 0$$

which implies using the expression for the partial correlation that

$$\rho(X, Y) = \rho(X, W)\rho(Y, W)$$

Since

$$|\rho(X, Y)| \leqslant 1 \;,\; |\rho(X, W)| \leqslant 1 \;,\; |\rho(Y, W)| \leqslant 1$$

this in turn implies that under the hypothesis of conditional independence

$$|\rho(X, Y)| < |\rho(X,W)| \quad \text{or} \quad |\rho(Y,W)| \qquad (**)$$

Hence if W is a random variable representing relevance then the correlation between it and either index term is greater than the correlation between the index terms.

Qualitatively I shall try and generalise this to functions other than correlation coefficients. Linfoot[27] defines a type of informational correlation measure by

$$r_{ij} = (1 - \exp(-2I(x_i, x_j)))^{\frac{1}{2}} \qquad 0 \leqslant r_{ij} \leqslant 1$$

or

$$I(x_i, x_j) = -\log \frac{(1 - r_{ij}^2)}{2}$$

where $I(x_i, x_j)$ is the now familiar expected mutual information measure. But r_{ij} reduces to the standard correlation coefficient $\rho(.,.)$ if (x_i, x_j) is normally distributed. So it is not unreasonable to assume that for non-normal distributions r_{ij} will behave approximately like $\rho(.,.)$ and will in fact satisfy (**) as well. But r_{ij} is strictly monotone with respect to $I(x_i, x_j)$ so it too will satisfy (**). Therefore we can now say that under conditional independence the information contained in one index term about another is less than the information contained in either term about the conditioning variable W. In symbols we have

$$I(x_i, x_j) < I(x_i, W) \quad \text{or} \quad I(x_j, W),$$

where $I(., W)$ is the information radius with its weights interpreted as prior probabilities. Remember that $I(., W)$ was suggested as the measure of discrimination power. I think this result deserves to be stated formally as an hypothesis when W is interpreted as relevance.

Discrimination Gain Hypothesis: Under the hypothesis of conditional independence the statistical information contained in one index term about another is less than the information contained in either index term about relevance.

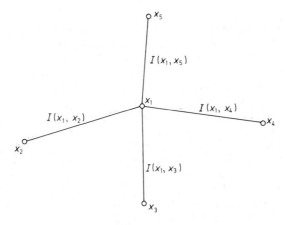

Figure 6.2.

I must emphasise that the above argument leading to the hypothesis is not a proof. The argument is only a qualitative one although I believe it could be tightened up. Despite this it provides (together with the hypothesis) some justification and theoretical basis for the use of the MST based on $I(x_i, x_j)$ to improve retrieval. The discrimination hypothesis is a way of firming up the Association Hypothesis under conditional independence.

One consequence of the discrimination hypothesis is that it provides a rationale for ranking the index terms connected to a query term in the dependence tree in order of I(term, query term) values to reflect the order of discrimination power values. The basis for this is that the more strongly connected an index term is to the query term (measured by EMIM) the more discriminatory it is likely to be. To see what is involved more clearly I have shown an example set-up in *Figure 6.2*. Let us suppose that x_1 is the variable corresponding to the query term and that $I(x_1, x_2) < I(x_1, x_3) < I(x_1, x_4) < I(x_1, x_5)$ then our hypothesis says that without knowing in advance how good a discriminator each of the index terms 2,3,4,5 is, it is reasonable to assume that $I(x_2, W) < I(x_3, W) < I(x_4, W) < I(x_5, W)$. Clearly we cannot guarantee that the index terms will satisfy the last ordering but it is the best we can do given our ignorance.

Bibliographic remarks

The basic background reading for this chapter is contained in but a few papers. One approach to probabilistic weighting based on relevance data derives from the work of Yu and his collaborators[28,29]. The other is contained in the already frequently cited paper of Robertson and Sparck Jones[1]. Unfortunately, both these approaches rely heavily on the assumption of stochastic independence. My own paper[2] and the one of Bookstein and Kraft[3] are the only ones I know of which try and construct a model without this assumption. Perhaps an earlier paper by Negoita should be mentioned here which discusses an attempt to use non-linear decision functions in IR[30]. Robertson's recent progress in documentation on models gives a useful summary of some of the more recent work[31].

According to Doyle[32] (p. 267), Maron and Kuhns[19] were the first to describe in the open literature the use of association (statistical co-occurrence) of index terms as a means of enlarging and sharpening the search. However, Doyle himself was already working on similar ideas in the late fifties[33] and produced a number of papers on 'associations' in the early sixties[34,35]. Stiles in 1961[36], already apparently aware of Maron and Kuhns work, gave an explicit procedure for using terms co-occurring significantly with search terms, and not unlike the method based on the dependence tree described in this chapter. He also used the χ^2 to measure association between index terms which is mathematically very similar to using the expected mutual information measure, although the latter is to be preferred when *measuring* dependence (see Goodman and Kruskal for a discussion on this point[37]). Stiles was very clear about the usefulness of using associations between index terms, he saw that through them one was 'able to locate documents relevant to a request *even though the document had not been indexed by the term used in the request*'[36].

The model in this chapter also connects with two other ideas in earlier research. One is the idea of *inverse document frequency weighting* already discussed in Chapter 2. The other is the idea of term clustering. Taking the weighting idea first, this in fact goes back to the early paper by Edmundson and Wyllys[38], we can write

$$P(\text{relevance/document}) \propto \frac{1}{P(\text{document})}$$

or in words, for any document the probability of relevance is inversely proportional the probability with which it will occur on a random basis. If the P(document) is assumed to be the product of the probabilities of the individual index terms being either present or absent in the document then after taking logs we have the inverse document frequency weighting principle. It assumes that the likelihood P(document/relevance) is constant for all documents. Why it is exactly

140

that this principle works so well is not yet clear (but see Yu and Salton's recent theoretical paper[39]).

The connection with term clustering was already made earlier on in the chapter. The spanning tree can be looked upon as a classification of the index terms. One of the important consequences of the model described in this chapter is that it lays down precisely how the tree should be used in retrieval. Earlier work in this area was rather *ad hoc* and did not lead to conclusive results[40].

It should be clear now that the quantitative model embodies within one theory such diverse topics as term clustering, early association analysis, document frequency weighting, and relevance weighting.

References

1. ROBERTSON, S. E. and SPARCK JONES, K., 'Relevance weighting of search terms', *Journal of the American Society for Information Science,* **27,** 129–146 (1976)
2. VAN RIJSBERGEN, C. J., 'A theoretical basis for the use of co-occurrence data in information retrieval', *Journal of Documentation,* **33,** 106–119 (1977)
3. BOOKSTEIN, A. and KRAFT, D., 'Operations research applied to document indexing and retrieval decisions', *Journal of the ACM,* **24,** 410–427 (1977)
4. MARON, M. E., 'Mechanized documentation: The logic behind a probabilistic interpretation', In: *Statistical Association Methods for Mechanized Documentation* (Edited by Stevens *et al.*) National Bureau of Standards, Washington, 9–13 (1965)
5. OSBORNE, M. L., *A Modification of Veto Logic for a Committee of Threshold Logic Units and the Use of 2-class Classifiers for Function Estimation,* Ph.D. Thesis, Oregon State University (1975)
6. GOOD, I. J., *Probability and the Weighing of Evidence,* Charles Griffin and Co. Ltd., London (1950)
7. ROBERTSON, S. E., 'The probability ranking principle in IR', *Journal of Documentation,* **33,** 294–304 (1977)
8. GOFFMAN, W., 'A searching procedure for information retrieval', *Information Storage and Retrieval,* **2,** 73–78 (1964)
9. WILLIAMS, J. H., 'Results of classifying documents with multiple discriminant functions', In: *Statistical Association Methods for Mechanized Documentation* (Edited by Stevens *et al.*) National Bureau of Standards, Washington, 217–224 (1965)
10. DE FINETTI, B., *Theory of Probability,* Vol. 1, 146–161, Wiley, London (1974)
11. KU, H. H. and KULLBACK, S., 'Approximating discrete probability distributions', *IEEE Transactions on Information Theory,* **IT-15,** 444–447 (1969)
12. KULLBACK, S., *Information Theory and Statistics,* Dover, New York (1968)
13. CHOW, C. K. and LIU, C. N., 'Approximating discrete probability distributions with dependence trees', *IEEE Transactions on Information Theory,* **IT-14,** 462–467 (1968)

14. COX, D. R., 'The analysis of multivariate binary data', *Applied Statistics*, **21**, 113–120 (1972)
15. BOX, G. E. P. and TIAO, G. C., *Bayesian Inference in Statistical Analysis*, 304–315, Addison-Wesley, Reading, Mass. (1973)
16. GOOD, I. J., *The Estimation of Probabilities: An Essay on Modern Bayesian Methods*, The M.I.T. Press, Cambridge, Mass. (1965)
17. HARPER, D. and VAN RIJSBERGEN, C. J., 'An evaluation of feedback in document retrieval using co-occurrence data', *Journal of Documentation*, **34**, (in the press)
18. HUGHES, G. F., 'On the mean accuracy of statistical pattern recognizers', *IEEE Transactions on Information Theory*, IT-14, 55–63 (1968)
19. MARON, M. E. and KUHNS, J. L., 'On relevance, probabilistic indexing and information retrieval', *Journal of the ACM*, 7, 216–244 (1960)
20. IVIE, E. L., *Search Procedures Based on Measures of Relatedness Between Documents*, Ph.D. Thesis, M.I.T., Report MAC-TR-29 (1966)
21. WHITNEY, V. K. M., 'Minimal spanning tree, Algorithm 422', *Communications of the ACM*, **15**, 273–274 (1972)
22. BENTLEY, J. L. and FRIEDMAN, J. H., *Fast Algorithm for Constructing Minimal Spanning Trees in Coordinate Spaces*, Stanford Report, STAN-CS-75-529 (1975)
23. CROFT, W. B., 'Clustering large files of documents using single link', *Journal of the American Society for Information Science*, **28**, 341–344 (1977)
24. SALTON, G., *Dynamic Information and Library Processing*, Prentice-Hall, Englewoods Cliffs, N.J., 441–445 (1975)
25. JARDINE, N. and SIBSON, R., *Mathematical Taxonomy*, pp. 12–15, Wiley, London and New York (1971)
26. KENDALL, M. G. and STUART, A., *Advanced Theory of Statistics*, Vol. 2, 2nd ed., Griffin, London (1967)
27. LINFOOT, E. H., 'An informational measure of correlation', *Information and Control*, 1, 85–89 (1957)
28. YU, C. T. and SALTON, G., 'Precision Weighting—An effective automatic indexing method', *Journal of the ACM*, **23**, 76–85 (1976)
29. YU, C. T., LUK, W. S. and CHEUNG, T. Y., 'A statistical model for relevance feedback in information retrieval', *Journal of the ACM*, **23**, 273–286 (1976)
30. NEGOITA, C. V., 'On the decision process in information retrieval', *Studii si cercetari de documentare*, **15**, 269–281 (1973)
31. ROBERTSON, S. E., 'Theories and models in information retrieval', *Journal of Documentation*, **33**, 126–148 (1977)
32. DOYLE, L. B., *Information Retrieval and Processing*, Melville Publishing Co., Los Angeles, California (1975)
33. DOYLE, L. B., 'Programmed interpretation of text as a basis for information retrieval systems', In: *Proceedings of the Western Joint Computer Conference* San Francisco,60–63 (1959)
34. DOYLE, L. B., 'Semantic road maps for literature searchers', *Journal of the ACM*, 8, 553–578 (1961)
35. DOYLE, L. B., 'Some compromises between word grouping and document grouping', In: *Statistical Association Methods for Mechanized Documentation* (Edited by Stevens *et al.*) National Bureau of Standards, Washington, 15–24 (1965)
36. STILES, H. F., 'The association factor in information retrieval', *Journal of the ACM*, 8, 271–279 (1961)
37. GOODMAN, L. and KRUSKAL, W., 'Measures of association for cross-classifications', *Journal of the American Statistical Association*, 49, 732–764 (1954)
142

38. EDMUNDSON, H. P. and WYLLYS, R. E., 'Automatic abstracting and indexing—Survey and recommendations', *Communications of the ACM*, **4**, 226–234 (1961)
39. YU, C. T. and SALTON, G., 'Effective information retrieval using term accuracy', *Communications of the ACM*, **20**, 135–142 (1977)
40. SPARCK JONES, K., *Automatic Keyword Classification for Information Retrieval*, Butterworths, London (1971)

Seven

EVALUATION

Introduction

Much effort and research has gone into solving the problem of evaluation of information retrieval systems. However, it is probably fair to say that most people active in the field of information storage and retrieval still feel that the problem is far from solved. One may get an idea of the extent of the effort by looking at the numerous survey articles that have been published on the topic (see the regular chapter in the *Annual Review* on evaluation). Nevertheless, new approaches to evaluation are constantly being published (e.g. Cooper[1]; Jardine and Van Rijsbergen[2]; Heine[3]).

In a book of this nature it will be impossible to cover all work to date about evaluation. Instead I shall attempt to explicate the conventional, most commonly used method of evaluation, followed by a survey of the more promising attempts to improve on the older methods of evaluation.

To put the problem of evaluation in perspective let me pose three questions: (1) Why evaluate? (2) What to evaluate? (3) How to evaluate? The answers to these questions pretty well cover the whole field of evaluation. There is much controversy about each and although I do not wish to add to the controversy I shall attempt an answer to each one in turn.

The answer to the first question is mainly a social and economic one. The social part is fairly intangible, but mainly relates to the desire to put a measure on the benefits (or disadvantages) to be got from information retrieval systems. I use 'benefit' here in a much wider sense than just the benefit accruing due to acquisition of relevant documents. For example, what benefit will users obtain (or what harm will be done) by replacing the traditional sources of information by a fully

144

automatic and interactive retrieval system? Studies to gauge this are going on but results are hard to interpret. For some kinds of retrieval systems the benefit may be more easily measured than for others (compare statute or case law retrieval with document retrieval). The economic answer amounts to a statement of how much it is going to cost you to use one of these systems, and coupled with this is the question 'is it worth it?'. Even a simple statement of cost is difficult to make. The computer costs may be easy to estimate, but the costs in terms of personal effort are much harder to ascertain. Then, whether it is worth it or not depends on the individual user.

It should be apparent now that in evaluating an information retrieval system we are mainly concerned with providing data so that users can make a decision as to (1) whether they want such a system (social question) and (2) whether it will be worth it. Furthermore, these methods of evaluation are used in a comparative way to measure whether certain changes will lead to an improvement in performance. In other words, when a claim is made for say a particular search strategy, the yardstick of evaluation can be applied to determine whether the claim is a valid one.

The second question (what to evaluate?) boils down to what can we measure that will reflect the ability of the system to satisfy the user. Since this book is mainly concerned with automatic document retrieval systems I shall answer it in this context. In fact, as early as 1966, Cleverdon gave an answer to this. He listed six main measurable quantities:

(1) the *coverage* of the collection, that is, the extent to which the system includes relevant matter;
(2) the *time lag,* that is, the average interval between the time the search request is made and the time an answer is given;
(3) the form of *presentation* of the output;
(4) the *effort* involved on the part of the user in obtaining answers to his search requests;
(5) the *recall* of the system, that is, the proportion of relevant material actually retrieved in answer to a search request;
(6) the *precision* of the system, that is, the proportion of retrieved material that is actually relevant.

It is claimed that (1)–(4) are readily assessed. It is recall and precision which attempt to measure what is now known as the *effectiveness* of the retrieval system. In other words it is a measure of the ability of the system to retrieve relevant documents while at the same time holding back non-relevant ones. It is assumed that the more effective the system the more it will satisfy the user. It is also assumed that precision and recall are sufficient for the measurement of effectiveness.

145

There has been much debate in the past as to whether precision and recall are in fact the appropriate quantities to use as measures of effectiveness. A popular alternative has been recall and fall-out (the proportion of non-relevant documents retrieved). However, all the alternatives still require the determination of relevance in some way. The relationship between the various measures and their dependence on relevance will be made more explicit later. Later in the chapter a theory of evaluation is presented based on precision and recall. The advantages of basing it on precision and recall are that they are:

(1) the most commonly used pair;
(2) fairly well understood quantities.

The final question (How to evaluate?) has a largely technical answer. In fact, most of the remainder of this chapter may be said to be concerned with this. It is interesting to note that the technique of measuring retrieval effectiveness has been largely influenced by the particular retrieval strategy adopted and the form of its output. For example, when the output is a ranking of documents an obvious parameter such as rank position is immediately available for control. Using the rank position as cut-off, a series of precision recall values could then be calculated, one pair for each cut-off value. The results could then be summarised in the form of a set of points joined by a smooth curve. The path along the curve would then have the immediate interpretation of varying effectiveness with the cut-off value. Unfortunately the kind of question this form of evaluation does not answer is, for example, how many queries did better than average and how many did worse? Nevertheless, we shall need to spend more time explaining this approach to the measurement of effectiveness since it is the most common approach and needs to be understood.

Before proceeding to the technical details relating to the measurement of effectiveness it is as well to examine more closely the concept of relevance which underlies it.

Relevance

Relevance is a *subjective* notion. Different users may differ about the relevance or non-relevance of particular documents to given questions. However, the difference is not large enough to invalidate experiments which have been made with document collections for which test questions with corresponding relevance assessments are available. These questions are usually elicited from bona fide users, that is, users in a particular discipline who have an information need. The relevance assessments are made by a panel of experts in that discipline. So we

146

now have the situation where a number of questions exist for which the 'correct' responses are known. It is a general assumption in the field of IR that should a retrieval strategy fare well under a large number of *experimental* conditions then it is likely to perform well in an *operational* situation where relevance is *not* known in advance.

There is a concept of relevance which can be said to be *objective* and which deserves mention as an interesting source of speculation. This notion of relevance has been explicated by Cooper[4]. It is properly termed 'logical relevance'. Its usefulness in present day retrieval systems is limited. However, it can be shown to be of some importance when it is related to the development of question-answering systems, such as the one recently designed by T. Winograd at Massachusetts Institute of Technology.

Logical relevance is most easily explicated if the questions are restricted to the yes–no type. This restriction may be lifted – for details see Cooper's original paper. Relevance is defined in terms of *logical consequence*. To make this possible a question is represented by a set of sentences. In the case of a yes–no question it is represented by two formal statements of the form 'p' and 'not-p'. For example, if the query were 'Is hydrogen a halogen element?', the pair of statements would be the formal language equivalent of 'Hydrogen is a halogen element' and 'Hydrogen is not a halogen element'. More complicated questions of the 'which' and 'whether' type can be transformed in this manner, for details the reader is referred to Belnap[5,6]. If the two statements representing the question are termed *component statements* then the subset of the set of stored sentences is a *premiss set* for a component statement if and only if the component statement is a logical consequence of that subset. (Note we are now temporarily talking about stored *sentences* rather than stored documents.) A *minimal premiss set* for a component statement is one that is as small as possible in the sense that if any of its members were deleted, the component statement would no longer be a logical consequence of the resulting set. Logical relevance is now defined as a two-place relation between stored sentences and information need representations (that is, the question represented as component statements). The final definition is as follows:

> A stored sentence is logically relevant to (a representation of) an information need if and only if it is a member of some minimal premiss set of stored sentences for some component statement of that need.

Although logical relevance is initially only defined between sentences it can easily be extended to apply to stored documents. A document is

147

relevant to an information need if and only if it contains at least one sentence which is relevant to that need.

Earlier on I stated that this notion of relevance was only of limited use at the moment. The main reason for this is that the kind of system which would be required to implement a retrieval strategy which would retrieve only the logically relevant documents has not been built yet. However, the components of such a system do exist to a certain extent. Firstly, theorem provers, which can prove theorems within formal languages such as the first-order predicate calculus, have reached quite a level of sophistication now (see, for example, Chang and Lee[7]). Secondly, Winograd's system is capable of answering questions about its simple universe of blocks in natural language. In principle this system could be extended to construct a universe of documents, that is, the content of a document is analysed and incorporated into the universe of currently 'understood' documents. It may be that the scale of a system of this kind will be too large for present day computers; only the future will tell.

Saracevic[8] has given a thorough review of the notion of relevance in information science. Robertson[9] has summarised some of the more recent work on probabilistic interpretations of relevance.

Precision and recall, and others

We now leave the speculations about relevance and return to the promised detailed discussion of the measurement of effectiveness. Relevance will once again be assumed to have its broader meaning of 'aboutness' and 'appropriateness', that is, a document is ultimately determined to be relevant or not by the user. Effectiveness is purely a measure of the ability of the system to satisfy the user in terms of the relevance of documents retrieved. Initially, I shall concentrate on measuring effectiveness by precision and recall; a similar analysis could be given for any pair of equivalent measures.

It is helpful at this point to introduce the famous 'contingency' table which is not really a contingency table at all.

	RELEVANT	NON-RELEVANT	
RETRIEVED	$A \cap B$	$\bar{A} \cap B$	B
NOT RETRIEVED	$A \cap \bar{B}$	$\bar{A} \cap \bar{B}$	$\bar{B}$
	A	$\bar{A}$	N

(N = number of documents in the system)

148

A large number of measures of effectiveness can be derived from this table. To list but a few:

$$\text{PRECISION} = \frac{|A \cap B|}{|B|}$$

$$\text{RECALL} \quad = \frac{|A \cap B|}{|A|}$$

$$\text{FALLOUT} = \frac{|\bar{A} \cap B|}{|\bar{A}|}$$

($| \, . \, |$ is the counting measure)

There is a functional relationship between all three involving a parameter called *generality* (G) which is a measure of the density of relevant documents in the collection. The relationship is:

$$P = \frac{R \times G}{(R \times G) + F(1 - G)} \quad^* \quad \text{where} \quad G = \frac{|A|}{N}$$

For each request submitted to a retrieval system one of these tables can be constructed. Based on each one of these tables a precision–recall

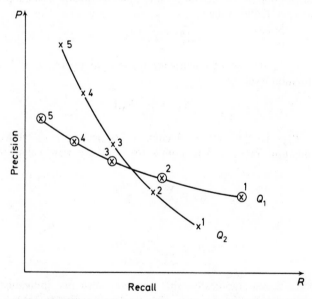

Figure 7.1. The precision–recall curves for two queries. The ordinals indicate the values of the control parameter λ

* For a derivation of this relation from Bayes' Theorem the reader should consult the author's recent paper on retrieval effectiveness[10].

149

value can be calculated. If the output of the retrieval strategy depends on a parameter, such as rank position or co-ordination level (the number of terms a query has in common with a document), it can be varied to give a different table for each value of the parameter and hence a different precision–recall value. If λ is the parameter, then P_λ denotes precision, R_λ recall, and a precision–recall value will be denoted by the ordered pair (R_λ, P_λ). The set of ordered pairs makes up the precision–recall graph. Geometrically when the points have been joined up in some way they make up the precision–recall curve. The performance of each request is usually given by a precision–recall curve (see *Figure 7.1*). To measure the overall performance of a system, the set of curves, one for each request, is combined in some way to produce an average curve.

Averaging techniques

The method of pooling or averaging of the individual *P–R* curves seems to have depended largely on the retrieval strategy employed. When retrieval is done by co-ordination level, *micro-evaluation* is adopted. If S is the set of requests then:

$$|\tilde{A}| = \sum_{s \in S} |A_s|$$

where A_s is the set of documents relevant to request s. If λ is the co-ordination level then:

$$|\tilde{B}_\lambda| = \sum_{s \in S} |B_{\lambda s}|$$

where $B_{\lambda s}$ is the set of documents retrieved at or above the co-ordination level λ. The points (R_λ, P_λ) are now calculated as follows:

$$R_\lambda = \sum_{s \in S} \frac{|A_s \cap B_{\lambda s}|}{|\tilde{A}|}$$

$$P_\lambda = \sum_{s \in S} \frac{|A_s \cap B_{\lambda s}|}{|\tilde{B}_\lambda|}$$

Figure 7.2 shows graphically what happens when two individual *P–R* curves are combined in this way. The raw data are given in Table 7.1.

An alternative approach to averaging is *macro-evaluation* which can be independent of any parameter such as co-ordination level. The average curve is obtained by specifying a set of *standard* recall values

150

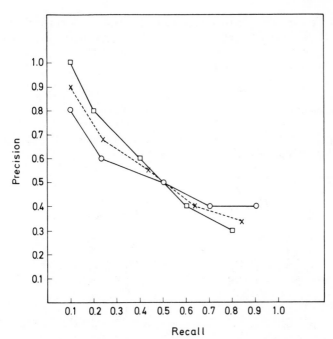

Figure 7.2. An example of 'averaging' in micro-evaluation

TABLE 7.1. THE RAW DATA FOR THE MICRO−EVALUATION IN *FIGURE 7.2*

QUERY 1 :

R	0.1	0.2	0.4	0.6	0.8
P	1.0	0.8	0.6	0.4	0.3

$A_1 = 100$

QUERY 2 :

R	0.1	0.3	0.5	0.7	0.9
P	0.8	0.6	0.5	0.4	0.4

$A_2 = 80$

λ	$|B_{\lambda 1}|$	$|A_1 \cap B_{\lambda 1}|$	$|B_{\lambda 2}|$	$|A_2 \cap B_{\lambda 2}|$	R_λ	P_λ
1	10	10	10	8	0.1	0.9
2	25	20	40	24	0.24	0.68
3	66	40	80	40	0.44	0.55
4	150	60	140	56	0.64	0.40
5	266	80	180	72	0.84	0.34

for which average precision values are calculated by averaging over all queries the individual precision values corresponding to the standard recall values. Often no unique precision value corresponds exactly so it becomes necessary to interpolate.

Interpolation

Many interpolation techniques have been suggested in the literature. See, for example, Keen[11].

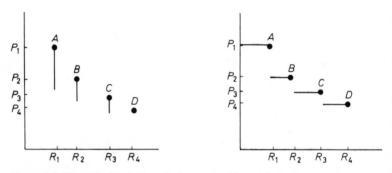

Figure 7.3. The right hand figure is the result of interpolating between the points A, B, C, D in the left hand figure

Figure 7.3 shows a typical *P-R* graph for a single query. The points *A*, *B*, *C* and *D*, I shall call the *observed* points, since these are the only points observed directly during an experiment the others may be inferred from these. Thus given that $A = (R_1, P_1)$ has been observed, then the next point *B* is the one corresponding to an increase in recall, which follows from a unit increase in the number of relevant documents retrieved. Between any two observed points the recall remains constant, since no more relevant documents are retrieved.

It is an experimental fact that *average* precision–recall graphs are monotonically decreasing. Consistent with this, a linear interpolation estimates the *best* possible performance between any two adjacent observed points. To avoid inflating the experimental results it is probably better to perform a more conservative interpolation as follows.

Let (R_λ, P_λ) be the set of precision–recall values obtained by varying some parameter λ. To obtain the set of observed points we specify a subset of the parameters λ. Thus (R_θ, P_θ) is an observed point

152

if θ corresponds to a value of λ at which an increase in recall is produced. We now have:

$$G_s = \{(R_{\theta s}, P_{\theta s})\}$$

the set of observed points for a request. To interpolate between any two points we define:

$$P_s(R) = \{\sup P : R' \geqslant R \text{ s.t. } (R', P) \in G_s\}$$

where R is a standard recall value. From this we obtain the average precision value at the standard recall value R by:

$$\tilde{P}(R) = \sum_{s \in S} \frac{P_s(R)}{|S|}$$

The set of observed points is such that the interpolated function is monotonically decreasing. *Figure 7.3* shows the effect of the interpolation procedure, essentially it turns the *P–R* curve into a step-function with the jumps at the observed points. A necessary consequence of its monotonicity is that the *average P–R* curve will also be monotonically decreasing. It is possible to define the set of observed points in such a way that the interpolated function is not monotonically decreasing. In practice, even for this case, we have that the average precision–recall curve is monotonically decreasing.

In *Figure 7.4* we illustrate the interpolation and averaging process.

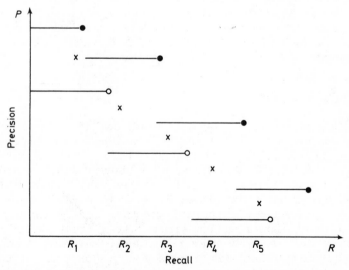

Figure 7.4. An example of macro-evaluation. The points indicated by crosses lie midway between the two enclosing horizontal bars and their abscissae are given by the standard recall values R_i

153

Composite measures

Dissatisfaction in the past with methods of measuring effectiveness by a pair of numbers (e.g. precision and recall) which may co-vary in a loosely specified way has led to attempts to invent *composite* measures. These are still based on the 'contingency' table but combine parts of it into a single number measure. Unfortunately many of these measures are rather *ad hoc* and cannot be justified in any rational way. The simplest example of this kind of measure is the sum of precision and recall.

$$S = P + R$$

This is simply related to a measure suggested by Borko.

$$BK = P + R - 1$$

More complicated ones are

$$Q = \frac{R - F}{R + F - 2RF} \qquad (F = \text{Fallout})$$

$$V = 1 - \frac{1}{2\left(\frac{1}{P}\right) + 2\left(\frac{1}{R}\right) - 3}$$

Vickery's measure V can be shown to be a special case of a general measure which will be derived below.

Some single-number measures have derivations which can be justified in a rational manner. Some of them will be given individual attention later on. Suffice it here to point out that it is the *model* underlying the derivation of these measures that is important.

The Swets model*

As early as 1963 Swets[12] expressed dissatisfaction with existing methods of measuring retrieval effectiveness. His background in signal detection led him to formulate an evaluation model based on statistical decision theory. In 1967 he evaluated some fifty different retrieval methods from the point of view of his model[13]. The results of his evaluation were encouraging but not conclusive. Subsequently, Brookes[14] suggested some reasonable modifications to Swets' measure of effectiveness, and Robertson[15] showed that the suggested modifications were in fact simply related to an alternative measure already suggested by Swets. It is interesting that although the Swets model is theoretically attractive

---

* Bookstein[16] has recently re-examined this model showing how Swets implicitly relied on an 'equal variance' assumption.

and links IR measurements to a ready made and well-developed statistical theory, it has not found general acceptance amongst workers in the field.

Before proceeding to an explanation of the Swets model, it is as well to quote in full the conditions that the desired measure of effectiveness is designed to meet. At the beginning of his 1967 report Swets states:

'A desirable measure of retrieval performance would have the following properties. *First*, it would express solely the ability of a retrieval system to distinguish between wanted and unwanted items — that is, it would be a measure of "effectiveness" only, leaving for separate consideration factors related to cost or "efficiency". *Second*, the desired measure would not be confounded by the relative willingness of the system to emit items — it would express discrimination power independent of any "acceptance criterion" employed, whether the criterion is characteristic of the system or adjusted by the user. *Third*, the measure would be a single number — in preference, for example, to a pair of numbers which may co-vary in a loosely specified way, or a curve representing a table of several pairs of numbers — so that it could be transmitted simply and immediately apprehended. *Fourth*, and finally, the measure would allow complete ordering of different performances, indicate the amount of difference separating any two performances, and assess the performance of any one system in absolute terms — that is, the metric would be a scale with a unit, a true zero, and a maximum value. Given a measure with these properties, we could be confident of having a pure and valid index of how well a retrieval system (or method) were performing the function it was primarily designed to accomplish, and we could reasonably ask questions of the form "Shall we pay X dollars for Y units of effectiveness". '

He then goes on to claim that 'The measure I proposed [in 1963], one drawn from statistical decision theory, has the *potential* [my italics] to satisfy all four desiderata'. So, what is this measure?

To arrive at the measure, we must first discuss the underlying model. Swets defines the basic variables Precision, Recall, and Fallout in probabilistic terms.

Recall = an estimate of the conditional probability that an item will be retrieved given that it is relevant [we denote this $P(B/A)$].

Precision = an estimate of the conditional probability that an item will be relevant given that it is retrieved [i.e. $P(A/B)$].

Fallout = an estimate of the conditional probability that an item will be retrieved given that it is non-relevant [i.e. $P(B/\bar{A})$].

He accepts the validity of measuring the effectiveness of retrieval by a curve either precision–recall or recall–fallout generated by the variation of some control variable λ (e.g. co-ordination level). He seeks to characterise each curve by a single number. He rejects precision–recall in favour of recall–fallout since he is unable to do it for the former but achieves limited success with the latter.

In the simplest case we assume that the variable λ is distributed normally on the set of relevant and non-relevant documents. The two distributions are given respectively by $N(\mu_1, \sigma_1)$ and $N(\mu_2, \sigma_2)$. The density functions are given by $f_1(\lambda|A)$ and $f_2(\lambda|\bar{A})$. We may picture the distribution as shown in *Figure 7.5.*

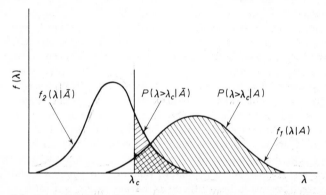

Figure 7.5. *Two normal distributions for* λ, *one,* $N(\mu_1, \sigma_1)$, *on the set of relevant documents* A *with density of* $f_1(\lambda_1|A)$, *the other,* $N(\mu_2, \sigma_2)$, *on the set of non-relevant documents* $\bar{A}$ *with density* $f_2(\lambda|\bar{A})$. *The size of the areas shaded in a* N–W *and* N–E *direction represents recall and fallout respectively.*

The usual set-up in IR is now to define a decision rule in terms of λ, to determine which documents are retrieved (the acceptance criterion). In other words we specify λ_c such that a document for which the associated λ exceeds λ_c is retrieved. We now measure the effectiveness of a retrieval strategy by measuring some appropriate variables (such as R and P, or R and F) at various values of λ_c. It turns out that the differently shaded areas under the curves in *Figure 7.5* correspond to recall and fallout. Moreover, we find the *operating characteristic* (OC) traced out by the point (F_λ, R_λ) due to variation in λ_c is a smooth curve fully determined by two points, in the general case of unequal variance, and by one point in the special case of equal variance. To see this one only needs to plot the (F_λ, R_λ) points on double probability paper (scaled linearly for the normal deviate) to find that the points lie on a straight line. A slope of $45°$ corresponds to equal variance, and

156

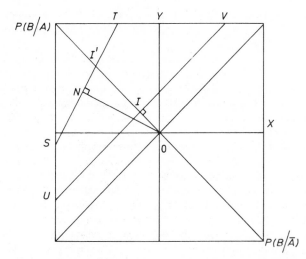

Figure 7.6. The two OC's are ST *and* UV. *Swets recommends using the distances* $\sqrt{2}OI$ *and* $\sqrt{2}OI'$ *to compare their effectiveness. Brookes suggests using the normal distances* OI *and* ON *instead. (Adapted from Brookes[14], page 51)*

otherwise the slope is given by the ratio of σ_1 and σ_2. *Figure 7.6* shows the two cases. Swets now suggests, regardless of slope, that the distance OI (actually $\sqrt{2}OI$) be used as a measure of effectiveness. This amounts to using:

$$S1 = \frac{\mu_2 - \mu_1}{\frac{1}{2}(\sigma_1 + \sigma_2)}$$

which is simply the difference between the means of the distribution normalised by the average standard deviation. Unfortunately this measure does rather hide the fact that a high $S1$ value may be due to a steep slope. The slope, and $S1$, would have to be given which fails to meet Swets' second condition. We, also, still have the problem of deciding between two strategies whose OC's intersect and hence have different $S1$ values and slopes.

Brookes[14] in an attempt to correct for the $S1$ bias towards systems with slopes much greater than unity suggested a modification to $S1$. Mathematically Brookes's measure is:

$$S2 = \frac{\mu_2 + \mu_1}{(\sigma_1^2 + \sigma_2^2)^{\frac{1}{2}}}$$

157

Brookes also gives statistical reasons for preferring $S2$ to $S1$ which need not concern us here. Geometrically $S2$ is the perpendicular distance from 0 to OC (see *Figure 7.6*).

Interestingly enough Robertson[15] showed that $S2$ is simply related to the area under the Recall–Fallout curve. In fact the area is a strictly increasing function of $S2$. It also has the appealing interpretation that it is equal to the percentage of correct choices a strategy will make when attempting to select from a pair of items, one drawn at random from the non-relevant set and one drawn from the relevant set. It does seem therefore that $S2$ goes a long way to meeting the requirements laid down by Swets. However, the appropriateness of the model is questionable on a number of grounds. Firstly, the linearity of the OC curve does not necessarily imply that λ is normally distributed in both populations, although they will be 'similarly' distributed. Secondly, λ is assumed to be continuous which certainly is not the case for the data checked out both by Swets and Brookes, in which the co-ordination level used assumed only integer values. Thirdly, there is no evidence to suggest that in the case of more sophisticated matching functions, as used by the SMART system, that the distributions will be similarly distributed let alone normally. Finally the choice of fallout rather than precision as second variable is hard to justify. The reason is that the *proportion* of non-relevant retrieved for large systems is going to behave much like the ratio of 'non-relevant' retrieved to 'total documents in system'. For comparative purposes 'total document' may be ignored leaving us with 'non-relevant retrieved' which is complementary to 'relevant retrieved'. But now we may as well use precision instead of fallout.

The Robertson model–the logistic transformation

Robertson in collaboration with Teather has developed a model for estimating the probabilities corresponding to recall and fallout[17]. The estimation procedure is unusual in that in making an estimate of these probabilities for a single query it takes account of two things: one, the amount of data used to arrive at the estimates, and two, the averages of the estimates over all queries. The effect of this is to 'pull' an estimate closer to the overall mean if it seems to be an outlyer whilst at the same time counterbalancing the 'pull' in proportion to the amount of data used to make the estimate in the first place. There is now some evidence to show that this pulling-in-to-the-mean is statistically a reasonable thing to do[18].

Using the *logit* transformation for probabilities, that is

$$\text{logit } \theta = \log \frac{\theta}{1-\theta} \qquad 0 < \theta < 1$$

the basic quantitative model for a single query j they propose is

$$\text{logit } \theta_{j1} = \alpha_j + \Delta_j$$

$$\text{logit } \theta_{j2} = \alpha_j - \Delta_j$$

Here θ_{j1} and θ_{j2} are probabilities corresponding to recall and fallout respectively as defined in the previous section. The parameters α_j and Δ_j are to be interpreted as follows:

α_j measures the *specificity* of the query formulation; Δ_j measures the *separation* of relevant and non-relevant documents.

For a given query j if the query i has been formulated in a more specific way than j, one would expect the recall and fallout to decrease, i.e.

$$\theta_{i1} < \theta_{j1} \quad \text{and} \quad \theta_{i2} < \theta_{j2}$$

Also, if for query i the system is better at separating the non-relevant from the relevant documents than it is for query j one would expect the recall to increase and the fallout to decrease, i.e.

$$\theta_{i1} > \theta_{j1} \quad \text{and} \quad \theta_{i2} < \theta_{j2}$$

Given that logit is a monotonic transformation, these interpretations are consistent with the simple quantitative model defined above.

To arrive at an estimation procedure for α_j and Δ_j is a difficult technical problem and the interested reader should consult Robertson's thesis[19]. It requires certain assumptions to be made about α_j and Δ_j, the most important of which is that the $\{\alpha_j\}$ and $\{\Delta_j\}$ are independent and normally distributed. These assumptions are rather difficult to validate. The only evidence produced so far derives the distribution of $\{\alpha_j\}$ for certain test data. Unfortunately these estimates, although they are unimodally and symmetrically distributed, themselves can only be arrived at by using the normality assumption. In the case of Δ_j it has been found that it is approximately constant across queries so that a common–Δ model is not unreasonable:

$$\text{logit } \theta_{j1} = \alpha_{j1} + \Delta$$

$$\text{logit } \theta_{j2} = \alpha_{j2} - \Delta$$

From them it would appear that Δ could be a candidate for a single number measure of effectiveness. However, Robertson has gone to some pains to warn against this. His main argument is that these parameters are related to the behavioural characteristics of an IR

159

system so that if we were to adopt Δ as a measure of effectiveness we could be throwing away vital information needed to make an extrapolation to the performance of other systems.

The Cooper model – expected search length

In 1968, Cooper[20] stated: 'The primary function of a retrieval system is conceived to be that of saving its users to as great an extent as is possible, the labour of perusing and discarding irrelevant documents, in their search for relevant ones'. It is this 'saving' which is measured and is claimed to be the *single* index of merit for retrieval systems. In general the index is applicable to retrieval systems with ordered (or ranked) output. It roughly measures the search effort which one would expect to save by using the retrieval system as opposed to searching the collection at random. An attempt is made to take into account the varying difficulty of finding relevant documents for different queries. The index is calculated for a query of a precisely specified *type*. It is assumed that users are able to quantify their information need according to one of the following types:

(1) only one relevant document is wanted;
(2) some arbitrary number n is wanted;
(3) all relevant documents are wanted;
(4) a given proportion of the relevant documents is wanted, etc.

Thus, the index is a measure of performance for a query of given type. Here we shall restrict ourselves to Type 2 queries. For further details the reader is referred to Cooper[20].

The output of a search strategy is assumed to be a *weak ordering* of documents. I have defined this concept on page 118 in a different context. We start by first considering a special case, namely a *simple ordering,* which is a weak ordering such that for any two distinct elements e_1 and e_2 it is never the case that $e_1 R e_2$ and $e_2 R e_1$ (where R is the order relation). This simply means that all the documents in the output are ordered linearly with no two or more documents at the same level of the ordering. The *search length* is now defined as the number of non-relevant documents a user must scan before his information need (in terms of the type quantification above) is satisfied. For example, consider a ranking of 20 documents in which the relevant ones are distributed as in *Figure 7.7.* A Type 2 query with $n = 2$ would have search length 2, with $n = 6$ it would have search length 3.

160

Rank	1	2	3	4	5	6	7	8	9	10	11	12	13	14	15	16	17	18	19	20
Relevance	N	Y	N	Y	Y	Y	Y	N	Y	N	N	N	Y	N	Y	N	N	N	N	N

Figure 7.7. An example of a simple ordering, that is, the ranks are unique, for 20 retrieval documents. Y indicates relevant and N indicates not relevant

Unfortunately the ranking generated by a matching function is rarely a simple ordering, but more commonly a weak ordering. This means that at any given level in the ranking, there is at least one document (probably more) which makes the search length inappropriate since the order of documents within a level is random. If the information need is met at a certain level in the ordering then depending on the arrangement of the relevant documents within that level we shall get different search lengths. Nevertheless we can use an analogous quantity which is the *expected search length*. For this we need to calculate the probability of each possible search length by juggling (mentally) the relevant and non-relevant documents in the level at which the user need is met. For example, consider the weak ordering in *Figure 7.8*. If the query is of Type 2 with $n = 6$ then the need is met at level 3. The possible search lengths are 3, 4, 5 or 6 depending on how many non-relevant documents precede the sixth relevant document. We can ignore the possible arrangements within levels 1 and 2; their contributions are always the same. To compute the expected search length we need the probability of each possible search length. We get at this by considering first the number of different ways in which two relevant documents could be distributed among five, it is $\binom{5}{2} = 10$. Of these 4 would result in a search length of 3, 3 in a search length of 4, 2 in a search length of 5 and 1 in a search length of 6. Their corresponding probabilities are therefore, 4/10, 3/10, 2/10 and 1/10. The expected search length is now:

$$(4/10) . 3 + (3/10) . 4 + (2/10) . 5 + (1/10). 6 = 4$$

The above procedure leads immediately to a convenient 'intuitive' derivation of a formula for the expected search length. It seems plausible that the *average* results of many random searches through the final level (level at which need is met) will be the same as for a single

Rank	1	1	1	2	2	2	2	2	3	3	3	3	3	4	4	4	4	4	4	4
Relevance	N	N	Y	Y	N	Y	Y	Y	N	Y	Y	N	N	N	N	N	N	N	Y	N

Figure 7.8. An example of a weak ordering, that is, with ties in the ranks, for 20 retrieval documents

161

search with the relevant documents spaced 'evenly' throughout that level. First we enumerate the variables:

(a) q is the query of given type;
(b) j is the total number of documents non-relevant to q in all levels preceding the final;
(c) r is the number of relevant documents in the final level;
(d) i is the number of non-relevant documents in the final level;
(e) s is the number of relevant documents required from the final level to satisfy the need according its type.

Now, to distribute the r relevant documents evenly among the non-relevant documents, we partition the non-relevant documents into $r + 1$ subsets each containing $i/(r + 1)$ documents. The expected search length is now:

$$\text{ESL}(q) = j + \frac{i.s.}{r + 1}$$

As a measure of effectiveness ESL is sufficient if the document collection and test queries are fixed. In that case the overall measure is the *mean expected search length*

$$\overline{\text{ESL}} = \frac{1}{|Q|} \sum_{q \in Q} \text{ESL}(q)$$

where Q is the set of queries. This statistic is chosen in preference to any other for the property that it is minimised when the total expected search length

$$\sum_{q \in Q} \text{ESL}(q) \text{ is minimised.}$$

To extend the applicability of the measure to deal with varying test queries and document collections, we need to normalise the ESL in some way to counter the bias introduced because:

(1) queries are satisfied by different numbers of documents according to the type of the query and therefore can be expected to have widely differing search lengths;
(2) the density of relevant documents for a query in one document collection may be significantly different from the density in another.

The first item suggests that the ESL per desired relevant document is really what is wanted as an index of merit. The second suggests

162

normalising the ESL by a factor proportional to the expected number of non-relevant documents collected for each relevant one. Luckily it turns out that the correction for variation in test queries and for variation in document collection can be made by comparing the ESL with the *expected random search length* (ERSL). This latter quantity can be arrived at by calculating the expected search length when the entire document collection is retrieved at one level. The final measure is therefore:

$$\frac{ERSL(q) - ESL(q)}{ERSL(q)}$$

which has been called the *expected search length reduction factor* by Cooper. Roughly it measures improvement over random retrieval. The explicit form for ERSL is given by:

$$ERSL(q) = \frac{S \cdot I}{R + 1}$$

where

(1) R is the total number of documents in the collection relevant to q;

(2) I is the total number of documents in the collection non-relevant to q;

(3) S is the total desired number of documents relevant to q.

The explicit form for ESL was given before. Finally, the overall measure for a set of queries Q is defined, consistent with the mean ESL, to be:

$$\frac{\overline{ERSL} - \overline{ESL}}{\overline{ERSL}}$$

which is known as the *mean expected search length reduction factor*.

Within the framework as stated at the head of this section this final measure meets the bill admirably. However, its acceptability as a measure of effectiveness is still debatable (see, for example, Senko[21]). It totally ignores the recall aspect of retrieval, unless queries are evaluated which express the need for a certain proportion of the relevant documents in the system. It therefore seems to be a good substitute for precision, one which takes into account order of retrieval and user need.

For a further defence of its subjective nature see Cooper[1]. A spirited attack on Cooper's position can be found in Soergel[22].

The SMART measures

In 1966, Rocchio gave a derivation of two overall indices of merit based on recall and precision. They were proposed for the evaluation of retrieval systems which ranked documents, and were designed to be independent of cut-off.

The first of these indices is *normalised recall*. It roughly measures the effectiveness of the ranking in relation to the best possible and worst possible ranking. The situation is illustrated in *Figure 7.9* for 25

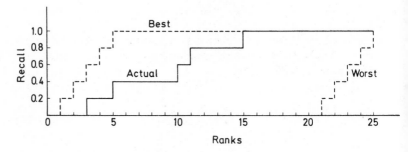

Figure 7.9. An illustration of how the normalised recall curve is bounded by the best and worst cases. (Adapted from Robertson[15], page 99)

documents where we plot recall on the y-axis and the ranks on the x-axis. Normalised recall (R_{norm}) is the area between the actual case and the worst as a proportion of the area between the best and the worst. If n is the number of relevant documents, and r_i the rank at which the ith document is retrieved, then the area between the best and actual case can be shown to be (after a bit of algebra):

$$A_b - A_a = \frac{\sum_{i=1}^{n} r_i - \sum_{i=1}^{n} i}{n} \quad \text{(see Salton[23], page 285)}$$

A convenient explicit form of normalised recall is:

$$R_{norm} = 1 - \frac{\Sigma r_i - \Sigma i}{n(N-n)}$$

where N is the number of documents in the system and $N - n$ the area between the best and the worst case (to see this substitute $r_i = N - i + 1$ in the formula for $A_b - A_a$). The form ensures that R_{norm} lies between 0 (for the worst case) and 1 (for the best case).

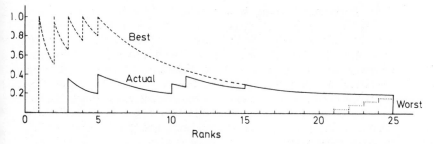

Figure 7.10. An illustration of how the normalised precision curve is bounded by the best and worst cases. (Adapted from Robertson[15], page 100)

In an analogous manner *normalised* precision is worked out. In *Figure 7.10* we once more have three curves showing (1) the best case, (2) the actual case, and (3) the worst case in terms of the precision values at different rank positions.

The calculation of the areas is a bit more messy but simple to do (see Salton[23], page 298). The area between the actual and best case is now given by:

$$A_b - A_a = \sum_{i=1}^{n} \log r_i - \sum_{i=1}^{n} \log i$$

The log function appears as a result of approximating $\sum 1/r$ by its continuous analogue $\int 1/r\, dr$, which is $\log r$ + constant.

The area between the worst and best case is obtained in the same way as before using the same substitution, and is:

$$\log \frac{N!}{(N-n)!\, n!}$$

The explicit form, with appropriate normalisation, for normalised precision is therefore:

$$P_{norm} = 1 - \frac{\sum \log r_i - \sum \log i}{\log\left(\dfrac{N!}{(N-n)!\, n!}\right)}$$

Once again it varies between 0 (worst) and 1 (best).

A few comments about these measures are now in order. Firstly their behaviour is consistent in the sense that if one of them is 0 (or 1) then the other is 0 (or 1). In other words they both agree on the best and worst performance. Secondly, they differ in the weights assigned to arbitrary positions of the precision–recall curve, and these weights may

165

differ considerably from those which the user feels are pertinent (Senko[21]). Or, as Salton[23] (page 289) puts it: 'the normalised precision measure assigns a much larger weight to the initial (low) document ranks than to the later ones, whereas the normalised recall measure assigns a uniform weight to all relevant documents'. Unfortunately the weighting is *arbitrary* and *given*. Thirdly, it can be shown that normalised recall and precision have interpretations as approximations to the average recall and precision values for all possible cut-off levels. That is, if $R(i)$ is the recall at rank position i, and $P(i)$ the corresponding precision value, then:

$$R_{norm} \sim \frac{1}{N} \sum_{i=1}^{N} R(i)$$

$$P_{norm} \sim \frac{1}{N} \sum_{i=1}^{N} P(i)$$

Fourthly, whereas Cooper has gone to some trouble to take account of the random element introduced by ties in the matching function, it is largely ignored in the derivation of P_{norm} and R_{norm}.

One further comment of interest is that Robertson[15] has shown that normalised recall has an interpretation as the area under the Recall–Fallout curve used by Swets.

Finally mention should be made of two similar but simpler measures used by the SMART system. They are:

$$\text{Rank Recall} = \frac{\sum_{i=1}^{n} i}{\sum_{i=1}^{n} r_i} \qquad\qquad \text{Log Precision} = \frac{\sum_{i=1}^{n} \ln i}{\sum_{i=1}^{n} \ln r_i}$$

and do not take into account the collection size N, n is here the number of relevant documents for the particular test query.

A normalised symmetric difference

Let us now return to basics and consider how it is that users could simply measure retrieval effectiveness. We are considering the common situation where a set of documents is retrieved in response to a query, the possible ordering of this set is ignored. Ideally the set should consist only of documents relevant to the request, that is giving 100 per cent precision and 100 per cent recall (and by implication 0 per cent fallout). In practice, however, this is rarely the case, and the retrieved set consists of both relevant and non-relevant documents. The situation may therefore be pictured as shown in *Figure 7.11,* where A is the set of relevant documents, B the set of retrieved documents, and $A \cap B$ the set of retrieved documents which are relevant.

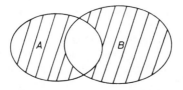

Figure 7.11. An illustration of the symmetric difference between two sets A and B. A Δ B is the shaded area

Now, an intuitive way of measuring the adequacy of the retrieved set is to measure the size of the shaded area. Or to put it differently, to measure to what extent the two sets do not match. The area is in fact the symmetric difference: $A \Delta B$ (or $A \cup B - A \cap B$). Since we are more interested in the proportion (rather than absolute number) of relevant and non-relevant documents retrieved we need to normalise this measure. A simple normalisation gives:

$$E = \frac{|A \Delta B|}{|A| + |B|}$$

In terms of P and R we have:

$$E = 1 - \frac{1}{\frac{1}{2}\left(\frac{1}{P}\right) + \frac{1}{2}\left(\frac{1}{R}\right)}$$

which is a simple composite measure.

The preceding argument in itself is not sufficient to justify the use of this particular composite measure. However, I shall now introduce a framework within which a general measure may be derived which among others has E as one of its special cases.

167

Foundation*

Problems of measurement have arisen in physics, psychology, and more recently, the social sciences. Clarification of these problems has been sought with the help of the *theory of measurement.* I shall attempt to do the same for information retrieval. My purpose is to construct a framework, based on the mathematical theory of measurement within which measures of effectiveness for retrieval systems can be derived. The basic mathematical notions underlying the measurement ideas will be introduced, but for their deeper understanding the reader is referred to the excellent book by Krantz *et al.*[24] It would be fair to say that the theory developed there is applied here. Also of interest are the books by Ellis[25] and Lieberman[26].

The problems of measurement in information retrieval differ from those encountered in the physical sciences in one important aspect. In the physical sciences there is usually an empirical ordering of the quantities we wish to measure. For example, we can establish empirically by means of a scale which masses are equal, and which are greater or less than others. Such a situation does not hold in information retrieval. In the case of the measurement of effectiveness by precision and recall, there is no *absolute* sense in which one can say that one particular pair of precision–recall values is better or worse than some other pair, or, for that matter, that they are comparable at all. However, to leave it at that is to admit defeat. There is no reason why we cannot postulate a particular ordering, or, to put it more mildly, why we cannot show that a certain model for the measurement of effectiveness has acceptable properties. The immediate consequence of proceeding in this fashion is that each property ascribed to the model may be challenged. The only defence one has against this is that:

(1) all properties ascribed are consistent;
(2) they bring out into the open all the assumptions made in measuring effectiveness;
(3) each property has an acceptable interpretation;
(4) the model leads to a plausible measure of effectiveness.

It is as well to point out here that it does not lead to a unique measure, but it does show that certain classes of measures can be regarded as being equivalent.

* The next three sections are substantially the same as those appearing in my paper: 'Foundations of evaluation', *Journal of Documentation,* **30**, 365-373 (1974). They have been included with the kind permission of the Managing Editor of Aslib.

The model

We start be examining the structure which it is reasonable to assume for the measurement of effectiveness. Put in other words, we examine the conditions that the factors determining effectiveness can be expected to satisfy. We limit the discussion here to two factors, namely precision and recall, although this is no restriction, different factors could be analysed, and, as will be indicated later, more than two factors can simplify the analysis.

If $\mathcal{R}$ is the set of possible recall values and $\mathcal{P}$ is the set of possible precision values then we are interested in the set $\mathcal{R} \times \mathcal{P}$ with a relation on it. We shall refer to this as a *relational structure* and denote it $< \mathcal{R} \times \mathcal{P}, \geqslant >$ where $\geqslant$ is the binary relation on $\mathcal{R} \times \mathcal{P}$. (We shall use the same symbol for less than or equal to, the context will make clear what the domain is.) All we are saying here is that for any given point (R, P) we wish to be able to say whether it indicates more, less or equal effectiveness than that indicated by some other point. The kind of order relation is a *weak order*. To be more precise:

Definition 1. The relational structure $< \mathcal{R} \times \mathcal{P}, \geqslant >$ is a *weak order* if and only if for $e_1, e_2, e_3 \in \mathcal{R} \times \mathcal{P}$ the following axioms are satisfied.

(1) Connectedness: either $e_1 \geqslant e_2$ or $e_2 \geqslant e_1$
(2) Transitivity: if $e_1 \geqslant e_2$ and $e_2 \geqslant e_3$ then $e_1 \geqslant e_3$

We insist that if two pairs can be ordered both ways then $(R_1, P_1) \sim (R_2, P_2)$, i.e. equivalent not necessarily equal. The transitivity condition is obviously desirable.

We now turn to a second condition which is commonly called *independence*. This notion captures the idea that the two components contribute their effects independently to the effectiveness.

Definition 2. A relation $\geqslant$ on $\mathcal{R} \times \mathcal{P}$ is independent if and only if, for $R_1, R_2 \in \mathcal{R}$, $(R_1, P) \geqslant (R_2, P)$ for some $P \in \mathcal{P}$ implies $(R_1, P') \geqslant (R_2, P')$ for every $P' \in \mathcal{P}$; and for $P_1, P_2 \in \mathcal{P}$, $(R, P_1) \geqslant (R, P_2)$ for some $R \in \mathcal{R}$ implies $(R', P_1) \geqslant (R', P_2)$ for every $R' \in \mathcal{R}$.

All we are saying here is, given that at a constant recall (precision) we find a difference in effectiveness for two values of precision (recall) then this difference cannot be removed or reversed by changing the constant value.

We now come to a condition which is not quite as obvious as the preceding ones. To make it more meaningful I shall need to use a diagram, *Figure 7.12,* which represents the ordering we have got so far with definitions 1 and 2. The lines l_1 and l_2 are lines of equal effectiveness, that is any two points (R, P), $(R', P') \in l_i$ are such that $(R, P) \sim (R', P')$ (where $\sim$ indicates *equal* effectiveness). Now let us

169

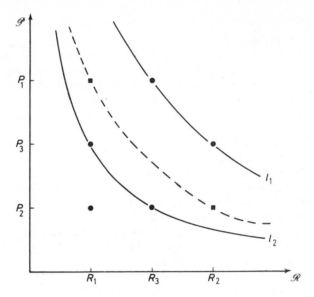

Figure 7.12. A diagram illustrating the Thomsen condition

assume that we have the points on l_1 and l_2 but wish to deduce the relative ordering in between these two lines. One may think of this as an interpolation procedure.

Definition 3 (Thomsen condition). For every R_1, R_2, $R_3 \in \mathfrak{R}$ and P_1, P_2, $P_3 \in \mathcal{P}$, $(R_1, P_3) \sim (R_3, P_2)$ and $(R_3, P_1) \sim (R_2, P_3)$ imply that $(R_1, P_1) \sim (R_2, P_2)$.

Intuitively this can be reasoned as follows. The intervals $R_1 R_3$ and $P_2 P_3$ are equivalent since an increase in the R-factor by $R_1 R_3$ and an increase in the P-factor by $P_2 P_3$ starting from (R_1, P_2) lead to the same effectiveness (points on l_2). It therefore follows that a decrease in each factor starting from equal effectiveness, in this case the two points (R_3, P_1) and (R_2, P_3) on l_1, should lead to equal effectiveness.

The fourth condition is one concerned with the continuity of each component. It makes precise what intuitively we would expect when considering the existence of intermediate values.

Definition 4 (Restricted Solvability). A relation $\geqslant$ on $\mathfrak{R} \times \mathcal{P}$ satisfies *restricted solvability* provided that:

(1) whenever R, $\bar{R}$, $\underline{R} \in \mathfrak{R}$ and $P, P' \in \mathcal{P}$ for which $(\bar{R}, P') \geqslant (R, P) \geqslant (\underline{R}, P')$ then there exists $R' \in \mathfrak{R}$ s.t. $(R', P') \sim (R, P)$;

(2) a similar condition holds on the second component.

170

In other words we are ensuring that the equation $(R', P') \sim (R, P)$ is soluble for R' provided that there exist $\bar{R}$, $\underline{R}$ such that $(\bar{R}, P') \geqslant (R, P') \geqslant (\underline{R}, P')$. An assumption of continuity of the precision and recall factors would ensure this.

The fifth condition is not limiting in any way but needs to be stated. It requires, in a precise way, that each component is essential.

Definition 5. Component $\mathcal{R}$ is *essential* if and only if there exist R_1, $R_2 \in \mathcal{R}$ and $P_1 \in \mathcal{P}$ such that it is *not* the case that $(R_1, P_1) \sim (R_2, P_1)$. A similar definition holds for $\mathcal{P}$.

Thus we require that variation in one while leaving the other constant gives a variation in effectiveness.

Finally we need a technical condition which will not be explained here, that is the *Archimedean property* for each component. It merely ensures that the intervals on a component are comparable. For details the reader is referred to Krantz *et al.*[24]

We now have six conditions on the relational structure $< \mathcal{R} \times \mathcal{P}, \geqslant >$ which in the theory of measurement are necessary and sufficient conditions* for it to be an *additive conjoint structure*. This is enough for us to state the main *representation theorem*. It is a theorem asserting that if a given relational structure satisfies certain conditions (axioms), then a homomorphism into a numerical relational structure can be constructed. A homomorphism into the real numbers is often referred to as a scale. Measurement may therefore be regarded as the construction of homomorphisms from empirical relational structures of interest into numerical relational structures that are useful.

In our case we can therefore expect to find real-valued functions Φ_1 on $\mathcal{R}$ and Φ_2 on $\mathcal{P}$ and a function F from $Re \times Re$ into Re, 1:1 in each variable, such that, for all $R, R' \in \mathcal{R}$ and $P, P' \in \mathcal{P}$ we have:

$$(R, P) \geqslant (R', P') \Leftrightarrow F[\Phi_1(R), \Phi_2(P)] \geqslant F[\Phi_1(R'), \Phi_2(P')]$$

(Note that although the same symbol $\geqslant$ is used, the first is a binary relation on $\mathcal{R} \times \mathcal{P}$, the second is the usual one on Re, the set of reals.)

In other words there are numerical scales Φ_i on the two components and a rule F for combining them such that the resultant measure preserves the qualitative ordering of effectiveness. When such a representation exists we say that the structure is *decomposable*. In this representation the components ($\mathcal{R}$ and $\mathcal{P}$) contribute to the effectiveness measure independently. It is not true that all relational

---

* It can be shown that (starting at the other end) given an additively independent representation the properties defined in 1 and 3, and the Archimedean property are necessary. The structural conditions 4 and 5 are sufficient.

structures are decomposable. What is true, however, is that non-decomposable structures are extremely difficult to analyse.

A further simplification of the measurement function may be achieved by requiring a special kind of non-interaction of the components which has become known as *additive independence*. This requires that the equation for decomposable structures is reduced to:

$$(R, P) \geqslant (R', P') \Leftrightarrow \Phi_1(R) + \Phi_2(P) \geqslant \Phi_1(R') + \Phi_2(P')$$

where F is simply the addition function. An example of a non-decomposable structure is given by:

$$(R, P) \geqslant (R', P') \Leftrightarrow \Phi_1(R) + \Phi_2(P) + \Phi_1(R)\Phi_2(P) \geqslant \Phi_1(R') +$$
$$+ \Phi_2(P') + \Phi_1(R')\Phi_2(P').$$

Here the term $\Phi_1 \Phi_2$ is referred to as the *interaction* term, its absence accounts for the non-interaction in the previous condition.

We are now in a position to state the main representation theorem.

Theorem

Suppose $< \Re \times \wp, \geqslant >$ is an additive conjoint structure, then there exist functions, Φ_1 from $\Re$, and Φ_2 from $\wp$ into the real numbers such that, for all $R, R' \in \Re$ and $P, P' \in \wp$:

$$(R, P) \geqslant (R', P') \Leftrightarrow \Phi_1(R) + \Phi_2(P) \geqslant \Phi_1(R') + \Phi_2(P')$$

If Φ_i' are two other functions with the same property, then there exist constants $\Theta > 0, \gamma_1$, and γ_2 such that

$$\Phi_1' = \Theta\Phi_1 + \gamma_1 \qquad \Phi_2' = \Theta\Phi_2 + \gamma_2$$

The proof of this theorem may be found in Krantz *et al.*[15]

Let us stop and take stock of the situation. So far we have discussed the properties of an additive conjoint structure and justified its use for the measurement of effectiveness based on precision and recall. We have also shown that an additively independent representation (unique up to a linear transformation) exists for this kind of relational structure. The explicit form of Φ_i has been left unspecified. To determine the form of Φ_i we need to introduce some extrinsic considerations. Although the representation theorem shows the existence of a numerical representation $F = \Phi_1 + \Phi_2$, this is not the most convenient form for expressing the further conditions we require of F, nor for its interpretation. So, in spite of the fact that we are seeking an additively independent representation we consider conditions on a general F. It will turn out that the F which is appropriate can be simply transformed into an additive representation. The transformation is $f(F) = -(F-1)^{-1}$ which is strictly monotonically increasing in the range $0 \leqslant F \leqslant 1$, which is the range of interest. In any case when measuring retrieval effectiveness any strictly monotone transformation of the measure will do just as well.

Explicit measures of effectiveness

I shall now argue for a specific form of Φ_i and F, based on a model for the user. In other words, the form Φ_i and F are partly determined by the user. We start by showing how the ordering on $\mathcal{R} \times \mathcal{P}$ in fact induces an ordering of intervals on each factor. From *Figure 7.13* we have that $(R_3, P_1) \geqslant (R_1, P_2)$, $(R_3, P_1) \geqslant (R_1, P_1)$ and $(R_1, P_2) \geqslant (R_1, P_1)$. Therefore the increment (interval) $R_1 R_3$ is preferred to the increment $P_1 P_2$. But $(R_2, P_2) \geqslant (R_4, P_1)$, which gives $P_1 P_2$ is preferred to $R_2 R_4$. Hence $R_1 R_3 \geqslant_1 R_2 R_4$ where $\geqslant_1$ is the induced order relation on $\mathcal{R}$. We now have a method of comparing each interval on $\mathcal{R}$ with a fixed interval on $\mathcal{P}$.

Since we have assumed that effectiveness is determined by precision and recall we have committed ourselves to the importance of *proportions* of documents rather than absolute numbers. Consistent with this is the assumption of *decreasing marginal effectiveness*. Let me illustrate this with an example. Suppose the user is willing to sacrifice

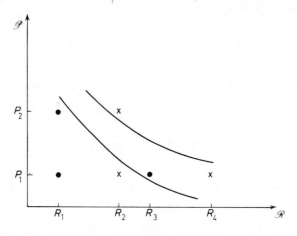

Figure 7.13. The diagram shows the relative positions of points with respect to two contours

173

one unit of precision for an increase of one unit of recall, but will not sacrifice another unit of precision for a further unit increase in recall, i.e.

$$(R + 1, P - 1) > (R, P)$$

but

$$(R + 1, P) > (R + 2, P - 1)$$

We conclude that the interval between $R + 1$ and R exceeds the interval between P and $P - 1$ whereas the interval between $R + 1$ and $R + 2$ is smaller. Hence the marginal effectiveness of recall is decreasing. (A similar argument can be given for precision.) The implication of this for the shape of the curves of equal effectiveness is that they are convex towards the origin.

Finally, we incorporate into our measurement procedure the fact that users may attach different relative importance to precision and recall. What we want is therefore a parameter (β) to characterise the measurement function in such a way that we can say: it measures the effectiveness of retrieval with respect to a user who attaches β times as much importance to recall as precision. The simplest way I know of quantifying this is to specify the P/R ratio at which the user is willing to trade an increment in precision for an equal loss in recall.

Definition 6. The relative importance a user attaches to precision and recall is the P/R ratio at which $\partial E/\partial R = \partial E/\partial P$, where $E = E(P, R)$ is the measure of effectiveness based on precision and recall.

Can we find a function satisfying all these conditions? If so, can we also interpret it in an intuitively simple way? The answer to both these questions is yes. It involves:

$$\alpha\left(\frac{1}{P}\right) + (1 - \alpha)\frac{1}{R} \qquad 0 \leqslant \alpha \leqslant 1$$

The scale functions are therefore, $\Phi_1(P) = \alpha(1/P)$, and $\Phi_2(R) = (1 - \alpha)(1/R)$. The 'combination' function F is now chosen to satisfy definition 6 without violating the additive independence. We get:

$$F(\Phi_1, \Phi_2) = 1 - \frac{1}{\Phi_1 + \Phi_2}$$

We now have the effectiveness measure. In terms of P and R it will be:

$$E = 1 - \frac{1}{\alpha\left(\dfrac{1}{P}\right) + (1 - \alpha)\dfrac{1}{R}}$$

To facilitate interpretation of the function, we transform according to $\alpha = 1/(\beta^2 + 1)$, and find that $\partial E/\partial R = \partial E/\partial P$ when $P/R = \beta$. If A is the set of relevant documents and B the set of retrieval documents, then:

$$P = \frac{|A \cap B|}{|B|} \quad \text{and} \quad R = \frac{|A \cap B|}{|A|}$$

E now gives rise to the following special cases:

(1) When $\alpha = 1/2$ $(\beta = 1)$ $E = |A \triangle B|/(|A| + |B|)$, a normalised symmetric difference between sets A and B $(A \triangle B = A \cup B - A \cap B)$. It corresponds to a user who attaches equal importance to precision and recall.

(2) $E \rightarrow 1 - R$ when $\alpha \rightarrow 0$ $(\beta \rightarrow \infty)$, which corresponds to a user who attaches no importance to precision.

(3) $E \rightarrow 1 - P$ when $\alpha \rightarrow 1 (\beta \rightarrow 0)$, which corresponds to a user who attaches no importance to recall.

It is now a simple matter to show that certain other measures given in the literature are special cases of the general form E. By the representation theorem, the Φ_i's are uniquely determined up to a linear transformation, that is, Φ_i' is defined by $\Phi_i' = \Theta\Phi_i + \gamma_i$ would serve equally well as scale functions. If we now set $\Phi_1' = 2\Phi_1 - 1/2$, $\Phi_2' = 2\Phi_2 - 1/2$, and $\beta = 1$ then we have:

$$E = 1 - \frac{1}{\dfrac{1}{P} + \dfrac{1}{R} - 1}$$

which is the measure recommended by Heine[3].

One final example is the measure suggested by Vickery in 1965 which was documented by Cleverdon et al.[27] Here we set:

$$\Phi_1' = 4\Phi_1 - \frac{3}{2}, \ \Phi_2' = 4\Phi_2 - \frac{3}{2}, \text{ and } \beta = 1 \text{ and obtain}$$

$$E = 1 - \frac{1}{2\left(\dfrac{1}{P}\right) + 2\left(\dfrac{1}{R}\right) - 3}$$

which is Vickery's measure (apart from a scale factor of 100).

To summarise, we have shown that it is reasonable to assume that effectiveness in terms of precision and recall determines an additive conjoint structure. This guarantees the existence of an additively independent representation. We then found the representation satisfying some user requirements and also having special cases which are simple to interpret.

The analysis is not limited to the two factors precision and recall, it could equally well be carried out for say the pair fallout and recall. Furthermore, it is not necessary to restrict the model to two factors. If appropriate variables need to be incorporated the model readily extends to n factors. In fact for more than two dimensions the Thomsen condition is not required for the representation theorem.

Presentation of experimental results

In my discussion of micro-, macro-evaluation, and expected search length, various ways of averaging the effectiveness measure of the set of queries arose in a natural way. I now want to examine the ways in which we can summarise our retrieval results when we have no *a priori* reason to suspect that taking means is legitimate.

In this section the discussion will be restricted to single number measures such as a normalised symmetric difference, normalised recall, etc. Let us use Z to denote any arbitrary measure. The test queries will be Q_i and n in number. Our aim in all this is to make statements about the relative merits of retrieval under different conditions $a,b,c,\ldots$ in terms of the measure of effectiveness Z. The 'conditions' $a,b,c,\ldots$ may be different search strategies, or information structures, etc. In other words we have the usual experimental set-up where we control a variable and measure how its change influences retrieval effectiveness. For the moment we restrict these comparisons to one set of queries and the same document collection.

The measurements we have therefore are $\{Z_a(Q_1), Z_a(Q_2), \ldots\}$, $\{Z_b(Q_1), Z_b(Q_2), \ldots\}$, $\{Z_c(Q_1), Z_c(Q_2), \ldots\}$, ... where $Z_x(Q_i)$ is the value of Z when measuring the effectiveness of the response to Q_i under condition x. If we now wish to make an *overall* comparison between these sets of measurements we could take *means* and compare these. Unfortunately the distributions of Z encountered are far from bell-shaped, or symmetric for that matter, so that the mean is not a particularly good 'average' indicator. The problem of summarising IR data has been a hurdle ever since the beginning of the subject. Because of the non-parametric nature of the data it is better not to quote a single statistic but instead to show the variation in effectiveness by plotting graphs. Should it be necessary to quote 'average' results it is important that they are quoted alongside the distribution from which they are derived.

There are a number of ways of representing sets of Z-values graphically. Probably the most obvious one is to use a scatter diagram, where the x-axis is scaled for Z_a and the y-axis for Z_b and each plotted point is the pair $(Z_a(Q_i), Z_b(Q_i))$. The number of points plotted will equal the number of queries. If we now draw a line at $45°$ to the x-axis from the origin we will be able to see what proportion of the queries did better under condition a than under condition b. There are two disadvantages to this method of representation: the comparison is limited to two conditions, and it is difficult to get an idea of the *extent* to which two conditions differ.

A more convenient way of showing retrieval results of this kind is to plot them as *cumulative frequency distributions,* or as they are frequently called by statisticians *empirical distribution functions.* Let $\{Z(Q_1), Z(Q_2), \ldots, Z(Q_n)\}$ be a set of retrieval results then the empirical distribution function $F(z)$ is a function of z which equals the proportion of $Z(Q_i)$'s which are less than or equal to z. To plot this function we divide the range of z into intervals. If we assume that $0 \leqslant z \leqslant 1$, then a convenient set of intervals is ten. The distributions will take the general shape as shown in *Figure 7.14.* When the measure Z is such that the smaller its value the more effective the retrieval, then the higher the curve the better. It is quite simple to read off the various quantiles. For example to find the median we only need to find the z-value corresponding to 0.5 on the $F(z)$ axis. In our diagrams they are 0.2 and 0.4 respectively for conditions a and b.

I have emphasised the measurement of effectiveness from the point of view of the user. If we now wish to compare retrieval on *different*

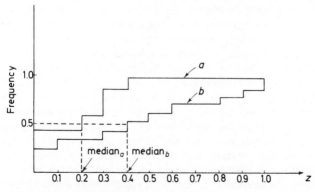

Figure 7.14. Two cumulative frequency distributions showing the difference in effectiveness under conditions a and b

document collections with *different* sets of queries then we can still use these measures to indicate which system satisfies the user more. On the other hand we cannot thereby establish which system is more effective in its retrieval operations. It may be that in system A the sets of relevant documents constitute a smaller proportion of the total set of documents than is the case in system B. In other words it is much harder to find the relevant documents in system B than in system A. So, any direct comparison must be weighted by the *generality* measure which gives the number of relevant documents as a proportion of the total number of documents. Alternatively one could use *fallout* which measures the proportion of non-relevant documents retrieved. The important point here is to be clear about whether we are measuring user satisfaction or system effectiveness.

Significance tests

Once we have our retrieval effectiveness figures we may wish to establish that the difference in effectiveness under two conditions is *statistically significant*. It is precisely for this purpose that many statistical tests have been designed. Unfortunately I have to agree with the findings of the Comparative Systems Laboratory[28] in 1968, that there are no known statistical tests applicable to IR. This may sound like a counsel of defeat but let me hasten to add that it is possible to select a test which violates only a few of the assumptions it makes. Two good sources which spell out the pre-conditions for non-parametric tests are Siegel[29] and Conover[30]. A much harder but also more rewarding book on non-parametrics is Lehmann[31].

Parametric tests are inappropriate because we do not know the form of the underlying distribution. In this class we must include the popular *t-test*. The assumptions underlying its use are given in some detail by Siegel (page 19), needless to say most of these are not met by IR data. One obvious failure is that the observations are not drawn from normally distributed populations.

On the face of it non-parametric tests might provide the answer. There are some tests for dealing with the case of related samples. In our experimental set-up we have one set of queries which is used in different retrieval environments. Therefore, without questioning whether we have *random* samples, it is clear that the sample under condition a is related to the sample under condition b. When in this situation a common test to use has been the *Wilcoxon Matched-Pairs test*. Unfortunately again some important assumptions are not met. The test is done on the differences $D_i = Z_a(Q_i) - Z_b(Q_i)$, but it is assumed

178

that D_i is continuous and that it is derived from a *symmetric* distribution, neither of which is normally met in IR data.

It seems therefore that some of the more sophisticated statistical tests are inappropriate. There is, however, one simple test which makes very few assumptions and which can be used providing its limitations are noted. This one is known in the literature as the *sign test* (Siegel[29], page 68 and Conover[30], page 121). It is applicable in the case of related samples. It makes *no* assumptions about the form of the underlying distribution. It does, however, assume that the data are derived from a *continuous* variable and that the $Z(Q_i)$ are *statistically independent*. These two conditions are unlikely to be met in a retrieval experiment. Nevertheless given that some of the conditions are not met it can be used *conservatively*.

The way it works is as follows. Let $\{Z_a(Q_1), Z_a(Q_2), \ldots,\}, \{Z_b(Q_1), Z_b(Q_2) \ldots,\}$ be our two sets of measurements under conditions a and b respectively. Within each pair $(Z_a(Q_i), Z_b(Q_i))$ a comparison is made, and each pair is classified as ' $+$ ' if $Z_a(Q_i) > Z_b(Q_i)$, as ' $-$ ' if $Z_a(Q_i) < Z_b(Q_i)$ or 'tie' if $Z_a(Q_i) = Z_a(Q_i)$. Pairs which are classified as 'tie' are removed from the analysis thereby reducing the effective number of measurements. The null hypothesis we wish to test is that:

$$P(Z_a > Z_b) = P(Z_a < Z_b) = \tfrac{1}{2}$$

Under this hypothesis we expect the number of pairs which have $Z_a > Z_b$ to equal the number of pairs which have $Z_a < Z_b$. Another way of stating this is that the two populations from which Z_a and Z_b are derived have the same median.

In IR this test is usually used as a one-tailed test, that is, the alternative hypothesis prescribes the superiority of retrieval under condition a over condition b, or vice versa. A table for small samples $n \leqslant 25$ giving the probability under the null hypothesis for each possible combination of '+'s and '−'s may be found in Siegel[29] (page 250). To give the reader a feel for the values involved: in a sample of 25 queries the null hypothesis will be rejected at the 5 per cent level if there are at least 14 differences in the direction predicted by the alternative hypothesis.

The use of the sign test raises a number of interesting points. The first of these is that unlike the Wilcoxon test it only assumes that the Z's are measured on an ordinal scale, that is, the magnitude of $|Z_a - Z_b|$ is *not* significant. This is a suitable feature since we are usually only seeking to find which strategy is better in an average sense and do not wish the result to be unduly influenced by excellent retrieval performance on one query. The second point is that some care needs to be taken when comparing Z_a and Z_b. Because our measure of

179

effectiveness can be calculated to infinite precision we may be insisting on a difference when in fact it only occurs in the tenth decimal place. It is therefore important to decide beforehand at what value of ϵ we will equate Z_a and Z_b when $|Z_a - Z_b| \leqslant \epsilon$.

Finally, although I have just explained the use of the sign test in terms of single number measures it is also used to detect a significant difference between precision–recall graphs. We now interpret the Z's as precision values at a set of standard recall values. Let this set be $SR = \{0.1, 0.2, \ldots, 1.0\}$, then corresponding to each $R\epsilon\ SR$ we have a pair $(P_a(R), P_b(R))$. The P_a's and P_b's are now treated in the same way as the Z_a's and Z_b's. Note that when doing the evaluation this way the precision–recall values will have already been averaged over the set of queries by one of the ways explained before.

Bibliographic remarks

Quite a number of references to the work on evaluation have already been given in the main body of the chapter. Nevertheless, there are still a few important ones worth mentioning.

Buried in the report by Keen and Digger[32] (Chapter 16) is an excellent discussion of the desirable properties of any measure of effectiveness. It also gives a checklist indicating which measure satisfies what. It is probably worth repeating here that Part I of Robertson's paper[33] contains a discussion of measures of effectiveness based on the 'contingency' table as well as a list showing who used what measure in their experiments. King and Bryant[34] have written a book on the evaluation of information services and products emphasising the commercial aspects. Goffman and Newill[35] describe a methodology for evaluation in general.

A parameter which I have mentioned in passing but which deserves closer study is *generality*. Salton[36] has recently done a study of its effect on precision and fallout for different sized document collections.

The trade-off between precision and recall has for a long time been the subject of debate. Cleverdon[37] who has always been involved in this debate has now restated his position. Heine[38] in response to this has attempted to further clarify the trade-off in terms of the Swets model.

Guazzo[39] and Cawkell[40] describe an approach to the measurement of retrieval effectiveness based on information theory.

The notion of relevance has at all times attracted much discussion. An interesting early philosophical paper on the subject is by Weiler[41]. Goffman[42] has done an investigation of relevance in terms of Measure Theory. And more recently Negoita[43] has examined the notion in terms of different kinds of logics.

180

A short paper by Good[44] which is in sympathy with the approach based on a theory of measurement given here, discusses the evaluation of retrieval systems in terms of expected utility.

One conspicuous omission from this chapter is any discussion of cost-effectiveness. The main reason for this is that so far very little of importance can be said about it. A couple of attempts to work out mathematical cost models for IR are Cooper[45] and Marschak[46].

References

1. COOPER, W. S., 'On selecting a measure of retrieval effectiveness', Part 1: 'The "subjective" philosophy of evaluation', Part 2: 'Implementation of the philosophy', *Journal of the American Society for Information Science,* **24,** 87–100 and 413–424 (1973)
2. JARDINE, N. and VAN RIJSBERGEN, C. J., 'The use of hierarchic clustering in information retrieval', *Information Storage and Retrieval,* 7, 217–240 (1971)
3. HEINE, M. H., 'Distance between sets as an objective measure of retrieval effectiveness', *Information Storage and Retrieval,* 9, 181–198 (1973)
4. COOPER, W. S., 'A definition of relevance for information retrieval', *Information Storage and Retrieval,* 7, 19–37 (1971)
5. BELNAP, N. P., An analysis of questions: Preliminary report, Scientific Report TM-1287, SDC, Santa Monica, California (1963)
6. BELNAP, N. D. and STEEL, T. B., *The Logic of Questions and Answers,* Yale University Press, New Haven and London (1976)
7. CHANG, C. L. and LEE, R. C. T., *Symbolic Logic and Mechanical Theorem Proving,* Academic Press, New York (1973)
8. SARACEVIC, T., 'Relevance: A review of and a framework for the thinking on the notion in information science', *Journal of the American Society for Information Science,* **26,** 321–343 (1975)
9. ROBERTSON, S. E., 'The probabilistic character of relevance', *Information Processing and Management,* **13,** 247–251 (1977)
10. VAN RIJSBERGEN, C. J., 'Retrieval effectiveness', In: *Progress in Communication Sciences,* **Vol. 1** (Edited by Melvin J. Voigt) (in the press)
11. KEEN, E. M., 'Evaluation parameters'. *In* Report ISR-13 to the National Science Foundation, Section II, Cornell University, Department of Computer Science (1967)
12. SWETS, J. A., 'Information retrieval systems', *Science,* **141,** 245–250 (1963)
13. SWETS, J. A., *Effectiveness of Information Retrieval Methods,* Bolt, Beranek and Newman, Cambridge, Massachusetts (1967)
14. BROOKES, B. C., 'The measure of information retrieval effectiveness proposed by Swets', *Journal of Documentation,* **24,** 41–54 (1968)
15. ROBERTSON, S. E., 'The parametric description of retrieval tests, Part 2: 'Overall measures', *Journal of Documentation,* **25,** 93–107 (1969)
16. BOOKSTEIN, A., 'When the most "pertinent" document should not be retrieved – an analysis of the Swets Model', *Information Processing and Management,* **13,** 377–383 (1977)
17. ROBERTSON, S. E. and TEATHER, D., 'A statistical analysis of retrieval tests: a Bayesian approach', *Journal of Documentation,* **30,** 273–282 (1974)
18. EFRON, B. and MORRIS, C., 'Stein's parador in statistics', *Scientific American,* **236,** 119–127 (1977)

19. ROBERTSON, S. E., *A Theoretical Model of the Retrieval Characteristics of Information Retrieval Systems*, Ph.D. Thesis, University College London (1975)
20. COOPER, W. S., 'Expected search length: A single measure of retrieval effectiveness based on weak ordering action of retrieval systems', *Journal of the American Society for Information Science*, **19**, 30–41 (1968)
21. SENKO, M. E., Information storage and retrieval systems, *In: Advances in Information Systems Science*, (Edited by J. Tou) Plenum Press, New York (1969)
22. SOERGEL, D., 'Is user satisfaction a hobgoblin?', *Journal of the American Society for Information Science*, **27**, 256–259 (1976)
23. SALTON, G., *Automatic Information Organization and Retrieval*, McGraw-Hill, New York (1968)
24. KRANTZ, D. H., LUCE, R. D., SUPPES, P. and TVERSKY, A., *Foundations of Measurement*, Volume 1, *Additive and Polynomial Representation*, Academic Press, London and New York (1971)
25. ELLIS, B., *Basic Concepts of Measurement*, Cambridge University Press, London (1966)
26. LIEBERMAN, B., *Contemporary Problems in Statistics*, Oxford University Press, New York (1971)
27. CLEVERDON, C. W., MILLS, J. and KEEN, M., *Factors Determining the Performance of Indexing Systems*, Volume I – Design, Volume II – Test Results, ASLIB Cranfield Project, Cranfield (1966)
28. Comparative Systems Laboratory, *An Inquiry into Testing of Information Retrieval Systems*, 3 Volumes, Case-Western Reserve University (1968)
29. SIEGEL, S., *Nonparametric Statistics for the Behavioural Sciences*, McGraw-Hill, New York (1956)
30. CONOVER, W. J., *Practical Nonparametric Statistics*, Wiley, New York (1971)
31. LEHMANN, E. L., *Nonparametrics: Statistical Methods Based on Ranks*, Holden-Day Inc., San Francisco, California (1975)
32. KEEN, E. M. and DIGGER, J. A., *Report of an Information Science Index Languages Test*, Aberystwyth College of Librarianship, Wales (1972)
33. ROBERTSON, S. E., 'The parametric description of retrieval tests', Part I: 'The basic parameters', *Journal of Documentation*, **25**, 1–27 (1969)
34. KING, D. W. and BRYANT, E. C., *The Evaluation of Information Services and Products*, Information Resources Press, Washington (1971)
35. GOFFMAN, W. and NEWILL, V. A., 'A methodology for test and evaluation of information retrieval systems', *Information Storage and Retrieval*, **3**, 19–25 (1966)
36. SALTON, G., 'The "generality" effect and the retrieval evaluation for large collections', *Journal of the American Society for Information Science*, **23**, 11–22 (1972)
37. CLEVERDON, C. W., 'On the inverse relationship of recall and precision', *Journal of Documentation*, **28**, 195–201 (1972)
38. HEINE, M. H., 'The inverse relationship of precision and recall in terms of the Swets' model', *Journal of Documentation*, **29**, 81–84 (1973)
39. GUAZZO, M., 'Retrieval performance and information theory', *Information Processing and Management*, **13**, 155–165 (1977)
40. CAWKELL, A. E., 'A measure of "Efficiency Factor" – communication theory applied to document selection systems', *Information Processing and Management*, **11**, 243–248 (1975)
41. WEILER, G., 'On relevance', *Mind*, **LXXI**, 487–493 (1962)

182

42. GOFFMAN, W., 'On relevance as a measure', *Information Storage and Retrieval,* **2,** 201–203 (1964)
43. NEGOITA, C. V., 'On the notion of relevance', *Kybernetes,* **2,** 161–165 (1973)
44. GOOD, I. J., 'The decision–theory approach to the evaluation of information retrieval systems', *Information Storage and Retrieval,* **3,** 31–34 (1967)
45. COOPER, M. D., 'A cost model for evaluating information retrieval systems', *Journal of the American Society for Information Science,* **23,** 306–312 (1972)
46. MARSCHAK, J., 'Economics of information systems', *Journal of the American Statistical Association,* **66,** 192–219 (1971)

Eight

THE FUTURE

Future research

In the preceding chapters I have tried to bring together some of the more elaborate tools that are used during the design of an experimental information retrieval system. Many of the tools themselves are only at the experimental stage and research is still needed, not only to develop a proper understanding of them, but also to work out their implications for IR systems present and future. Perhaps I can briefly indicate some of the topics which invite further research.

1. Automatic classification

Substantial evidence that large document collections can be handled successfully by means of automatic classification will encourage new work into ways of structuring such collections. It could also be expected to boost commercial interest and along with it the support for further development.

It is therefore of some importance that using the kind of data already in existence, that is using document descriptions in terms of keywords, we establish that document clustering on large document collections can be both effective and efficient. This means more research is needed to devise ways of speeding up clustering algorithms without sacrificing too much structure in the data. It may be possible to design probabilistic algorithms for clustering procedures which will compute a classification on the average in less time than it may require for the worst case. For example, it may be possible to cut down the $O(n^2)$ computation time to *expected* $O(n\log n)$, although for some pathological cases it would still require $O(n^2)$. Another way of

184

approaching this problem of speeding up clustering is to look for what one might call *almost* classifications. It may be possible to compute classification structures which are close to the theoretical structure sought, but are only close approximations which can be computed more efficiently than the ideal.

A big question, that has not yet received much attention, concerns the extent to which retrieval effectiveness is limited by the type of document description used. The use of keywords to describe documents has affected the way in which the design of an automatic classification system has been approached. It is possible that in the future, documents will be represented inside a computer entirely differently. Will grouping of documents still be of interest? I think that it will.

Document classification is a special case of a more general process which would also attempt to exploit relationships between documents. It so happens that dissimilarity coefficients have been used to express a distance-like relationship. Quantifying the relationship in this way has in part been dictated by the nature of the language in which the documents are described. However, were it the case that documents were represented not by keywords but in some other way, perhaps in a more complex language, then relationships between documents would probably best be measured differently as well. Consequently, the structure to represent the relationships might not be a simple hierarchy, except perhaps as a special case. In other words, one should approach document clustering as a process of finding structure in the data which can be exploited to make retrieval both effective and efficient.

An argument parallel to the one in the last paragraph could be given for automatic keyword classification, which in the more general context might be called automatic 'content unit' classification. The methods of handling keywords, which are being and have already been developed, will also address themselves to the automatic construction of classes of 'content units' to be exploited during retrieval. Keyword classification will then remain as a special case.

H. A. Simon in his book *The Sciences of the Artificial* defined an interesting structure closely related to a classificatory system, namely, that of a *nearly decomposable system.* Such a system is one consisting of subsystems for which the interactions *among* subsystems is of a different order of magnitude from that of the interactions *within* subsystems. The analogy with a classification is obvious if one looks upon classes as subsystems. Simon conceived of nearly decomposable systems as ways of describing dynamic systems. The relevant properties are (a) in a nearly decomposable system, the short-run behaviour of each of the component subsystems is approximately independent of the short-run behaviour of the other components; (b) in the long run, the

185

behaviour of any one of the components depends in only an aggregate way on the behaviour of the other components. Now it mày be that this is an appropriate analogy for looking at the *dynamic* behaviour (e.g. updating, change of vocabulary) of document or keyword classifications. Very little is in fact known about the behaviour of classification structures in dynamic environments.

2. File structures

On the file structure chosen and the way it is used depends the efficiency of an information retrieval system.

Inverted files have been rather popular in IR systems. Certainly, in systems based on unweighted keywords especially where queries are formulated in Boolean expressions, an inverted file can give very fast response. Unfortunately it is not possible to achieve an efficient adaptation of an inverted file to deal with the matching of more elaborate document and query descriptions such as weighted keywords. Research into file structures which could efficiently cope with the more complicated document and query descriptions is still needed. The only way of getting at this may be to start with a document classification and investigate file structures appropriate for it. Along this line it might well prove fruitful to investigate the relationship between document clustering and relational data bases which organise their data according to n-ary relations.

There are many more problems in this area which are of interest to IR systems. For example, the physical organisation of large hierarchic structures appropriate to information retrieval is an interesting one. How is one to optimise allocation of storage to a hierarchy if it is to be stored on devices which have different speeds of access?

3. Search strategies

So far fairly simple search strategies have been tried. They have varied between simple serial searches and the cluster-based strategies described in Chapter 5. Tied up with each cluster-based strategy is its method of cluster representation. By changing the cluster representative, the decision and stopping rules of search strategies can usually also be changed. One approach that does not seem to have been tried would involve having a number of cluster representatives each perhaps derived from the data according to different principles.

Probabilistic search strategies have not been investigated much either*, although such strategies have been tried with some effect in the fields of pattern recognition and automatic medical diagnosis. Of course in these fields the object descriptions are more detailed than are the document descriptions in IR, which may mean that for these strategies to work in IR we may require the document descriptions to increase in detail.

In Chapter 5 I mentioned that bottom-up search strategies are apparently more successful than the more traditional top-down searches. This leads me to speculate that it may well be that a *spanning tree* on the documents could be an effective structure for guiding a search for relevant documents. A search strategy based on a spanning tree for the documents may well be able to use the *dependence* information derived from the spanning tree for the index terms. An interesting research problem would be to see if by allowing some kind of interaction between the two spanning trees one could improve retrieval effectiveness.

4. Simulation

The three areas of research discussed so far could fruitfully be explored through a simulation model. We now have sufficiently detailed knowledge to enable us to specify a reasonable simulation model of an IR system. For example, the shape of the distributions of keywords throughout a document collection is known to influence retrieval effectiveness. By varying these distributions what can one expect to happen to document or keyword classifications? It may be possible to devise more efficient file structures by studying the performance of various file structures while simulating different keyword distributions.

One major open problem is the simulation of relevance. To my knowledge no one has been able to simulate the characteristics of relevant documents successfully. Once this problem has been cracked it opens the way to studying such hypotheses as the Cluster and Association hypothesis by simulation.

5. Evaluation

This has been the most troublesome area in IR. It is now generally agreed that one should be able to do some sort of cost-benefit, or efficiency–effectiveness analysis, of a retrieval system.

* The work described in Chapter 6 goes some way to remedying this situation.

In basing a theory of evaluation on the theory of measurement, is it possible to devise a measure of effectiveness not starting with precision and recall but simply with the set of relevant documents and the set of retrieved documents? If so, can we generalise such a measure to take account of degree of relevance? An alternative derivation of an E-type measure could be done in terms of recall and fallout. Is there any advantage to doing this?

Up to now the measurement of effectiveness has proved fairly intractable to statistical analysis. This has been mainly because no reasonable underlying statistical model can be found, however, that is not to say that one does not exist!*

There may be 'laws' of retrieval such as the well known trade-off between precision and recall that are worth establishing either empirically or by theoretical argument. It has been shown that the trade-off does in fact follow from more basic assumptions about the retrieval model. Similar arguments are needed to establish the upper bounds to retrieval under certain models.

6. Content analysis

There is a need for more intensive research into the problems of what to use to represent the content of documents in a computer.

Information retrieval systems, both operational and experimental, have been keyword based. Some have become quite sophisticated in their use of keywords, for example, they may include a form of normalisation and some sort of weighting. Some use distributional information to measure the strength of relationships between keywords or between the keyword descriptions of documents. The limit of our ingenuity with keywords seemed to have been reached when a few semantic relationships between words were defined and exploited.

The major reason for this rather simple-minded approach to document retrieval is a very good one. Most of the experimental evidence over the last decade has pointed to the superiority of this approach over the possible alternatives. Nevertheless there is room for more spectacular improvements. It seems that at the root of retrieval effectiveness lies the adequacy (or inadequacy) of the computer representation of documents. No doubt this was recognised to be true in the early days but attempts at that time to move away from keyword representation met with little success. Despite this I would like to see research in IR take another good look at the problem of what should be stored inside the computer.

* I think the Robertson model described in Chapter 7 goes some way to being considered as a reasonable statistical model.

188

The time is ripe for another attempt at using natural language to represent documents inside a computer. There is reason for optimism now that a lot more is known about the syntax and semantics of language. We have new sources of ideas in the advances which have been made in other disciplines. In artificial intelligence, work has been directed towards programming a computer to understand natural language. Mechanical procedures for processing (and understanding) natural language are being devised. Similarly, in psycho-linguistics the mechanism by which the human brain understands language is being investigated. Admittedly the way in which developments in these fields can be applied to IR is not immediately obvious, but clearly they are relevant and therefore deserve consideration.

It has never been assumed that a retrieval system should attempt to 'understand' the content of a document. Most IR systems at the moment merely aim at a bibliographic search. Documents are deemed to be relevant on the basis of a superficial description. I do not suggest that it is going to be a simple matter to program a computer to understand documents. What is suggested is that some attempt should be made to construct something like a naïve model, using more than just keywords, of the content of each document in the system. The more sophisticated question–answering systems do something very similar. They have a model of their universe of discourse and can answer questions about it, and can incorporate new facts and rules as they become available.

Such an approach would make 'feedback' a major tool. Feedback, as used currently, is based on the assumption that a user will be able to establish the relevance of a document on the basis of data, like its title, its abstract, and/or the list of terms by which it has been indexed. This works to an extent but is inadequate. If the content of the document were understood by the machine, its relevance could easily be discovered by the user. When he retrieved a document, he could ask some simple questions about it and thus establish its relevance and importance with confidence.

Future developments

Much of the work in IR has suffered from the difficulty of comparing retrieval results. Experiments have been done with a large variety of document collections, and rarely has the same document collection been used in quite the same form in more than one piece of research. Therefore one is always left with the suspicion that worker A's results may be data specific and that were he to test them on worker B's data they would not hold.

189

The lesson that is to be learnt is that should new research get underway it will be very important to have a suitable data-base ready. I have in mind a natural-language document collection, probably using the full text of each document. It should be constructed with many applications in mind and then be made universally available.*

Information retrieval systems are likely to play an ever increasing part in the community. They are likely to be on-line and interactive. The hardware to accomplish this is already available but its universal implementation will only follow after it has been made commercially viable.

One major recent development is that computers and data-bases are becoming linked into networks. It is foreseeable that individuals will have access to these networks through their private telephones and use normal television sets as output devices. The main impact of this for IR systems will be that they will have to be simple to communicate with, which means they will have to use ordinary language, and they will have to be competent in their ability to provide relevant information. The VIEWDATA system provided by the British Post Office is a good example of a system that will need to satisfy these demands.

By extending the user population to include the non-specialist, it is likely that an IR system will be expected to provide not just a citation, but a display of the text, or part of it, and perhaps answer simple questions about the retrieved documents. Even specialists may well desire of an IR system that it do more than just retrieve citations.

To bring all this about the document retrieval system will have to be interfaced and integrated with data retrieval systems, to give access to facts related to those in the documents. An obvious application lies in a chemical or medical retrieval system. Suppose a person has retrieved a set of documents about a specific chemical compound, and that perhaps some spectral data was given. He may like to consult a data retrieval system giving him details about related compounds. Or he may want to go on-line to, say, DENDRAL which will give him a list of possible compounds consistent with the spectral data. Finally, he may wish to do some statistical analysis of the data contained in the documents. For this he will need access to a set of statistical programs.

Another example can be found in the context of computer-aided instruction, where it is clearly a good idea to give a student access to a document retrieval system which will provide him with further reading on a topic of his immediate interest. The main thrust of these examples is that an important consideration in the design of a retrieval system should be the manner in which it can be interfaced with other systems.

* A study recommending the provision of such an experimental test bed has recently been completed, see Sparck Jones, and van Rijsbergen, 'Information retrieval test collections', *Journal of Documentation*, **32**, 59–75 (1976)

Although the networking of medium sized computers has made headline news, and individuals and institutions have been urged to buy into a network as a way of achieving access to a number of computers, it is by no means clear that this will always be the best strategy. Quite recently a revolution has taken place in the mini-computer market. It is now possible to buy a moderately powerful computer for a relatively small outlay. Since information channels are likely to be routed through libraries for some time to come, it is interesting to think about the way in which the cheaper hardware may affect their future role. Libraries have been keen to provide users with access to large data-bases, stored and controlled somewhere else often situated at a great distance, possibly even in another country. One option libraries have is the one I have just mentioned, that is, they could connect a console into a large network. An alternative, and more flexible approach, would be for them to have a mini-computer maintaining access to a small, recently published chunk of the document collection. They would be able to change it periodically. The mini would be part of the network but the user would have the option of invoking the local or global system. The local system could then be tailored to local needs which would give it an important advantage. Such things as personal files, containing say user profiles could be maintained on the mini. In addition, if the local library's catalogue and subject index were available on-line, it would prove very useful in conjunction with the document retrieval system. A user could quickly check whether the library had copies of the documents retrieved as well as any related books.

Another hardware development likely to influence the development of IR systems is the marketing of cheap micro-processors. Because these cost so little now, many people have been thinking of designing 'intelligent' terminals to IR systems, that is, ones which are able to do some of the processing instead of leaving it all to the main computer. One effect of this may well be that some of the so-called more expensive operations can now be carried out at the terminal, whereas previously they would have been prohibited.

As automation advances, much lip service is paid to the likely benefit to society. It is an unfortunate fact that so much modern technology is established before we can actually assess whether or not we want it. In the case of information retrieval systems, there is still time to predict and investigate their impact. If we think that IR systems will make an important contribution, we ought to be clear about what it is we are going to provide and why it will be an improvement on the conventional methods of retrieving information.

191

BIBLIOGRAPHY

AITCHISON, T. M., HALL, A. M., LAVELLE, K. H. and TRACY, J. M., *Comparative Evaluation of Index Languages,* Part I, *Design,* Part II, *Results,* Project INSPEC, Institution of Electrical Engineers, London (1970)

ANDERBERG, M. R., *Cluster Analysis for Applications,* Academic Press, London and New York (1973)

ANDREWS, K., 'The development of a fast conflation algorithm for English'. Dissertation submitted for the Diploma in Computer Science, University of Cambridge (unpublished) (1971)

ANGIONE, P. V. 'On the equivalence of Boolean and weighted searching based on the convertibility of query forms', *Journal of the American Society for Information Science,* **26,** 112–124 (1975)

ARNAUDOV, D. D. and GOVORUN, N. N., *Some Aspects of the File Organization and Retrieval Strategy in Large Databases,* Joint Institute for Nuclear Research, Dubna (1977)

AUGUSTSON, J. G. and MINKER, J., 'An analysis of some graph-theoretic cluster techniques', *Journal of the ACM,* **17,** 571–588 (1970)

BAKER, F. B., 'Information retrieval based upon latent class analysis', *Journal of the ACM,* **9,** 512–521 (1962)

BALL, G. H., 'Data-analysis in the social sciences: What about the details?', *Proceedings of the Fall Joint Computer Conference,* **27,** 533–559 (1966)

BARBER, A. S., BARRACLOUGH, E. D. and GRAY, W. A., 'On-line information retrieval as a scientist's tool', *Information Storage and Retrieval,* **9,** 429–440 (1973)

BAR-HILLEL, Y., *Language and Information. Selected Essays on their Theory and Application,* Addison-Wesley, Reading, Massachusetts (1964)

BARRACLOUGH, E. D., MEDLARS on-line search formulation and indexing, Technical Report Series, No. 34, Computing Laboratory, University of Newcastle upon Tyne.

BARRACLOUGH, E. D., 'On-line searching in information retrieval', *Journal of Documentation,* **33,** 220–238 (1977)

BATTY, C. D., 'Automatic generation of indexing languages', *Journal of Documentation,* **25,** 142–151 (1969)

BECKNER, M., *The Biological Way of Thought,* Columbia University Press, New York, 22 (1959)

BELL, C. J., ALDRED, B. K. and ROGERS, T. W., 'Adaptability to change in large data base information retrieval systems'. Report No. UKSC-0027, UK Scientific Centre, IBM United Kingdom Limited, Neville Road, Peterlee, County Durham, U.K. (1972)

192

BELL, J. R. and KAMAN, C. H., 'The linear quotinent hash code', *Communications of the ACM*, **13**, 675–677 (1970)

BELKIN, N. J., 'Information concepts for information science', *Journal of Documentation*, **34**, 55–85 (1978)

BELNAP, N. P., 'An analysis of questions: Preliminary report', Scientific Report TM-1287, SDC, Santa Monica, California (1963)

BELNAP, N. P. and STEEL, T. B., *The Logic of Questions and Answers*, Yale University Press, New Haven and London (1976)

BENTLEY, J. L., 'Multidimensional binary search trees used for associative searching', *Communications of the ACM*, **13**, 675–677 (1975)

BENTLEY, J. L. and FRIEDMAN, J. H., *Fast Algorithm for Constructing Minimal Spanning Trees in Coordinate Spaces*, Stanford Report, STAN-CS-75-529 (1975)

BERGE, C., *The Theory of Graphs and its Applications*, Methuen, London (1966)

BERTZISS, A. T., *Data Structures: Theory and Practice*, Academic Press, London and New York (1971)

BONNER, R. E., 'On some clustering techniques', *IBM Journal of Research and Development*, **8**, 22–32 (1964)

BONO, P. R., 'Adaptive procedures for automatic document retrieval', Ph.D. Thesis, University of Michigan (1972)

BOOKSTEIN, A. 'When the most "pertinent" document should not be retrieved – an analysis of the Swets Model', *Information Processing and Management*, **13**, 377–383 (1977)

BOOKSTEIN, A. and KRAFT, D., 'Operations research applied to document indexing and retrieval decisions', *Journal of the ACM*, **24**, 410–427 (1977)

BOOKSTEIN, A. and SWANSON, D. R., 'Probabilistic models for automatic indexing', *Journal of the American Society for Information Science*, **25**, 312–318 (1974)

BOOKSTEIN, A. and SWANSON, D. R., 'A decision theoretic foundation for indexing', *Journal of the American Society for Information Science*, **26**, 45–50 (1975)

BORKO, H. and BERNICK, M., 'Automatic document classification', *Journal of the ACM*, **10**, 151–162 (1963)

BORKO, H., *Automated Language Processing*, Wiley, New York (1967)

BORKO, H., 'Toward a theory of indexing', *Information Processing and Management*, **13**, 355–365 (1977)

BOULTON, D. M. and WALLACE, C. S., 'A program for numerical classification', *The Computer Journal*, **13**, 63–69 (1970)

BOULTON, D. M. and WALLACE, C S., 'An information measure for single link classification', *The Computer Journal*, **18**, 236–238 (1975)

BOX, G. E. P. and TIAO, G. C., *Bayesian Inference in Statistical Analysis*, 304–315, Addison-Wesley, Reading, Mass. (1973)

BROOKES, B. C., 'The measure of information retrieval effectiveness proposed by Swets', *Journal of Documentation*, **24**, 41–54 (1968)

BURKHARD, W. A., 'Partial match queries and file designs', *Proceedings of the International Conference on Very Large Data Bases*, 523–525 (1975)

BURKHARD, W. A. and KELLER, R. M., 'Some approaches to best-match file searching', *Communications of the ACM*, **16**, 230–236 (1973)

CARROLL, J. M. and DEBRUYN, J. G., 'On the importance of root-stem truncation in word-frequency analysis', *Journal of the American Society for Information Science*, **21**, 368–369 (1970)

CAWKELL, A. E., 'A measure of "Efficiency Factor"–communication theory applied to document selection systems', *Information Processing and Management*, **11**, 243–248 (1975)

CHAN, F. K., 'Document classification through use of fuzzy relations and determination of significant features', M.Sc. Thesis, Department of Computer Science, University of Alberta, Canada (1973)

CHANG, C. L. and LEE, R. C. T., *Symbolic Logic and Mechanical Theorem Proving,* Academic Press, New York (1973)

CHOU, C. K., 'Algorithms for hash coding and document classification', Ph.D. Thesis, University of Illinois (1972)

CHOW, C. K. and LIU, C. N., 'Approximating discrete probability distributions with dependence trees', *IEEE Transactions on Information Theory,* IT-14, 462–467 (1968)

CLEVERDON, C. W., 'Progress in documentation. Evaluation of information retrieval systems', *Journal of Documentation,* 26, 55–67 (1970)

CLEVERDON, C. W. 'On the inverse relationship of recall and precision', *Journal of Documentation,* 28, 195–201 (1972)

CLEVERDON, C. W., MILLS, J. and KEEN, M., *Factors Determining the Performance of Indexing Systems,* Vol. I, *Design,* Vol. II, *Test Results,* ASLIB Cranfield Project, Cranfield (1966)

CLIFFORD, H. T. and STEPHENSON, W., *An Introduction to Numerical Classification,* Academic Press, New York (1975)

COATES, E. J., 'Some properties of relationships in the structure of indexing languages', *Journal of Documentation,* 29, 390–404 (1973)

CODD, E. F., 'A relational model of data for large shared data banks', *Communications of the ACM,* 13, 377–387 (1970)

COLE, A. J., *Numerical Taxonomy,* Academic Press, New York (1969)

Comparative Systems Laboratory, *An Inquiry into Testing of Information Retrieval Systems,* 3 Vols, Case-Western Reserve University (1968)

CONOVER, W. J., *Practical Nonparametric Statistics,* Wiley, New York (1971)

COOPER, M. D., 'A cost model for evaluating information retrieval systems', *Journal of the American Society for Information Science,* 23, 306–312 (1972)

COOPER, W. S., 'Expected search length: A single measure of retrieval effectiveness based on weak ordering action of retrieval systems', *Journal of the American Society for Information Science,* 19, 30–41 (1968)

COOPER, W. S., 'A definition of relevance for information retrieval', *Information Storage and Retrieval,* 7, 19–37 (1971)

COOPER, W. S., 'On selecting a measure of retrieval effectiveness', Part 1: 'The "subjective" philosophy of evaluation', Part 2: 'Implementation of the philosophy', *Journal of the American Society for Information Science,* 24, 87–100 and 413–424 (1973)

COOPER, W. S. and MARON, M. E., 'Foundations of probabilistic and utility-theoretic indexing', *Journal of the ACM,* 25, 67–80 (1978)

CORMACK, R. M., 'A review of classification', *Journal of the Royal Statistical Society,* Series A, 134, 321–353 (1971)

COX, D. R., 'The analysis of multivariate binary data', *Applied Statistics,* 21, 113–120 (1972)

CROFT, W. B., 'Document clustering', M.Sc. Thesis, Department of Computer Science, Monash University, Australia (1975)

CROFT, W. B., 'Clustering large files of documents using single link', *Journal of the American Society for Information Science,* 28, 341–344 (1977)

CROFT, W. B., *Organizing and Searching Large Files of Document Descriptions,* Ph.D. Thesis, University of Cambridge (in preparation)

CROUCH, D., 'A clustering algorithm for large and dynamic document collections', Ph.D. Thesis, Southern Methodist University (1972)

CUADRA, A. C. and KATTER, R. V., 'Opening the black box of "relevance" ', *Journal of Documentation,* 23, 291–303 (1967)

194

DAMERAU, F. J., 'An experiment in automatic indexing', *American Documentation*, **16**, 283–289 (1965)

DAMERAU, F. J., 'Automated language processing', *Annual Review of Information Science and Technology*, **11**, 107–161 (1976)

DATE, C. J., *An Introduction to Data Base Systems*, Addison-Wesley, Reading, Mass (1975)

DATTOLA, R. T., 'A fast algorithm for automatic classification', *In* Report ISR-14 to the National Science Foundation, Section V, Cornell University, Department of Computer Science (1968)

DATTOLA, R. T., *Automatic Classification in Document Retrieval Systems*, Ph.D. Thesis, Cornell University (1973)

DE FINETTI, B., *Theory of Probability*, Vol. 1, 146–161, Wiley, London (1974)

DENNIS, S. F., 'The design and testing of a fully automatic indexing – searching system for documents consisting of expository test', In: *Information Retrieval: A Critical Review* (Edited by G. Schecter), Thompson Book Co., Washington D.C., 67–94 (1967)

DISISS, Design of information systems in the social sciences. Clustering of journal titles according to citation data: preparatory work, design; data collection and preliminary analysis. Bath, Bath University Library, Working Paper No. 11 (1973)

DODD, G. G., 'Elements of data management systems', *Computing Surveys*, **1**, 117–133 (1969)

DOROFEYUK, A. A., 'Automatic Classification Algorithms (Review)', *Automation and Remote Control*, **32**, 1928–1958 (1971)

DOYLE, L. B., 'Programmed interpretation of text as a basis for information retrieval systems', In: *Proceedings of the Western Joint Computer Conference* San Francisco, 60–63 (1959)

DOYLE, L. B., 'Semantic road maps for literature searchers', *Journal of the ACM*, **8**, 553–578 (1961)

DOYLE, L. B., 'The microstatistics of text', *Information Storage and Retrieval*, **1**, 189–214 (1963)

DOYLE, L. B., 'Is automatic classification a reasonable application of statistical analysis of text?', *Journal of the ACM*, **12**, 473–489 (1965)

DOYLE, L. B., 'Some compromises between word grouping and document grouping', In: *Statistical Association Methods for Mechanized Documentation* (Edited by Stevens *et al.*) National Bureau of Standards, Washington, 15–24 (1965)

DOYLE, L. B., *Information Retrieval and Processing*, Melville Publishing Co., Los Angeles, California (1975)

DUDA, R. O. and HART, P. E., *Pattern Classification and Scene Analysis*, Wiley, New York (1973)

EDMUNDSON, H. P. and WYLLYS, R. E., 'Automatic abstracting and indexing survey and recommendations', *Communications of the ACM*, **4**, 226–234 (1961)

EFRON, B. and MORRIS, C., 'Stein's paradox in statistics', *Scientific American*, **236**, 119–127 (1977)

EIN-DOR, P., 'The comparative efficiency of two dictionary structures for document retrieval', *Infor Journal*, **12**, 87–108 (1974)

ELLIS, B., *Basic Concepts of Measurement*, Cambridge University Press, London (1966)

ETZWEILER, L. and MARTIN, C., 'Binary cluster division and its application to a modified single pass clustering algorithm', *In* Report No. ISR-21 to the National Library of Medicine (1972)

EVERITT, B., *Cluster Analysis*, Heineman Educational Books, London (1974)

FAIRTHORNE, R. A., 'The mathematics of classification'. *Towards Information Retrieval*, Butterworths, London, 1–10 (1961)

FARRADANE, J., RUSSELL, J. M. and YATES-MERCER, A., 'Problems in information retrieval. Logical jumps in the expression of information', *Information Storage and Retrieval*, **9**, 65–77 (1973)

FISHER, L. and VAN NESS, J. W., 'Admissible clustering procedures', *Biometrika*, **58**, 91–104 (1971)

FOSTER, J. M., *List Processing*, Macdonald, London; and American Elsevier Inc., New York (1967)

FREDKIN, E., 'Trie memory', *Communications of the ACM*, **3**, 490–499 (1960)

FRITZCHE, M., 'Automatic clustering techniques in information retrieval', Diplomarbeit, Institut für Informatik der Universität Stuttgart (1973)

GARVIN, P. L., *Natural Language and the Computer*, McGraw-Hill, New York (1963)

GHOSE, A. and DHAWLE, A. S., 'Problems of thesaurus construction', *Journal of the American Society for Information Science*, **28**, 211–217 (1977)

GOFFMAN, W., 'A searching procedure for information retrieval', *Information Storage and Retrieval*, **2**, 73–78 (1964)

GOFFMAN, W., 'On relevance as a measure', *Information Storage and Retrieval*, **2**, 201–203 (1964)

GOFFMAN, W., 'An indirect method of information retrieval', *Information Storage and Retrieval*, **4**, 361–373 (1969)

GOFFMAN, W. and NEWILL, V. A., 'A methodology for test and evaluation of information retrieval systems', *Information Storage and Retrieval*, **3**, 19–25 (1966)

GOOD, I. J., *Probability and the Weighing of Evidence*, Charles Griffin and Co. Ltd., London (1950)

GOOD, I. J., 'Speculations concerning information retrieval', Research Report PC-78, IBM Research Centre, Yorktown Heights, New York (1958)

GOOD, I. J., 'Categorization of classification', *In Mathematics and Computer Science in Biology and Medicine*, HMSO, London, 115–125 (1965)

GOOD, I. J., *The Estimation of Probabilities: An Essay on Modern Bayesian Methods*, The M.I.T. Press, Cambridge, Mass. (1965)

GOOD, I. J., 'The decision–theory approach to the evaluation of information retrieval systems', *Information Storage and Retrieval*, **3**, 31–34 (1967)

GOODMAN, L. and KRUSKAL, W., 'Measures of association for cross-classifications', *Journal of the American Statistical Association*, **49**, 732–764 (1954)

GOODMAN, L. and KRUSKAL, W., 'Measures of association for cross-classification II: Further discussions and references', *Journal of the American Statistical Association*, **54**, 123–163 (1959)

GOWER, J. C., 'Maximal predictive classification', *Biometrics*, **30**, 643–654 (1974)

GOWER, J. C. and ROSS, G. J. S., 'Minimum spanning trees and single-linkage cluster analysis', *Applied Statistics*, **18**, 54–64 (1969)

GRAY, J. C., 'Compound data structure for computer aided design: a survey', *Proceedings ACM National Meeting*, 355–365 (1967)

GUAZZO, M., 'Retrieval performance and information theory', *Information Processing and Management*, **13**, 155–165 (1977)

HARARY, F., NORMAN, R. Z. and CARTWRIGHT, D., *Structural Models: An Introduction to the Theory of Directed Graphs*, Wiley, New York (1966)

HARPER, D. and VAN RIJSBERGEN, C. J., 'An evaluation of feedback in document retrieval using co-occurrence data', *Journal of Documentation*, **34** (in the press)

HARTER, S. P., 'A probabilistic approach to automatic keyword indexing, Part 1: On the distribution of speciality words in a technical literature, Part 2: An

196

algorithm for probabilistic indexing', *Journal of the American Society for Information Science*, **26**, 197–206 and 280–289 (1975)

HARTIGAN, J. A., *Clustering Algorithms*, Wiley, New York and London (1975)

HATFIELD, D. J. and GERALD, J., 'Program restructuring for virtual memory', *IBM Systems Journal*, **10**, 168–192 (1971)

HAYES, R. M., 'Mathematical models in information retrieval', *In Natural Language and the Computer* (Edited by P. L. Garvin), McGraw-Hill, New York, 287 (1963)

HAYES, R. M. and BECKER, J., *Handbook of Data Processing for Libraries*, Melville Publishing Co., Los Angeles, California (1974)

HEINE, M. H., 'The inverse relationship of precision and recall in terms of the Swets' model', *Journal of Documentation*, **29**, 81–84 (1973)

HEINE, M. H., 'Distance between sets as an objective measure of retrieval effectiveness', *Information Storage and Retrieval*, **9**, 181–198 (1973)

HEMPEL, C. G., *Aspects of scientific explanation and other essays in the philosophy of science*, The Free Press, New York, 137–154 (1965)

HIGGINS, L. D. and SMITH, F. J., 'Disc access algorithms', *Computer Journal*, **14**, 249–253 (1971)

HILL, D. R., 'A vector clustering technique', *In Mechanised Information Storage, Retrieval and Dissemination* (Edited by Samuelson), North-Holland, Amsterdam (1968)

HSIAO, D., 'A generalized record organization', *IEEE Transactions on Computers*, **C-20**, 1490–1495 (1971)

HSIAO, D. and HARARY, F., 'A formal system for information retrieval from files', *Communications of the ACM*, **13**, 67–73 (1970)

HUGHES, G. F., 'On the mean accuracy of statistical pattern recognizers', *IEEE Transactions on Information Theory*, **IT-14**, 55–63 (1968)

HYVARINEN, L., 'Classification of qualitative data', *BIT, Nordisk Tidskrift för Informationsbehandling*, **2**, 83–89 (1962)

IVIE, E. L., 'Search procedures based on measures of relatedness between documents', Ph.D. Thesis, M.I.T., Report MAC-TR-29 (1966)

JARDINE, N. and SIBSON, R., *Mathematical Taxonomy*, Wiley, London and New York (1971)

JARDINE, N. and VAN RIJSBERGEN, C. J., 'The use of hierarchic clustering in information retrieval', *Information Storage and Retrieval*, **7**, 217–240 (1971)

JOHNSON, D. B. and LAFUENTE, J. M., 'A controlled single pass classification algorithm with application to multilevel clustering', *In* Report ISR-18 to the National Science Foundation and the National Library of Medicine (1970)

JONKERS, H. L., 'A straightforward and flexible design method for complex data base management systems', *Information Storage and Retrieval*, **9**, 401–415 (1973)

KANG, A. N. C., LEE, R. C. T., CHANG, C.-L. and CHANG, S.-K., 'Storage reduction through minimal spanning trees and spanning forests', *IEEE Transactions on Computers*, **C-26**, 425–434 (1977)

KEEN, E. M., 'Evaluation parameters', *In* Report ISR-13 to the National Science Foundation, Section II, Cornell University, Department of Computer Science (1967)

KEEN, E. M. and DIGGER, J. A., Report of an Information Science Index Languages Test, Aberyswyth College of Librarianship, Wales (1972)

KEENAN, E. L., 'On semantically based grammar', *Linguistic Inquiry*, **3**, 413–461 (1972)

KEENAN, E. L., *Formal Semantics of Natural Language*, Cambridge University Press (1975)

197

KENDALL, M. G., *In Multivariate Analysis* (Edited by P. R. Krishnaiah), Academic Press, London and New York, 165–184 (1966)

KENDALL, M. G. and STUART, A., *Advanced Theory of Statistics,* Vol. 2, 2nd ed., Griffin, London (1967)

KERCHNER, M. D., 'Dynamic document processing in clustered collections', Ph.D. Thesis, Cornell University. Report ISR-19 to National Science Foundation and to the National Library of Medicine (1971)

KING, D. W. and BRYANT, E. C., *The Evaluation of Information Services and Products,* Information Resources Press, Washington (1971)

KNUTH, D. E., *The Art of Computer Programming,* Vol. 1, *Fundamental Algorithms,* Addison-Wesley, Reading, Massachusetts (1968)

KNUTH, D. E., *The Art of Computer Programming,* Vol. 3, *Sorting and Searching,* Addison-Wesley, Reading, Massachusetts (1973)

KOCHEN, M., *The Growth of Knowledge – Readings on Organisation and Retrieval of Information,* Wiley, New York (1967)

KOCHEN, M., *Principles of Information Retrieval,* Melville Publishing Co., Los Angeles, California (1974)

KRANTZ, D. H., LUCE, R. D., SUPPES, P. and TVERSKY, A., *Foundations of Measurement,* Volume 1 *Additive and Polynomial Representation,* Academic Press, London and New York (1971)

KU, H. H. and KULLBACK, S., 'Approximating discrete probability distributions', *IEEE Transactions on Information Theory,* IT-15, 444–447 (1969)

KUHNS, J. L., 'The continuum of coefficients of association', *In Statistical Association Methods for Mechanised Documentation* (Edited by Stevens *et al.*), National Bureau of Standards, Washington, 33–39 (1965)

KULLBACK, S., *Information Theory and Statistics,* Dover, New York (1968)

LANCASTER, F. W., *Information Retrieval Systems: Characteristics, Testing and Evaluation,* Wiley, New York (1968)

LANCASTER, F. W. and FAYEN, E. G., *Information Retrieval On-line,* Melville Publishing Co., Los Angeles, California (1973)

LEFKOVITZ, D., *File structures for on-line systems,* Spartan Books, New York (1969)

LEHMANN, E. L., *Nonparametrics: Statistical Methods Based on Ranks,* Holden-Day Inc., San Francisco, California (1975)

LERMAN, I. C., *Les Bases de la Classification Automatique,* Gauthier-Villars, Paris (1970)

LESK, M. E. and SALTON, G., 'Relevance assessments and retrieval system evaluation', *Information Storage and Retrieval,* 4, 343–359 (1969)

LEVIEN, R., 'Relational data file II: Implementation', In: *Information Retrieval* (Edited by Schecter), 6, 225–241 (1967)

LIEBERMAN, B., *Contemporary Problems in Statistics,* Oxford University Press, New York (1971)

LINFOOT, E. H., 'An informational measure of correlation', *Information and Control,* 1, 85–89 (1957)

LITOFSKY, B., 'Utility of automatic classification systems for information storage and retrieval', Ph.D. Thesis, University of Pennsylvania (1969)

LOVINS, B. J., 'Development of a stemming algorithm', *Mechnical Translation and Computational Liguistics,* 11, 22–31 (1968)

LOVINS, B. J., 'Error evaluation for stemming algorithms as clustering algorithms', *Journal of the American Society for Information Science,* 22, 28–40 (1971)

LUHN, H. P., 'A statistical approach to mechanised encoding and searching of library information', *IBM Journal of Research and Development,* 1, 309–317 (1957)

198

LUHN, H. P., 'The automatic creation of literature abstracts', *IBM Journal of Research and Development,* **2,** 159–165 (1958)

LUM, V. Y., LING, H. and SENKO, M. E., 'Analysis of a complex data management access method by simulation modelling', *Proceedings AFIP Fall Joint Computer Conference,* 211–222 (1970)

LUM, V. Y., YUEN, P. S. T., and DODD, M., 'Key-to-address transform techniques: a fundamental performance study on large existing formatted files', *Communications of the ACM,* **14,** 228–239 (1971)

McCARN, D. B. and LEITER, J., 'On-line services in medicine and beyond', *Science,* **181,** 318–324 (1973)

McDONELL, K. J. and MONTGOMERY, A. Y., 'The design of indexed sequential files', *The Australian Computer Journal,* **5,** 115–126 (1973)

MACNAUGHTON-SMITH, P., *Some Statistical and Other Numerical Techniques for Classifying Individuals,* Studies in the causes of deliquency and the treatment of offenders. Report No. 6, HMSO, London (1965)

MACQUEEN, J. 'Some methods for classification and analysis of multivariate observations', *In Proceedings of the Fifth Berkeley Symposium on Mathematical Statistics and Probability, 1965,* University of California Press, 281–297 (1967)

MANOLA, F. and HSIAO, D. K., 'A model for keyword based file structures and access', *NRL Memorandum Report 2544,* Naval Research Laboratory, Washington D.C. (1973)

MARON, M. E., 'Automatic indexing: an experimental enquiry', *Journal of the ACM,* **8,** 404–417 (1961)

MARON, M. E., 'Mechanized documentation: The logic behind a probabilistic interpretation', In: *Statistical Association Methods for Mechanized Documentation* (Edited by Stevens *et al.*) National Bureau of Standards, Washington, 9–13 (1965)

MARON, M. E., 'Relational data file I: Design philosophy', In: *Information Retrieval* (Edited by Schecter), **6,** 211–223 (1967)

MARON, M. E., 'On indexing, retrieval and the meaning of about', *Journal of the American Society for Information Science,* **28,** 38–43 (1977)

MARON, M. E. and KUHNS, J. L., 'On relevance, probabilistic indexing and information retrieval', *Journal of the ACM,* **7,** 216–244 (1960)

MARSCHAK, J., 'Economics of information systems', *Journal of the American Statistical Association,* **66,** 192–219 (1971)

MEALEY, G. H., 'Another look at data', *Proceedings AFIP Fall Joint Computer Conference,* 525–534 (1967)

Medline Reference Manual, MEDLARS Management Section, Bibliographic Services Division, National Library of Medicine.

MILLER, W. L., 'A probabilistic search strategy for MEDLARS', *Journal of Documentation,* **27,** 254–266 (1971)

MINKER, J., WILSON, G. A. and ZIMMERMAN, B. H., 'An evaluation of query expansion by the addition of clustered terms for a document retrieval system', *Information Storage and Retrieval,* **8,** 329–348 (1972)

MINSKY, M., *Semantic Information Processing,* MIT Press, Cambridge, Massachusetts (1968)

MONTGOMERY, C. A., 'Linguistics and Information Science', *Journal of the American Society for Information Science,* **23,** 195–219 (1972)

MORRIS, R., 'Scatter storage techniques', *Communications of the ACM,* **11,** 35–38(1968)

MURRAY, D. M., 'A scatter storage scheme for dictionary lookups', *In* Report ISR-16 to the National Science Foundation, Section II, Cornell University, Department of Computer Science (1969)

MURRAY, D. M., 'Document retrieval based on clustered files', Ph.D. Thesis,

Cornell University. Report ISR-20 to National Science Foundation and to the National Library of Medicine (1972)

NEEDHAM, R. M., 'The application of digital computers to classification and grouping', Ph.D. Thesis, University of Cambridge (1961)

NEEDHAM, R. M., 'Problems of sclae in automatic classification', *In Statistical Association Methods for Mechanised Documentation* (abstract) (Edited by M. E. Stevens *et al.*), National Bureau of Standards, Washington (1965)

NEGOITA, C. V., 'On the application of the fuzzy sets separation theorem for automatic classification in information retrieval systems', *Information Sciences*, **5**, 279–286 (1973)

NEGOITA, C. V., 'On the notion of relevance', *Kybernetes*, **2**, 161–165 (1973)

NEGOITA, C. V., 'On the decision process in information retrieval', *Studii si cercetari de documentare*, **15**, 269–281 (1973)

NEGUS, A. E. and HALL, J. L., 'Towards an effective on-line reference retrieval system', Library Memo CLM-LM2/71, U.K. Atomic Energy Authority, Research Group (1971)

NILSSON, N. J., *Learning Machines – Foundations of Trainable Pattern Classifying Systems*, McGraw-Hill, New York (1965)

ODDY, R. N., 'Information retrieval through man-machine dialogue, *Journal of Documentation*, **33**, 1– 14 (1977)

ÖRE, O., *Graphs and Their Uses*, Random House, New York (1963)

OSBORNE, M. L., *A modification of Veto Logic for a Committee of Threshold Logic Units and the Use of 2-class Classifiers for Function Estimation*, Ph.D. Thesis, Oregon State University (1975)

OSTEYEE, D. B. and GOOD, I. J., *Information, Weight of Evidence, the Singularity between Probability Measures and Signal Detection*, Springer Verlag, Berlin (1974)

PAGE, E. S. and WILSON, L. B., *Information Representation and Manipulation in a Computer*, Cambridge University Press, Cambridge (1973)

PAICE, C. D., *Information Retrieval and the Computer*, Macdonald and Jane's, London (1977)

PATT, Y. N., 'Minimum search tree structure for data partitioned into pages', IEEE Transactions on Computers, C-21, 961–967 (1972)

PREPARATA, F. F. and CHIEN, R. T., 'On clustering techniques of citation graphs', Report R-349, Co-ordinated Science Laboratory, University of Illinois, Urbana, Illinois (1967)

PRYWES, N. S. and SMITH, D. P., 'Organization of information', *Annual Review of Information Science and Technology*, **7**, 103–158 (1972)

RADECKI, T., 'Mathematical model of time-effective information retrieval system based on the theory of fuzzy sets, *Information Processing and Management*, **13**, 109–116 (1977)

RAJSKI, C., 'A metric space of discrete probability distributions', *Information and Control*, **4**, 371–377 (1961)

RICKMAN, J. T., 'Design consideration for a boolean search system with automatic relevance feedback processing', *Proceedings of the ACM 1972 Annual Conference*, 478–481 (1972)

RIEBER, S. and MARATHE, U. P., 'The single pass clustering method', *In* Report ISR-16 to the National Science Foundation, Cornell University, Department of Computer Science (1969)

RIVEST, R., *Analysis of Associative Retrieval Algorithms*, Ph.D. Thesis, Stanford University, Computer Science (1974)

ROBERTS, D. C., 'File Organization Techniques'. *Advances in Computers*, **12**, 115–174 (1972)

ROBERTSON, S. E., 'The parameter description of retrieval tests', Part 1; The basic paramaters, *Journal of Documentation,* **25,** 1–27 (1969)

ROBERTSON, S. E., 'The parametric description of retrieval tests', Part 2; Overall measures, *Journal of Documentation,* **25,** 93–107 (1969)

ROBERTSON, S. E., *A Theoretical Model of the Retrieval Characteristics of Information Retrieval Systems,* Ph.D. Thesis, University College, London (1975)

ROBERTSON, S. E., 'The probabilistic character of relevance', *Information Processing and Management,* **13,** 247–251 (1977)

ROBERTSON, S. E., 'Theories and models in information retrieval', *Journal of Documentation,* **33,** 126–148 (1977)

ROBERTSON, S. E., 'The probability ranking principle in IR', *Journal of Documentation,* **33,** 294–304 (1977)

ROBERTSON, S. E. and TEATHER, D., 'A statistical analysis of retrieval tests: a Bayesian approach', *Journal of Documentation,* **30,** 273–282 (1974)

ROBERTSON, S. E. and SPARCK JONES, K., 'Relevance weighting of search terms', *Journal of the American Society for Information Science,* **27,** 129–146 (1976)

ROCCHIO, J. J., 'Document retrieval systems – Optimization and evaluation', Ph.D. Thesis, Harvard University, Report ISR-10 to National Science Foundation, Harvard Computation Laboratory (1966)

ROHLF, J., 'Graphs implied by the Jardine-Sibson Overlapping clustering methods, B_k', *Journal of the American Statistical Association,* **69,** 705–710 (1974)

SALTON, G., 'Manipulation of trees in information retrieval', *Communications of the ACM,* **5,** 103–114 (1962)

SALTON, G., *Automatic Information Organization and Retrieval,* McGraw-Hill, New York (1968)

SALTON, G., Automatic text analysis', *Science,* **168,** 335–343 (1970)

SALTON, G., *The SMART Retrieval System – Experiment in Automatic Document Processing,* Prentice-Hall, Englewood Cliffs, New Jersey (1971)

SALTON, G., 'Experiments in automatic thesaurus construction for information retrieval', Proceedings IFIP Congress 1971, **TA-2,** 43–49 (1971)

SALTON, G., 'The "generality" effect and the retrieval evaluation for large collections', *Journal of the American Society for Information Science,* **23,** 11–22 (1972)

SALTON, G., Paper given at the 1972 NATO Advanced Study Institute for on-line mechanised information retrieval systems (1972)

SALTON, G., 'Comment on "an evaluation of query expansion by the addition of clustered terms for a document retrieval system".' *Computing Reviews,* **14,** 232 (1973)

SALTON, G., *A Theory of Indexing,* Technical report No. TR74-203, Department of Computer Science, Cornell University, Ithaca, New York (1974)

SALTON, G., *Dynamic Information and Library Processing,* Prentice-Hall, Englewood Cliffs, N.J. (1975)

SALTON, G., WONG, A. and YANG, C. S., 'A vector space model for automatic indexing', *Communications of the ACM,* **18,** 613–620 (1975)

SALTON, G., WONG, A. and YU, C. T., 'Automatic indexing using term discrimination and term precision measurements', *Information Processing and Management,* **12,** 43–51 (1976)

SALTON, G. and YANG, C. S., 'On the specification of term values in automatic indexing', *Journal of Documentation,* **29,** 351–372 (1973)

SALTON, G., YANG, C. S. and YU, C. T., 'A theory of term importance in automatic text analysis', *Journal of the American Society for Information Science,* **26,** 33–44 (1975)

201

SARACEVIC, T., *Introduction to Information Science,* P. R. Bowker, New York and London (1970)

SARACEVIC, T., 'Relevance: A review of and a framework for the thinking on the notion in information science', *Journal of the American Society for Information Science,* **26,** 321–343 (1975)

SCHECTER, G., *Information Retrieval: A Critical View,* Academic Press, London (1967)

SCHULTZ, C. K., *H. P. Luhn: Pioneer of Information Science – Selected Works,* Macmillan, London (1968)

SENKO, M. E., 'Information storage and retrieval system', *In Advances in Information Systems Science* (Edited by J. Tou), Plenum Press, New York (1969)

SENKO, M. E., 'File organization and management information systems', *Annual Review of Information Science and Technology,* **4,** 111–134 (1969)

SENKO, M. E., 'Information systems: records, relations, sets, entities, and things, *Information Systems,* **1,** 3–13 (1975)

SEVERANCE, D. G., 'A parametric model of alternative file structures', *Information Systems,* **1,** 51–55 (1975)

SHANNON, C. E. and WEAVER, W., *The Mathematical Theory of Communication,* University of Illinois Press, Urbana (1964)

SIBLEY, E. H., 'Special Issue: Data base management systems', *Computing Surveys,* **8,** No. 1 (1976)

SIBSON, R., 'Some observations of a paper by Lance and Williams', *The Computer Journal,* **14,** 156–157 (1971)

SIBSON, R., 'Order invariant methods for data analysis', *Journal of the Royal Statistical Society,* Series B, **34,** No. 3, 311–349 (1972)

SIEGEL, S., *Nonparametric Statistics for the Behavioural Sciences,* McGraw-Hill, New York (1956)

SIMON, H. A., 'On a class of skew distributions', *Biometrika,* **42,** 425–440 (1955)

SIMON, J. C. and GUIHO, G., 'On algorithms preserving neighbourhood to file and retrieve information in a memory', *International Journal Computer Information Sciences,* **1,** 3–15 (CR 23923) (1972)

SMITH, L. C., 'Artificial intelligence in information retrieval systems', *Information Processing and Management,* **12,** 189–222 (1976)

SNEATH, P. H. A. and SOKAL, R. R., *Numerical Taxonomy: The Principles and Practice of Numerical Classification,* W. H. Freeman and Company, San Francisco (1973)

SOERGEL, D., 'Is user satisfaction a hobgoblin?', *Journal of the American Society for Information Science,* **27,** 256–259 (1976)

SPARCK JONES, K., 'Some thoughts on classification for retrieval', *Journal of Documentation,* **26,** 89–101 (1970)

SPARCK JONES, K., *Automatic Keyword Classification for Information Retrieval,* Butterworths, London (1971)

SPARCK JONES, K., 'A statistical interpretation of term specificity and its application in retrieval', *Journal of Documentation,* **28,** 11–21 (1972)

SPARCK JONES, K., 'Index term weighting', *Information Storage and Retrieval,* **9,** 619–633 (1973)

SPARCK JONES, K., 'Does indexing exhaustivity matter?', *Journal of the American Society for Information Science,* **24,** 313–316 (1973)

SPARCK JONES, K., *Automatic Indexing: A State of the Art Review,* review commissioned by the Office for Scientific and Technical Information, London (1974)

SPARCK JONES, K. and JACKSON, D. M., 'The use of automatically-obtained keyword classifications for information retrieval', *Information Storage and Retrieval,* **5,** 175–201 (1970)

SPARCK JONES, K. and KAY, M., *Linguistics and Information Science,* Academic Press, New York and London (1973)

STANFEL, L. E., 'Sequential adaptation of retrieval systems based on user inputs', *Information Storage and Retrieval,* 7, 69–78 (1971)

STANFEL, L. E., 'Practical aspects of doubly chained trees for retrieval', *Journal of the ACM,* 19, 425–436 (1972)

STANFEL, L. E., 'Optimal trees for a class of information retrieval problems', *Information Storage and Retrieval,* 9, 43–59 (1973)

STEVENS, M. E., *Automatic Indexing: A State of the Art Report,* Monograph 91, National Bureau of Standards, Washington (1965)

STEVENS, M. E., GIULIANO, V. E. and HEILPRIN, L. B., *Statistical Association Methods for Mechanised Documentation,* National Bureau of Standards, Washington (1964)

STILES, H. F., 'The association factor in information retrieval', *Journal of the ACM,* 8, 271–279 (1961)

STONE, D. C. and RUBINOFF, M., 'Statistical generation of a technical vocabulary', *American Documentation,* 19, 411–412 (1968)

SUSSENGUTH, E. H., 'Use of tree structures for processing files', *Communications of the ACM,* 6, 272–279 (1963)

SWETS, J. A., 'Information retrieval systems', *Science,* 141, 245–250 (1963)

SWETS, J. A., *Effectiveness of Information Retrieval Methods,* Bolt, Beranek and Newman, Cambridge, Massachusetts (1967)

VAN RIJSBERGEN, C. J., 'A clustering algorithm', *Computer Journal,* 13, 113–115 (1970)

VAN RIJSBERGEN, C. J., 'An algorithm for information structuring and retrieval', *The Computer Journal,* 14, 407–412 (1971)

VAN RIJSBERGEN, C. J., 'Further experiments with hierarchic clustering in document retrieval', *Information Storage and Retrieval,* 10, 1–14 (1974)

VAN RIJSBERGEN, C. J., 'The best-match problem in document retrieval', *Communications of the ACM,* 17, 648-649 (1974)

VAN RIJSBERGEN, C. J., 'File organization in library automation and information retrieval', *Journal of Documentation,* 32, 294–317 (1976)

VAN RIJSBERGEN, C. J., 'A theoretical basis for the use of co-occurrence data in information retrieval', *Journal of Documentation,* 33, 106–119 (1977)

VAN RIJSBERGEN, C. J., 'Retrieval effectiveness', In: *Progress in Communication Sciences,* Vol. 1 (Edited by Melvin J. Voigt) (in the press)

VAN RIJSBERGEN, C. J. and SPARCK JONES, K., 'A test for the separation of relevant and non-relevant documents in experimental retrieval collections', *Journal of Documentation,* 29, 251–257 (1973)

VAN RYZIN, J., *Classification and Clustering,* Academic Press, New York (1977)

VASWANI, P. K. T. and CAMERON, J. B., *The National Physical Laboratory Experiments in Statistical Word Associations and their Use in Document Indexing and Retrieval,* Publication 42, National Physical Laboratory, Division of Computer Science (1970)

VERHOEFF, J., GOFFMAN, W. and BELZER, J., 'Inefficiency of the use of boolean functions for information retrieval systems', *Communications of the ACM,* 4, 557–558, 594 (1961)

VICKERY, B. C., *Techniques of Information Retrieval,* Butterworths, London (1970)

WARHEIT, I. A., 'File organization of library records', *Journal of Library Automation,* 2, 20–30 (1969)

WATANABE, S., *Knowing and Guessing,* Wiley, New York (1969)

WEILER, G., 'On relevance', *Mind,* LXXI, 487–493 (1962)

203

WHITNEY, V. K. M., 'Minimal spanning tree, Algorithm 422', *Communications of the ACM,* **15,** 273–274 (1972)

WILLIAMS, J. H., 'Results of classifying documents with multiple discriminant functions', In: *Statistical Association Methods for Mechanized Documentation* (Edited by Stevens *et al.*) National Bureau of Standards, Washington, 217–224 (1965)

WINDLEY, P. F., 'Trees, forests and rearranging', *Computer Journal,* **3,** 84–88 (1960)

WINOGRAD, T., *Understanding Natural Language,* Edinburgh University Press, Edinburgh (1972)

WISHART, D., *FORTRAN II program for 8 methods of cluster analysis (CLUSTAN I)* Computer Contribution 38 State Geological Survey. The University of Kansas, Lawrence, Kansas, U.S.A. (1969)

YU, C. T. and LUK, W. S., 'Analysis of effectiveness of retrieval in clustered files'. *Journal of the ACM,* **24,** 607–622 (1977)

YU, C. T., LUK, W. S. and CHEUNG, T. Y., 'A statistical model for relevance feedback in information retrieval', *Journal of the ACM,* **23,** 273–286 (1976)

YU, C. T., LUK, W. S. and SIU, M. K., 'On the estimation of the number of desired records with respect to a given query' (in preparation)

YU, C. T. and SALTON, G., 'Precision weighting – an effective automatic indexing method', *Journal of the ACM,* **23,** 76–85 (1976)

YU, C. T. and SALTON, G., 'Effective information retrieval using term accuracy', *Communications of the ACM,* **20,** 135–142 (1977)

ZADEH, L. A., Fuzzy sets', *Information and Control,* 8, 338–353 (1965)

ZADEH, L. A., 'Similarity relations and fuzzy orderings', *Information Sciences,* **3,** 177–200 (1971)

ZIPF, H. P., *Human Behavior and the Principle of Least Effort,* Addison-Wesley, Cambridge, Massachusetts (1949)

INDEX

INDEX